Economics in Real Time

ADVANCES IN HETERODOX ECONOMICS

Fred Lee, University of Missouri–Kansas City, Series Editor
Rob Garnett, Texas Christian University, Associate Editor

The Advances in Heterodox Economics series promotes the development of heterodox economics beyond existing individual heterodox approaches: post Keynesian, institutional-evolutionary, Marxian-radical, feminist, sraffian, social, Austrian, and others. The series aims to publish books in the following areas: (1) the synthesis of two or more heterodox theories/approaches in the general fields of microeconomics and macroeconomics or in specialized fields such as industrial economics, ecological economics, international economics, and so forth; (2) the historical development of heterodox economics, including intellectual biographies of heterodox economists, histories of relevant theoretical controversies, and histories of the institutional development of heterodox economics; (3) the development of novel heterodox theories, such as the feminist theory of international trade; and (4) anthologies of heterodox work from all approaches in a specific field or area. The editor and associate editor work closely with individual authors and editors to ensure the quality of all published works.

Economics in Real Time

A Theoretical Reconstruction

John McDermott

THE UNIVERSITY OF MICHIGAN PRESS | Ann Arbor

338,50118
M13e

2007   2006   2005   2004   4   3   2   1

A CIP catalog record for this book is available from the British Library.

Library of Congress Cataloging-in-Publication Data

McDermott, John.
    Economics in real time : a theoretical reconstruction / John
McDermott.
        p.   cm.
    Includes bibliographical references and index.
    ISBN 0-472-11357-7 (cloth : alk. paper)
    1. Microeconomics.   2. Time and economic reactions.   3. Prices.
    4. Value.   5. Human capital.   I. Title.
    HB172 .M127   2004
    338.5'01'18—dc21   2003012785

To my wife, best friend, lover, muse,
listener (both voluntary and involuntary),
critic, supporter, contributor, life's companion,
and so much more, ❧

FRANCES DOROTHEA ALDRICH MAHER

"FRIN"
I dedicate this book,
With all my love.

Acknowledgments

Many friends and colleagues have read versions of this manuscript over the past half dozen years. My deep thanks for such generous assistance and steady encouragement.

Michael Meeropol, author in his own right of a fine history of U.S. economic policy, 1979–97 (*Surrender: How the Clinton Administration Completed the Reagan Revolution,* University of Michigan Press, 1998) also wrote an "invisible chapter" for the present volume. His contributions are so numerous and insightful as to be beyond citation.

Behzad Yaghmaian read a very early version, on the spectacular beach at Malaga, as he reported. It's an ill wind that blows no good at all, for just such a wind carried off the last chapter. The implication that it was not worth chasing down, along with his stern comments on the rest, had the desired effect; that the present book contains a formalized theory of micro-economics-in-time is largely his doing.

Christopher Gunn had read all or part of several versions, proposed numerous changes, suggested potential publishers, revived flagging morale, steadily insisting that the book be finished and "gotten out there" into the debate.

Michael Keaney urged more material from the institutionalist tradition and on value theory. I've stinted on institutionalism but I hope he will find the modified value theory chapters up to the mark.

For perhaps thirty years now I've gone to Rick Wolff for advice on economics but none so much as for materials bearing on the present volume. I feel deeply indebted to him in both the practical and the theoretical realms.

Gil Skillman commented on the very difficult first chapter of the book. His observations no less than his reservations helped very considerably in the rewriting of it.

Bertell Ollman may perhaps be dubious about my revisions of Marx but he helped to reformulate many arguments and—not less—directed the book to several publishers.

I have had a small correspondence on these subjects with both Daniel Bell and Robert Heilbroner. For their courtesy and assistance to a stranger, I want to extend my thanks.

I have served since 1988 on the Editorial Board of *The Review of Radical Political Economics,* under three Managing Editors, Bill James, David Houston, and Hazel Dayton Gunn, who, along with a few score co-referees and *Review* contributors, have provided an irreplaceable learning experience.

Many other friends and colleagues have contributed to the book, sometimes in notes and letters, more often in conversations: John Annette, Ros Baxandall, Abby Cheever, Linda Ditmar, Matt Drennan, Gerard Dumenil, Anthony Econom, Don Goldstein, Lennie Goodings, Suzy Goodman, Ed Greer, David Gullette, Margaret Morganroth Gullette, Laurie Johnson, Emily Kales, Betty Kruse, David Laibman, Winston Langley, Fred Lee, Tony Leiman, Norman Levy, Judy Lieberman, Dick Martin, John Miller, Gary Mongiovi, Nicoli Nattrass, Paule Ollman, Andrea Petersen, Jonathan Ree', Ellen Rosen, Richard Rosen, Bob Ross, Carole Silver, Kathy Stone, and Frank Thompson.

My thanks also to Ellen McCarthy, Senior Editor for Social Sciences, her associate, Ann Schultz, Marcia LaBrenz, and other colleagues at the University of Michigan Press. I hope this book will prove worthy of the time and effort they have given it.

As befits a theoretical work, whose merit rests ultimately on the quality of its own arguments, I have made only a few references to only a small handful of economics authorities. The experienced reader will recognize, however, many other distinguished writers not cited here, sometimes by an inadvertent borrowing, here and there by an objection, more often by the problems I've undertaken to address or ignore. Two names, however, stand out as my teachers. Mark Sherefkin, then of Cornell, was my first mentor in economics. I hope I've not strayed too far from that good start. My continuing mentor has been the late Joseph Schumpeter. I never studied with Professor Schumpeter, indeed never even met him, but I feel keenly his creative influence on my work. I cannot imagine that he would agree with the views I've presented in the present volume but think that he would heartily approve of this as of every effort to raise new questions and propose new answers to our ever unfolding economic experience.

Contents

Introduction: Microeconomic Time

The present volume argues for a microeconomics of sale/purchase-in-time, which is to say a microeconomics in which exchanges, heretofore treated as instantaneous events, are understood to occupy positive intervals of time instead. This makes possible a partial synthesis of the classical and the neoclassical traditions in economics. That is, sale/purchase-in-time alters the purely tautological stipulations of neoclassical demand theory into possibly verifiable historical-materialist terms and thereby completes part of the classical, particularly Marxist, tradition by articulating a theory of final demand.

This change is part of my larger project, which is to theorize how a modern labor force is produced, altered, and deployed as a producer commodity and, in brief subtext, with what social effect.

Chapter 1 conceives that the exchange relationship between producers/sellers and purchasers/consumers normally occupies positive intervals of time, contrasting this to the mainstream view along the following lines. If, in the familiar manner of both the classicals (Smith, Ricardo, Marx, Sraffa) and the neoclassicals (Jevons, Walras, Marshall, Arrow and Hahn, etc.), a sale/purchase is instead understood to occur in that instantaneous time when agreement is reached, the relationship is well characterized as being between a single seller and a single purchaser, a one-to-one relation in which both, formally free to make the agreement or not, and hence formally equal, fully and instantaneously transfer the services of one private property in exchange for another.

Then all formally identical, instantaneous sale/purchase relationships are readily aggregable, as if they were occurring at the same instant, yielding the logical possibility of a general equilibrium model of the entire economy, which under suitable conditions can yield an orderly economic universe of fully comparable prices, possibly instancing a Pareto optimum with respect to the final distribution of goods (and services).

The present study, however, argues that contemporary sale/purchase occupies positive durations or intervals of time. At least four classes of distinctly contemporary goods and services appear to require sale/purchase-in-time. These include (1) automobiles and other mechanical appliances, (2) electronic goods such as personal computers (PCs), (3) semiprepared foods, and (4) medical and retirement plans. Conventionally, we conceive a good or commodity to be comprised of a definite ensemble of services or use-values.

Analysis of the relationship between the producer/seller and purchaser/(final) consumer reveals that, for at least these classes of goods or commodities, all of their services—for example, the services of the personal computer—do not pass instantaneously across the sale/purchase relationship since the PC is engineered (and priced) to accept future software changes and may be adaptable to upgraded modems, printers, scanners, and so on. These potential services, or use-values, are typically acquired and activated only in the future. Here the transfer of the entirety of the PC's normal services from seller to purchaser normally occupies a positive interval or intervals of time.

It also follows that the relationship between seller and purchaser is not one-to-one but many-to-one since the producer/sellers of the software, printer, scanner, or discs need not be and often are not identical to the PC manufacturer and yet are intrinsically involved in the passage of the PC's potential services to the purchaser and thus, paradoxically, are a material party to the initial sale/purchase.

At the initiation of the sale/purchase the purchaser/consumer pays for the potential services of the PC, but some of those services or use-values do not pass to him or her until later in the sale/purchase interval, for example, when one goes on-line or acquires the latest laser printer. Here the purchaser has not exchanged money for integral services but has instead made an advance, that is, advanced money to the seller for what are still only potential services. Such services pass to the purchaser later, typically by means of some further expenditure of money.

Hence, this advance also entails a kind of effectual lien on at least some of the future earnings of the purchaser/consumer, for example, for gasoline, repairs, and insurance for a car; on-line services for a PC; or, more prominently, regular payments to a health plan provider.

A full alienation of property does not occur until the completion of the sale/purchase interval, with at least some of the services that together comprise the goods in question remaining effectively within the proprietary ambit of one or more of the sellers. The simple identity between sale/purchase and exchange of property does not hold; taken as a whole the services of the good in question are not well described as being transferred to the purchaser; instead their transfer is distributed over time, and the process is more accurately characterized as a complex distribution than a simple exchange.

Insofar as the services of the good in question, say, a microwave oven or compact disc (CD) player, must be complemented with semiprepared foods and microwavable dishes or CDs, respectively, to at least some degree the purchaser is dependent on the future behavior of the foods or discs manufacturers. Hence, the sale/purchase cannot be abstractly characterized as taking place between equals. Duration of time alone introduces a degree of inequality into the relationship.

Having purchased the car or the health plan, one gains a stake in its services, and the preservation of the stake requires that one remain within the sale/purchase state relationship. Hence, within the initial relationship many of its complementary sale/purchase relationships are formally unfree, that is, the purchaser faces an unequal choice of whether to make them or not.

With this addition of positive intervals of time into microanalysis, it follows that the familiar extrapolation to a general equilibrium model is no longer warranted. Hence, prices are not in principle fully comparable, having only a possibly situational comparability. From the purely methodological point of view, there seems to be no reason to believe that any Pareto optima remain unaltered across even small durations of time.

Finally, with respect to the microeconomics of sale/purchase-in-time, classical and neoclassical microeconomics correspond to the subcase when $t = 0$, a subcase in which all concrete relationships between producer/seller and purchaser/consumer are abstracted away, its virtues as an explanatory apparatus stemming logically from its tradeoff between fully abstract generality and time. But from the analytical point of view the familiar instantaneous microeconomics can be consistently maintained only as a boundary (analogous to a mathematical limit) of possible economic behavior. Alternately, to conceive of exchange in zero time as an actual or applicable subcase of sale/purchase is to introduce formal inconsistency into basic theory.

Thus, in sale/purchase-in-time, the services or use-values of the good in question are passed from the producer/seller to the purchaser/consumer within a positive interval of time. Sale/purchase is modally a many-to-one relationship in which the purchaser advances at least some money to the seller(s) and accepts in turn some liens on his or her future earnings. This is a distributive process, not an exchange, and in that distribution the purchaser remains to a degree dependent on the actions of one or more of the sellers and in a somewhat unequal relationship with them.

These different intervals of sale/purchase-in-time are not identical, though obviously there are overlaps. Hence, they do not yield to equilibrium analysis and their prices are therefore not fully and unconditionally comparable. A Pareto optimal distribution is not methodologically indicated. The historical microeconomic doctrine of sale/purchase in instantaneous time, familiar to us all, constitutes the limiting temporal case for the sale/purchase relationship and not a possible instance of it.

In chapter 2, Marx's analysis of commodity exchange is modified so as to incorporate it within both the logic and the practices of sale/purchase-in-time. The chapter contains both analytical and historical material bearing on this modification.

In chapter 3, the preceding apparatus is employed to show (1) that consumers' so-called final consumption normally occurs under at least a degree of economically imposed constraint, and (2) that this constraint operates at least in part to make of it a form of productive consumption, mainly but not exclusively with a view toward altering the productive qualities of the work force.

Following a critical reflection on the changed microeconomics entailed by the previous analysis (in chapter 4), the concept of a social labor-power is defined in chapter 5, put forward in place of both the mainstream's "the labor force" and Marx's (unqualified) "labor-power." The social labor-power is portrayed as a single structured ensemble of the potential productive efforts of all persons in a society. The concept emphasizes that those individual labor-powers are not replicas of one another, as in Marx, nor can they be reduced to a uniform standard, but instead complement each other to form a kind of organic whole. Moreover, the term comprises the labor-power of the unemployed as well as the employed, of those who are not in the formal labor force as well as of those who are and, equally, the labor-power of children and students and their mentors and parents.

The social labor-power is further divided into several distinct life courses, here called Courses. The concept is developed from that of a "career" but (1) covering all persons in the social labor-power, not solely a privileged segment; and (2) extending backward in time to bring in the young person's or child's preparatory years. Courses are then shown to be analyzable as distinct, serial ensembles of timed sales/purchases. This makes possible, in chapter 6, the development of the concept of "human capital" from an individual to a social phenomenon. It is in this discussion that a dynamic model of a modern economy is realized.

Chapter 7 demonstrates that *value* in both the classical and neoclassical traditions—that is, labor or labor-power and utility or preferencing, respectively—is only a disguised synonym for *price*. An alternate theory of value is sketched, and (in chapter 8) some of its salient implications are pursued for price theory, the contemporary relationship between money and credit, the changed nature of property, and the relationship between capital and the social labor-power.

A microeconomics of instantaneous sale/purchase lies at the intellectual foundation of the claim by Hayek and Popper that a "free market" is the indispensable condition for the existence of an "Open Society." Analysis of sale/purchase-in-time shows, however, that a significant degree of constraint is normally exercised over (final) consumers by modern producing/selling institutions. Within the limits appropriate to a dominantly theoretical study, the views of Hayek and Popper are examined and the counterargument made that our modern private economy neither expands nor protects the "Open Society" but puts in its place social and other arrangements that are secularly shaped to suit the interests of the institutional economic mechanism.

1 | Rethinking Economic Behavior

Economics, Microeconomics, and Ideology

There are pressing reasons to call for a microeconomics of greater empirical veracity and more methodological scrupulousness, thus of greater descriptive as well as analytical power. In this study I present and develop an alternative paradigm for general economic theory, which will, I hope, contribute to that double aim.

In the first instance such a microeconomics is needed in order to characterize an economy and an economics in which the productive qualities of the work force are not simply a given factor of production but are produced within the economy, produced, that is, in no way fundamentally different from other producer commodities. Of itself, this point is deeply inconsistent with much of the way in which we theorize a modern capitalist economy.

One of the main implications of this point is that the structure of consumer demand is itself altered by the production of a work force subject to qualitatively and quantitatively different social and other investments. Accordingly, I present a microeconomic analysis that rejects customary atomic and prescriptive individualism, substituting in its place an archetypal analysis of the production of the work force that is both social and materialist in character. Analytically speaking, I want to introduce a logic of partially constrained behavior into the theory of final or consumer demand. Crudely, people may freely choose how and when to spend today's income, but they are constrained by its size (and security), whatever debts and obligations they have previously incurred, their own social and cultural views and values, and institutional constraints of various kinds.[1]

There has been a revival since the last decades of the nineteenth century of "free market" ideology and its associated political/social concept, the "Open Society." But if the economies of the advanced countries are as

I characterize them in this study then the "freedom" and social spontaneity that market and Open Society theorists claim to discover are critically illusory. Accordingly, I point up as appropriate the general tendency in modern societies for "free" and spontaneous phenomena to recede before those that are essentially fabricated according to the program and needs of one or more large institutions. Or, more simply, I underline the multiple ways in which general social, cultural, and political relations are being absorbed into and reorganized by relations of production emanating from very large institutions, preeminently the transnational corporate firms and their allied states.

That this vast subject can be dealt with only fragmentarily in these pages shouldn't belie its importance for economics and, indeed, for social theory and politics generally. The emergence of an institutionally fabricated society or, as I've expressed it elsewhere, of a "postsociety industry," is among the dominant tendencies of contemporary history. Mainstream microeconomics, with its doctrines of consumer sovereignty and "free choice in a free market," serves powerfully to erase the very existence of this development, and to that extent, too, it must be faulted.

A Socially Fabricated Work Force: Implications

It is, of course, widely understood that it is precisely in the most advanced and successful economies that the production and alteration of the productive qualities of the work force are most marked. We accept that it is not the quantity of commodities consumed nor the opulence of their physical infrastructures that distinguishes the advanced from the developing economies but the relative size, amplitude, and variety of the skills and knowledge deployed, the health, the ethos and morale, and the adaptability of their respective work forces. And, to a greater rather than a lesser degree, these productive qualities have largely developed, been maintained, and been altered over time in the advanced countries as a result of deliberation and intent, not as a product of market or other forms of spontaneity. But, if this great fact is well understood, its implications for economic analysis are not.

The existence of a work force with more or less socially fabricated productive characteristics carries at least nine implications for both economics and economic science, each of which is quite substantial and none of which fit particularly well within the dominant economic paradigm, that is, neoclassical "microeconomics" as promulgated in the major universities and economics associations:

1. There is an economic system or order in the production of the work force. Interestingly, this is a major subject of interest in development economics and a major topic in the economic policy sciences, but it has not entered into fundamental theory. There the standpoint is only static and subsocial: (a) static in that the productive qualities of the work force are taken as a given in the analysis, as exogenous inputs solely, and not conceived within an interactive circuit with other productive forces and relations; and (b) subsocial in that one is concerned primarily with the productive qualities of a firm or industry's work force and not of the economy per se.

2. This in turn implies that human capital theory ought to be raised to the social level and not, as it is now, treated from the standpoint of this or that individual acquiring personal human capital that he or she may individually deploy. We perforce need an analytical treatment of human capital formation as it occurs at both the macro- and microlevels of economic analysis.

3. But this in turn implies that the very concepts of a "labor force" or "work force" are inadequate. Both concepts assume, and hence obscure the processes that determine which parts of the population will be trained, socialized, and employed, in what relative numbers, with what rewards, and with what menus of skills and knowledge. We need a more basic or generic concept that can then be analytically developed as needed. From Marx I've borrowed the (excessively generic) concept of "labor-power" but with the aim of developing the more concrete concept of "the Social Labor-Power." The latter refers to all of the potential labor exertions of a society that could or do contribute to the production of goods or services or, equally, that help to alter the productive characteristics, directly or indirectly, of other producing persons. Obviously, parenting and teaching must be included in the activities that constitute the social labor-power. It follows that points (1) and (2) will have to be discussed in terms of the social production of the social labor-power.

4. To produce a social labor-power is, of course, to produce some elaborate system of division of labor. And in a capitalist economy that division of labor, rather than another, ought to offer a special advantage to the process of private capital accumulation. That is, the produced division of labor, one would imagine, ought to offer a greater advantage to the capitalist economy than other notional possibilities or historical divisions do. In short, we need to analyze the social labor-power and its division of labor as forms of productive capital that interact within the wider circuit of productive capital taken as a whole.

5. If in the production of a modern capitalist work force we assume

that differential investments are made to produce the different parts of the division of labor, then these investment patterns will divide consumer preference patterns into various types. This, of course, implies an analysis of consumer or final demand that differs somewhat from what we find in textbooks and the familiar "micro" course; in place of the essentially "free" or unconstrained nature of consumer demand, which we see in the textbooks, we must explore the implications of partially constrained demand, that is, constrained at least to the degree that it supports the reproduction of a diversely skilled and equipped division of labor.

6. Further, if at least some consumer preferences, expenditures, and consumption behavior are socially constrained, however indirectly and mildly, with a view toward producing a worker who is in some sense "better" than his or her predecessors, it follows that at least some consumer or final consumption has a productive character and is a form of productive consumption. Then the question becomes: What social forms does this productive consumption take and how do they reveal empirically that they are in fact a form of productive consumption?

7. In neoclassical economics, the demand for producer goods is a derived demand—derived, that is, from consumer preferences. These preferences are conceived of as autonomous and sovereign within the economy. But a socially fabricated work force implies, as we have seen, that consumer preferences themselves will be altered in patterned ways by investments made in light of the needs or desires of the existing and prospective economy. Accordingly, we must conceive of a dynamic microeconomics in which, so to speak, supply and demand more or less continually refashion each other. We must not, I hasten to add, conceive of a microeconomic analysis that, say, traces an equilibrium state that gives way to disequilibrium and then moves toward a new equilibrium. Instead we require an analysis in which equilibrium conceptions have no place. In short, an intrinsically dynamic analysis seems called for, an analysis in which qualitative change over time is the "normal" situation. Among the requirements that this imposes on the theorist is that duration of time must be positively introduced into, rather than assumed out of, fundamental microeconomic analysis. This introduction of so-called real time into microeconomics is the most important paradigmatic root of the present study.

8. From the previous point it follows that we must alter our concept of price and the price system. Briefly, to a modern economist of virtually any persuasion the price system is both a univocal indicator of underlying economic "reality" and a measure of the relative worth of each good denominated within it. The key terms here are *univocal* and *measure*. The

price at which a given good or service is exchanged is understood—at least "in principle"—to be uniquely determined by underlying economic processes. And that price is, "all things holding equal," conceived to be a genuine measure of relative worth and not merely a useful index. It is difficult to understand how these claims can be justified in an economy that is intrinsically dynamic.[2] As we pursue the matter further, it will prove both necessary and fruitful to conceive of the "price" of any good or service as having no more than situational validity and of being but one among several equally significant indices of relative worth. In the terminology I adopt, we will speak of a relativist rather than a determinist microeconomics, of price nominalism rather than the (present day) microeconomics of price realism.

9. In the main, economists have treated the distribution of goods and services under the rubric of "The Market," a notional space in which free persons *exchange* equal amounts of goods and services in instantaneous time. If the medium of money is introduced into the analysis, it is assumed to have equal marginal utility for each participant. Since Walras, the narrative image called to mind in the categorical schema is that of an auction in which both would-be purchasers and would-be sellers bid against one another (Walras [1926] 1977: 83ff.; 169ff.). However, a pattern of differential investments made to produce and alter the labor force implies that some modes of distribution of goods and services are not well or, more to the point, accurately depicted in this bid/ask schema. One of the logical requirements on a new microeconomics is that it must analyze and develop forms other than the "free" forms of price-denominated buying, selling, and other kinds of distribution.

It seems clear that we need to revamp microeconomic analysis. But it follows, especially from point (6), that this "micro" be in the descriptive and epistemological senses a richer one than that presented in the current textbooks. In short, we need a microeconomic analysis that takes into account all the ways in which an existing economic organism skews different consumer preferences and so-called final consumption with a view toward producing a social labor-power with differing productive—hence earning and thus consuming—characteristics. Obviously, the treatment of time within microeconomics must be reconsidered.

Bringing Time into Microeconomics: Alternate Approaches

In the neoclassical mainstream, one theoretically introduces duration of time through the rate of interest or some other parameter representing the cost of capital. Then fundamental theory is developed on the basis of microeconomic propositions holding only for instantaneous time. It is possible, however, to formulate an alternate microeconomics that incorporates positive durations or intervals of time in the analysis. This "microeconomics in real time" does not have the theoretical elegance of the neoclassical edifice (see note 6, however). But it does appear to offer other advantages. First, the new analytical apparatus can be shown to generate every valid proposition of the neoclassical view. Second, it points up in a newly compelling way certain conundrums associated with the mainstream "microeconomics." Third, as intended, it allows us to bring into microeconomic analysis the production and reproduction, the uses and rewards, of the social labor-power and its various subsets, including, of course, the labor force.

The development of a microeconomics in real time will be easier to follow if we recall the salient features of the instantaneous micro now dominant. If, in the familiar mainstream manner, the modal *exchange* relationship between seller and purchaser is understood to occur in *instantaneous time,* then:

1. The relationship is characterized as occurring between a single seller and a single purchaser, a *one-to-one* relation.
2. In this relationship both seller and purchaser are *free* to make the exchange or not.
3. They are both *equal* in the exchange relationship.
4. They are able *to fully transfer* properties, goods for goods in a barter transaction, and money for goods in a sale/purchase exchange.

Then all *exchange relationships* in a given economy in a given instant may be conceived as follows.

5. They are readily conceived as parts of single *system* of exchanges that mutually condition each another, as described, for example, in the market narrative.[3]
6. They yield the logical possibility of a *general equilibrium model* of the entire economy.
7. Under suitable conditions, this economy can yield an orderly cosmos of ratios of exchange, that is, *comparable prices.*
8. This possibly may result in a *Pareto optimum* with respect to the final distribution of goods (and services.).[4]

Both the narrative plausibility and the inferential power of each of these 1 + 8 propositions are crucially dependent on the assumption of instantaneous exchange, that is, the assumption that exchange per se occupies no positive interval of time.

The first, conditional claim—that is, *exchange*—is of course merely a definition. In a narrative mode one would speak of an "agreement," with the moment of agreement between seller and purchaser constituting the reality of the exchange. From a purely analytical standpoint what is central is that exchange is here logically imagined to occupy no positive duration of time.

Proposition 1 (*one-to-one*) is simply part of that definition, that is, that an exchange is defined as a relationship occurring between two parties. Of course, in actual exchange relationships one or more of the parties may consist of a group (e.g., a partnership or consortium) or institution (e.g., a corporation or government agency) or there may be three, four, or more parties acting as middlemen (brokers, factors, estate executors, etc.) or even principals. In the neoclassical representation of these things, an empirical multiplicity of different parties in an exchange or linked sets of exchanges can be reduced in principle, without distortion, to a set of discrete one-to-one exchanges, each with no further analytical content than that a unit-set party has freely exchanged something with another unit-set party. Here the assumption of instantaneousness provides the reduction with both narrative and analytical plausibility.

Propositions 2 (*free*) and 3 (*equal*) overlap their meanings. In the analytical mode, the assumption of instantaneous time is essential here, for it gives a formal character to the freedom and equality of the exchangers, that is, it excises from the exchange relationship any possible material disparities in need between the parties or in their relative power—say, in their bargaining power. All that is analytically essential here is that the exchange relationship is understood to be symmetrical in its logical form, that x E(xchanges with) y is equivalent to y E x.

In proposition 4, the weight of the assertion is not on legal property per se but on the *full transfer,* that is, whatever services are alienated in an exchange are fully alienated. If a good, G, is transferred from seller to purchaser, all of G's services are thereby transferred. This stipulation doesn't exclude the buying and selling of, say, leases, futures, or shares in a company. What it does exclude is the possibility that the seller, in spite of the sale of some service of G, nevertheless retains a proprietary claim in that same service.[5]

As to propositions 5 (*system*) and 6 (*general equilibrium*), the latter's analytic equivalent 7 (*comparable prices*), and 8 (*Pareto optimum*), their narratives are too familiar to bear repeating. However, none hold in the neoclassical "micro" unless one assumes only instantaneous time.[6]

Logically, the situation in proposition set *Inst* {1 + 8} is as follows. The proposition subset, 1–4 constitutes the necessary condition for the validity or "truth" of propositions 5, 6, 7, and 8. Moreover, the truth of proposition 5 is the necessary condition for 6, proposition 6 is analytically equivalent to 7, and proposition 7 is the necessary condition for 8.[7]

Introducing Positive Time

At the narrative level, at least five classes of contemporary goods and services appear to require "exchange in time" in order to render their microeconomic properties without essential distortion. We have already pointed to the role of time in the shaping of the productive qualities of the social labor-power. We will take up that subject later. Here I want to focus on four classes of goods that we normally conceive to be meant for "final consumption." These include (1) automobiles and other mechanical appliances, (2) electronic goods such as personal computers, (3) semi-prepared foods, and (4) medical, retirement, and kindred plans. Because I want to conceive of such microeconomic transactions in these goods as occurring in positive time, the narrative will be clarified if we speak of sale/purchase rather than exchange. The reason for the terminological shift will become apparent shortly.

Before going on, three other observations should be taken into account. First, we must make explicit the implicit assumption of *Inst* {1 + 8} that, as is conventionally assumed, a good or commodity is comprised of some definite ensemble of services (or Marxist use-values) and that it is these that are transferred in the exchange. Second, we should note in passing that these four classes of goods are distinguished by the fact that they, unlike Victorian cotton cloth or classroom "widgets," represent goods that are both qualitatively characteristic of a modern economy and of quantitative significance within it. Finally, in the neoclassical edifice it is held that the role of final consumers is ultimately decisive. Accordingly, in the discussion below I initially conceive of the sale/purchase in each case as occurring between the producer/seller and the purchaser/(final)consumer.

We can begin by noting that for at least these classes of goods or commodities all of their services (e.g., those of the personal computer) are not passed to the purchaser via the initial purchase (i.e., they are not instantaneously and fully alienated in an exchange). In part, the PC, of course, is like a piece of capital equipment, which yields a stream of services over time. But there is more to it than that. One buys certain potential services of the PC at the initial sale/purchase—typically that it will be adaptable to future peripheral add-ons and software changes—but at least some of those services are not transferred to the buyer, nor can they be, at the point of sale. They will be transferred later, when that equipment or software is invented, produced, and marketed. Thus, the transfer of the entirety of the PC's normal services to the purchaser here occupies a positive interval or intervals of time. This interpretation is supported, moreover, by the observation that the PC is engineered to be adaptable to future software and equipment, that is, to future markets that can only be conceived as generic, not specific. These are possible future markets for as yet undesigned equipment or software and not identifiable markets for goods or services of established characteristics.[8]

A new car purchase has perhaps somewhat the same character since it will involve subsequent purchases of parts, repair services, and auxiliary equipment. However, it is not uncommon for those who wish to drive new vehicles to lease the car, with the lease including arrangements that relieve the lessee of proprietary responsibility to service and repair the car. Even the risk of a "lemon" is obviated by such contracts. Obviously, then, there are no impassable barriers preventing PC makers from offering similar leasing arrangements to their customers, and it is theoretically possible to conceive of all new car and PC purchases *as if* they were covered by such futures contracts, thus bringing this area of sale/purchase under *Inst* {1+ 8}.

One can analogously deal with health, dental, life insurance, and retirement plans: One contracts instantaneously in the present to make a stream of timed payments in exchange for a stream of timed services. Of course, as we know from the headlines today, the vendor may impose changes in the plan via bankruptcy or by unilaterally changing coverage, delaying retirement age, or reducing benefits. But on the model, say, of trip cancellation insurance, one could conceive of various insurance schemes with an actuarial basis that would compensate for such eventualities. Of course, there is a certain paradox in representing theoretically a free, unregulated market system within which uncertainty and risk have been insured out of existence. Be that as it may, from a theoretical standpoint the axioms represented by *Inst* {1 + 8} need not be jettisoned on account of any of these new varieties of buying and selling, although they do begin to put greater theoretical strain on the other levels of the neoclassical model, particularly on how we "interpret" the model.

This observation is further reinforced by the fact that the relationship between seller and purchaser for these classes of goods is not modally one-to-one but *many-to-one* since the producer/sellers of the software or printer, scanner, or discs need not be and often are not identical to the PC manufacturer and yet become necessarily involved, at the point of the initial sale/purchase in the (eventual) passage of the PC's services, or use-values, to the purchaser. Similarly, one enters into real but similarly tacit future relations with the petroleum and tire industries when one purchases a car; with doctors, nurses, and hospitals when one buys a health plan; and with semiprepared food producers when one purchases a microwave.

Here we face a theoretical quandary of sorts. One could treat the purchase of the car, repairs, and gasoline as autonomous economic purchases in one-to-one, unrelated relationships with as many different sellers. Prima facie this gambit would analytically bring the automobile purchase securely within the neoclassical "micro," although it makes no narrative sense to imagine that, say, gasoline prices and availability have no significant effect on auto purchases. We'll return to this issue shortly.

Even more stressful for *Inst* {1 + 8} is the fact that at the initiation of the sale/purchase the purchaser/consumer of a PC, for example, actually pays a bit extra for the potential services of the PC, although some of those services may not pass to him or her until later in the sale/purchase interval, for example, when he or she goes on-line or acquires the latest laser printer. To this extent, then, the purchaser has not merely exchanged money for goods but has made an *advance* (i.e., advanced money) to the seller for what are still only potential services, with the latter passing to the purchaser only later and typically by means of some further expenditure of money to one or more producers/sellers.

Here we begin to run seriously afoul of proposition 4 of *Inst* {1 + 8}. Looking again at the PC: the buyer buys it, takes it home, and uses it when and as he or she likes. It's his or her property. Or is it? Clearly not all the normal services that the buyer paid for and presumably wanted to possess have passed to his or her proprietary control via the initial sale/purchase; the buyer has to make payments to another producer/seller to get laser printing, go on the Web, or "enjoy" e-mail.

We can adjust our conception of what is and is not our "property" to cover this sort of case under proposition 4 (*transfer*) of *Inst* {1 + 8}, but in doing so we are stretching the meaning of *property* into areas that are relatively unfamiliar even to the most permissive property theorist, the most litigious property lawyer, the most avant-garde copyright specialist, and so forth. At any rate, the PC, considered as an ensemble of services, is not "mine" at the point of initial sale in anything like the same sense that, say, a pencil or typewriter is mine. And, of course, I have made a payment for services I can't yet enjoy, quite literally an advance payment.

This advance, with the consequent need to realize its value with further expenditures later, entails a kind of effectual *lien* on at least some of the future earnings of the purchaser/consumer for gasoline, repairs, and insurance for the car; on-line services for the PC; or, more prominently, regular payments into the health plan.

Following this logic, full transfer or alienation of this classic private property does not occur until the completion of the sale/purchase interval, with at least some of the services that comprise the goods in question remaining effectively within the proprietary ambit of one or more of the sellers. The simple identity between sale/purchase and full transfer of services does not hold. Taken as a whole the services of the good in question are not well described as being exchanged to the purchaser. As their transfer is distributed over time, the process is more accurately characterized as a complex, serial *distribution* of the PC's services than as a simple, instantaneous exchange.

Insofar as the services of the good in question (say, the microwave oven or CD player) must be complemented with semiprepared foods and microwavable dishes or CDs, respectively, the purchaser to that degree is dependent on the future behavior of the food or disc manufacturer, which is to say on producers/sellers with whom one has no sale/purchase relationship within the overt terms of the initial sale/purchase. At this point the assumption of full freedom and equality between seller and purchaser begins to become not merely theoretically strained but importantly counterfactual. There is *material inequality* within the sale/purchase relationship, with implications for the future sale/purchase relationships into which the parties will enter.[9]

It follows that having purchased the car or the health plan one gains a stake in enjoying its services. Preservation of the stake skews the decision to make certain complementary sales/purchases such as servicing the car or continuing with the health plan. To that precise extent these complementary sale/purchase relationships are *partially constrained,* that is, the purchaser faces an unequal choice in deciding whether to undertake them or not.

In the larger theoretical picture, it is at least arguable that while many of the features of contemporary sale/purchase can be incorporated within *Inst* {1 + 8} we can see via the preceding analyses that the actuarial basis to do so is becoming increasingly attenuated. Moreover, in order to stay within the stipulations of *Inst* {1 + 8} one must make further ad hoc theoretical adjustments, which, to this observer, seem very like those clever epicycles that long preserved the Ptolemaic system of the heavens against the flood of later, apparently discordant evidence. One thus preserves the parsimony of the neoclassical edifice but paradoxically only by means of extra theoretical improvisations.

It follows that if we allow positive intervals of time into microanalysis then the familiar extrapolation to a general equilibrium model is no longer warranted. Hence, all prices are not mutually/simultaneously determining in principle, and therefore they have only a possibly situational comparability.

Methodologically speaking, by conceiving of sale/purchase as occurring through positive intervals of time, one thereby accepts (and introduces) nonactuarial uncertainty into the microeconomic analysis itself as well as the possibility (indeed, the likelihood) of discontinuous demand functions, hence of discontinuity on the supply side. Under those circumstances, one appears to logically nullify one of the necessary conditions under which a Pareto optimum can hold.[10]

Thus, one can characterize modern sale/purchase for at least some classes of goods and services as occupying positive intervals of time within which the sellers retain various proprietary rights in the goods and/or services ostensibly sold. Here the seller/purchaser relationship is modally a many-to-one relationship, sometimes materially unequal, and/or one in which the purchaser/consumer is sometimes under a degree of material constraint. The purchaser often makes advances against the good's or service's use-value and to the same degree accepts liens on his or her future income. Hence, we should speak of sale/purchase not as an exchange relationship but as a distribution in time. The initial sale/purchase relationship is not concluded until all of the expected, normal, and conventional potential services of the good in question have been serially alienated to the buyer. It follows that in general sales/purchases-in-time are not mutually determining with a general equilibrium model in mind, that their prices would be at best only situationally comparable, and that no Pareto optimum is indicated by the analysis.

To bring out the contrast with the propositions of *Inst* {1 + 8}, and for convenience of reference, we can speak of the proposition set *Dur* {1 + 10}, referring, respectively, to *distribution + many-one, partially constrained, not formally equal, serial transfer, advances, liens, nonsystem, nonequilibrium, price relativity,* and *nonoptimal,* as indicated in the narration just concluded.[11]

Before going on we should observe that sale/purchase between modern firms has some of the features of the consumer purchases we've just discussed, especially that it occurs over some duration in time. For example, air transportation service is a joint product of, say, American

Airlines (organization and human services), Boeing (the aircraft), General Electric (the engines), and one or more communications services (booking and payment). These are not ad hoc or one-off relationships between the firms but are semipermanent and integrated into their business dealings. Boeing, for example, develops follow-on aircraft in continuous consultation with General Electric and the air carriers. These are seldom only occasional, top-level consultations—as in conventional "monopoly" theory—but are carried out continuously by midlevel "tech" representatives (sometimes also called technical observers). As was indicated earlier, I've stressed sale/purchase relations with final consumers because of the theoretical importance assigned to the sovereign consumer in the neoclassical theory, not because the relations are so fundamentally different in form from vertical supplier/user relations in industry or horizontal ones involving firms that traditionally cooperate.[12]

What Is the Relationship between the Two Microeconomics?

In looking at this question, we want to put aside their different narratives but at the same time see how their formal/analytical properties serve both to represent and then possibly to investigate "real world" economic behavior. We can limit the discussion to the "interpretation" of *Inst* {1 + 8} and *Dur* {1 + 10}, as in the interpretation of a model. Taking the question in those terms, there are several possibilities.

One can consider *Inst* {1 + 8} as the model or paradigm for microbehavior in general, while in *Dur* {1 + 10} we relax certain stipulations in the interest of not microeconomics per se but a variant interpretation apt to marketing structures for at least the four special classes of goods we've commented on and any others that are kindred to them.

Reversing that primacy, we can readily conceive that as the duration of a transaction under *Dur* {1 + 10} narrows—for example, buying a soft drink instead of a PC—the potential richness of the sale/purchase relationships described in micro-in-time gradually simplify. In that procedure, the proposition set *Inst* {1 + 8} could be taken as the subcase of *Dur* {1 + 10} for the condition that the time duration approaches a limit of zero. Only a very slight modification in the formulation of either *Dur* {1 + 10} or *Inst* {1 + 8} would be required to allow for this. To the extent that this time restriction was imposed, it would follow as a simple corollary that every true proposition in economics generated by the proposition set *Inst* {1 + 8} would be generated by the more inclusive proposition set *Dur*

{1 + 10}. Something like this is true—that "something" is clarified later—and to that extent it confirms point (I) presented earlier.

Ideal Types and Conundrums

There is another option that is only superficially similar to the one just discussed. Maybe *Inst* {1 + 8} and *Dur* {1 + 10} are altogether different, with the first representing exchange as an ideal type and the other representing possible "real world" scenarios—one, in the spirit of Schumpeter, a "logic of pure exchange" and the other a more or less economic anthropology of certain concrete kinds of exchange.

In a challenging essay written a few years back, Daniel Bell (1981) argued, in effect, that exchange (or sale/purchase), as it is characterized and represented here by *Inst* {1 + 8}, has an ideal, fictive, or "as if" character and should not be considered—contra, say, Marshall—a set of generalizations about human behavior (Bell 1981: 69, 53, 70, 69, respectively). Bell's argument is too complex to summarize here, but his conclusion will suffice for our present purposes. He writes that

> economic theory should not be taken as a "model" or template of how human beings behave, for these will always be inadequate, but as a "Utopia", a set of ideal standards against which one can debate and judge different policy actions and their consequences. (80)

This view seems consistent with the idea that proposition set *Inst* {1 + 8} embodies an "ideal type" for exchange in general, which can then be interpreted to fit a variety of real world scenarios, of which *Dur* {1 + 10} is one instance. While this seems to be a convenient and intuitively satisfactory characterization of *Inst* {1 + 8}, and apparently one in accord with Bell's own views of economics theorizing, it is not as plausible on analytical grounds as a narrative account of it might seem to indicate. At that purely formal level, the differences between proposition set *Inst* {1 + 8} and *Dur* {1 + 10} are at least twofold, and each poses theoretical hurdles to Bell's view.

For a start, the elemental exchange relationship, to which all exchanges are theoretically reducible, must be formally one-to-one and symmetrical, but the sale/purchase relationship is possibly (and often) many-to-one and nonsymmetrical. The left-hand member of the elemental exchange relationship must be a unit set; in sale/purchase-in-time it need not be and often isn't. Whatever else may hold between them it is clear that *Inst* {1 + 8} cannot be an "ideal type" for the buyer/seller relationships characterized in *Dur* {1 + 10}.[13]

The second problem is at once more subtle and farther reaching. I think it is consistent with Bell's argument to say that of course real buying and selling occurs in real time durations but we can conceptually shrink those durations toward zero time so as to isolate not the real empirical nature of exchange but its analytical character, that is, to focus on the concept of exchange as it functions in the analytical and inferential realm of economic theory per se. Or, in Bell's words, exchange is a "logical action" (1981: 69), not an empirical representation. In other words, we here conceive zero time as if it were a mathematical limit, and by doing so we can plausibly explicate the theory implicit in proposition set *Inst* {1 + 8}, which itself then functions as an ideal typification for microtheory in general, and so on, as in the mainstream texts.

The problem here is that the limit of a function is not among the values that the function assumes. To say that an exchange approaches zero time is not to say that it occurs in zero time, but unless we allow that it occurs in zero time the interpretation of the model will not be consistent with the formal analytical characteristics of the neoclassical "micro." That is, proposition subset *Inst* {1, 2, 3, 4} logically requires instantaneous time; small intervals just won't do. And the truth of proposition subset *Inst* {5, 6, 7, 8}, the crowning achievement of neoclassical microeconomics, hinges on the same stipulation of instantaneous time.[14]

There is an analogous problem when one uses the familiar classroom term *perfect competition*. Conceptually, one asserts in this usage that there is a (mathematically continuous) order or scale in which competitive situations can be ranked in terms of a set of conditions that specify what one means by *competitiveness*. Thus, for every two possible exchanges, no matter how complex and multifaceted, there is an algorithm that in principle ranks one as more competitive than the other, less so, or equally so. Hence, all exchanges can be ranked in the order of their greater or lesser competitiveness, and thanks to that order one can identify the most and least competitive situation—but not more! There is no such animal as "perfect" competition on that scale. Perfect competition functions here somewhat like a mathematical limit, that is, one extrapolates to it. Like the mathematical limit of zero time, perfect competition is a value in relation to the scale (or function) taken as a whole, but it is not a value on the scale. The latter is needed for the interpretation of the ideal type of "perfectly competitive economy" to be consistent with the proposition subset *Inst* {5, 6, 7, 8}.

If this argument is correct, as I think it is, exchange in zero time is not a possible instance of an exchange and neither is perfect competition a kind or species of competition. Forgetting the narratives we make in explaining them, a mathematical limit of zero time and an instanced zero time, or a comparative extrapolation to most competitive and an instanced perfect competition, are not formally interchangeable; their inferential properties are manifestly different, for one will support, and the other won't, the proposition set Inst {1 + 8}. These are two of the conundrums mentioned under the second point earlier.

A Further Conundrum

Although it is not readily apparent, this discussion has wider logical significance. The issue has to do with using contrary-to-fact assumptions. Here one has to distinguish between using contrary-to-fact assumptions as an investigative tool and, a quite different case, using them at the level of pure theory, as with zero time or perfect competition.

One might hypothesize, to take a simple instance, that, say, the domestic steel market will exhibit a stable equilibrium in the next quarter and construct a model to express that, taking into explicit account all the seemingly relevant factors such as inflation rates, domestic production capacity and utilization, wages, imports, capital markets, demand for steel, and so forth. That assumption would lead to the expectation (conclusion) that steel prices will remain relatively stable. If, in the event, steel prices were to fall or rise substantially, that would call into question the truth of the initial assumptions. Either one or more of the assumptions were incorrect or some other factor or factors, not hitherto taken into account, were falsifying the initial expectation from the model.

This commonsensical procedure actually reflects a wider point in formal inference, namely, that assumptions held to be true should inferentially generate only true conclusions. Hence, a false conclusion falsifies the set of assumptions, and this provides the signal that the investigator should check out his or her assumptions, not only their truth or falsity but their completeness or incompleteness. All of this is perfectly straightforward and achingly familiar.

The situation is different when one is doing purely theoretical work because of an elementary theorem in modern logic. One can readily show that in a formal system of inference the addition of even a single false proposition to a set of assumptions will generate as true (i.e., as a theorem) every proposition expressible in the language of the system. In other words, one will thereby validly generate all the genuine theorems but also validly generate as theorems all the false propositions and all the propositions whose truth or falsity is indeterminate. The point is that in such a situation the fact that something is validly deduced ceases to bear any import as to its truth.[15]

One routinely says in microeconomics that there is no such thing as perfect competition or, here, zero time; that is, a proposition asserting perfect competition or zero time is false. Nevertheless, one just as routinely assumes such propositions and draws inferences from them. But, as in the study of formal inferences, the inferred propositions, however valid the inference, may be true, false, or indeterminate. More or less typically, if the conclusion does not prima facie appear to hold, or in order to "cover all bets," one adds the phrase "all things holding equal" or its equivalent. But those expressions merely assert that there is some set of conditions, not specified in the axioms and claimed to exist in the transformation rules or the rules of interpretation, under which the ostensibly false propositions would be true or that would provide a supplemental assumption or assumptions to make them true.

It is the lack of specification that is at issue here. In the earlier, investigative case one uses the falsity of an inference as a signal indicating that one must reconstruct one's assumptions and thereby add to our knowledge of the question at issue. That very obviously is what one does not do with expressions such as "all things holding equal" or "pari passu." They in fact insulate the initial assumption about perfect competition or zero time from having to be adjusted under any circumstances. Methodologically and as they stand, the initial false assumption of perfect competition or zero time will always be rescued by "ceteris paribus." That is, the assumption will be made *as if* true and thus will also guarantee the truth of whatever one validly infers from it. This is another conundrum generated, in this case, by Bell's interpretation of a familiar mode of economics theorizing. It seems plausible to narratively describe such ideal types, as he does, as fictive devices, but their inferential qualities are either positively inconsistent with the inferential purposes that shaped their creation or appear to represent a kind of possibly paradoxical inferential overkill.

What Is Lost in a Micro That Encompasses Real Time?

We've already answered this question. Nothing is lost. Or, more technically, while the propositions of instantaneousness function in *Inst* {1 + 8} as the necessary conditions for propositions 5, 6, 7, and 8 (*system, general equilibrium, fully comparative prices,* and *Pareto optimum*), one can use analogues of those four characteristics without assuming instantaneous time. There is in general no barrier to assuming that some sets of economic phenomena should be aggregated, treated as a temporary or partial equilibrium with fully comparable prices and exhibiting some sort of optimally efficient allocation of resources. There is no barrier if one is in the investigative mode, that is, prepared to test and adjust those assumptions in accordance with their consonance with their implicates (i.e., empirical or analytical findings). Obviously, specification of time is key here, and, with different investigations in mind, one may assume a positive time interval to be as long or as short as is appropriate. A concept of zero time is never needed in actual investigative work; an assumption that some phenomena are invariant for a specified duration is more than adequate and serves methodologically all of the normal theoretical or investigatory uses that one requires from an assumption of partial or even general equilibrium.

But to say this is to reiterate the argument that *Dur* {1 + 10} provides an inferential apparatus for micro in general and that a modified *Inst* {1 + 8} represents the special subcase in which one holds invariant not time per se but changes over time in the operative factors in a problem under investigation.

That understanding of the relationship of the two micros has the additional merit of being conundrum free, which, as the earlier discussion seems to indicate, is not the case if we assume that *Inst* {1 + 8} is the appropriate model for microeconomics in general, even when we interpret it via the sort of methodologically sophisticated theory of ideal or fictive types of economic "logical actions" that Bell proposes.

The microeconomics currently dominant claims that it subjects a particular area of human behavior to scientific analysis, but, if my arguments hold, it is strained both as science and as analysis. On the other hand, a microeconomics rooted in the conception of sale/purchase states-in-time has stronger expressive qualities. To give a trivial illustration, which we've already addressed from another vantage point: if, where appropriate, we allow the duration of the some sale/purchase states to approach zero, we can incorporate without change every conundrum-free proposition of neoclassical microeconomics.[16]

Free Markets and Free Society?

The dominant theory of consumer demand has been used in intellectual support of a genre of social/political theories of which the archetype is

Karl Popper's Open Society. By this he means a society characterized—analogous to "the market"—by spontaneous, self-correcting competition for influence from many, many individuals, subgroups and institutions so that none of them—no political party or state apparatus, for example—can exercise a monopoly of power or even a significant measure of control over the others.

Popper himself has written, approvingly, that "only a minority of social institutions are consciously designed while the vast majority have just 'grown' as the undersigned results of human action" ([1957] 1967: 65). This position seems to me to be grossly inadequate in a society whose labor force is socially constructed by a vast education industry and by, say, the media, hence whose demand (and therefore many other social) characteristics cannot be conceived as unchanging and of purely "natural" or spontaneous origin.

Hayek, too, maintains "The fundamental principle that in ordering our affairs we should make as much use as possible of the spontaneous forces of society." He continues, in an oft-cited passage, stating that "the limits of our powers of imagination make it impossible to include in our scale of values more than a sector of the needs of the whole society . . . since, strictly speaking, scales of value can exist only in individual minds. . . . It is this recognition of the individual as the ultimate judge of his ends, the belief that as far as possible his own views ought to govern his actions, that forms the essence of the individualist position" (1944: 17, 59, respectively). But to accept this as a political position one must also imagine that the "individual" in question has a socially and historically transcendent character. He or she ("it," really), must be conceived as not in any fundamental sense being influenced by "its" place in the economy and society.

Unlike Mr. Robinson Crusoe, who daily faced a fictional natural wilderness, persons who live in modern societies are surrounded by physical objects, material environments, and social relationships that predate their own lives and today are almost wholly of human fabrication. For example, virtually every consumer item now in everyday use has been invented and its societywide utilization brought about by the action of identifiable corporate firms. Moreover, we live within social arrangements that Gramsci termed "Americanism," a kind of social, economic, and cultural system in which a person's fate and fortune are decided not by nature, tradition, or premodern social and other structures but by his or her role in the economy or, for the young, by their prospective place in it.[17]

Can we speak, like Popper and Hayek, of a "society" existing apart from and more or less autonomous with respect to the modern economy? In our society it does appear that spontaneous phenomena are in decline and socially constructed ones on the increase. In my view, the transcendent economic "individual" of the Jevonian/Walrasian variety is not only poor science but a blinding fiction.[18]

Clearly, we've raised a very large question. What is the limit, if any, to this remaking of society in the name of property, if so we may term it? In some past time it did seem empirically plausible to treat society as having a largely spontaneous character subject to multifaceted and indecipherable sources of change. Then Popper's and Hayek's views could be read as an extrapolation of experience, namely, that the history and evolution of different human societies tended of their own accord to purge, alter, or encourage, as the case may be, the sort of human institutions that were found within them. "Society," that mysterious, infinitely faceted, rich, obscure reality, was conceived as an "all" more potent by far than the sum of its parts. But this no longer seems to be a supportable view.

As Gramsci's concept of "Americanism" hints, there is a totalizing influence within modern society that stems from its economic activities. If there are limits to this "Americanist" totalizing, we have yet to see them. But what follows? Surely to view the future as populated with corporately fabricated people is at least as unattractive (and more plausible) than to see the future in the hands of massed Brown Shirts or ranks of obedient Komsomols. Moreover, if this is even an approximately correct reading of the trajectory of the present, what if anything can be done to prevent, deflect, or even moderate it if society, that once infinite reservoir of difference and variety, is being overwhelmed by all-consuming property?[19]

This reflection points up the social and political imperative to develop an economics, especially a microeconomics, of greater and more benevolent realism. The social and political implications of that altered economic science cannot be explored within the present study, but we should remain aware of the "deep" social and political importance of the theoretical and methodological issues to which we now return.

2 | What Is a "Commodity"?

To this point in the analysis we have stayed within or at least very close to a neoclassical framework, at least, that is, insofar as we have centered our analysis and exposition on the phenomenon of sale/purchase or exchange per se. Yet even that relatively narrow approach has demonstrated that sales/purchases are themselves embedded in and sharply conditioned by other microeconomic dimensions. As we've seen, these include, among other things, the customary or intended uses of the purchased item; the identity of other parties to the sale/purchase, including the initial producer; the stream and form of payments, the technical properties of the item itself; and, of course, the social/institutional organization of the processes of production, marketing, and final consumption. To progress further into these subjects requires that we bring in theoretical material from the other great tradition of historical economics, the classical school, most notably some of the work of Marx. Of particular interest here is his microeconomics of commodities.

Microcoeconomics and Commodity Form

Marx's "commodity," the topical subject of his major work *Capital,* is also at the center of his microeconomic analysis. But it is not conventionally seen in this light for three reasons. First, the enormous intellectual alienation between the Marxist economics tradition and that of what is called the neoclassical school obscures parallels between their work. Microeconomics as we understand its role and scope today is a product of the neoclassical school (also sometimes referred to as the subjective value or marginal utility school), deriving from the roughly simultaneous discovery of the marginal principle by Jevons and Walras, as well as Menger, Marshall, and Clark, in the last decades of the nineteenth century. Neither the Marxists nor their foes have been particularly interested in comparing the

Jevonian/Walrasian and Marxist accounts as microeconomic analyses per se with a view to perhaps encouraging some fruitful interaction. I find this unfortunate and have come to believe that it has materially hindered the development of the discipline of economics.

Marx's treatment of the subject in the first volume of *Capital* is not particularly well presented. Into this lacuna have leapt several modern Marxist interpretations that obscure the microeconomic aspect. These interpretations, as I'll demonstrate shortly, have more in common with the metaphysics of Aristotle than with the materialism of Marx. They tend in particular to disguise the point that for Marx the most important point about a "commodity" is that it is a constellation of human social practices, which is to say that it is a microeconomics through and through.

But, third, it is a "micro" with very different properties than that of the Jevons/Walras tradition, so much so that they appear to be apples and oranges. The neoclassical micro rests, as we saw, on a theory of a historically transcendent human nature, a nature not essentially modified by society and culture. Marx's micro is an analysis of historically conditioned human social behavior. Ironically, Marx has much less determinist views about human economic and other social behavior than do his critics in the neoclassical camp.

Marx's microeconomics is, accordingly, multidimensional. One cannot deduce economic propositions in linear fashion from a few simple postulates about the nature of human nature. The key "deep" proposition of the subjective value school is that human nature is normally characterized by "utility-maximizing" behavior. To students especially, different (pseudo-) psychological or (pseudo-) historical narratives are typically offered to "explain" this. As was argued in chapter 1, we should put those aside. From the methodological and analytical standpoints, individualist utility maximizing is the little logical engine that makes the neoclassical paradigm go; it is the inferential pivot of that remarkably elegant theory, and that elegance is not a small factor in its widespread acceptance by professional economists. The Marxist microeconomic paradigm, by the very fact of its multidimensional analysis of human behavior, does not lend itself nearly so neatly to an architecture of "pure theory," although, as we'll see, it has its own intellectual merits.[1]

The contemporary expression of a Marxist microeconomics takes the form of commodities distributed via sale/purchase-in-time. But in order to show that we need to clear away some of the underbrush that has grown up around Marx's views about the characteristics, production, circulation, and consumption of commodities.

Commodity Form

Capital is a study of the production and circulation of "commodities." In the first instance the concept is meant to include virtually all the goods and services that are produced and sold within a capitalist economy.[2]

I do not find Marx's exposition of commodity theory as clear and trouble free as one would like; in fact, he later expressed reservations about his initial presentation as it appeared in the opening chapter of the first edition of *Capital*.[3]

Accordingly, I hope the following development of the subject will prove easier to follow and will result in a better grasp of the theory than would be the case if we followed the traditional exposition. It will also help in the reconstruction of the theory that will be necessary if we are to apply it to the microeconomic behavior characteristic of a modern economy.

For Marx, every commodity must be analyzed along four interacting, historically evolving dimensions or linked perspectives. Commodities don't issue from four "factors" or comprise four "components," nor can they be analyzed at four different "levels." Factors are often autonomous; as are components; different levels might suggest different levels of importance. Each such usage would introduce a distortion into Marx's greatly nuanced discussion of commodities. To say that we must analyze a commodity along four dimensions is to imply that each dimension is intrinsically linked to all the others, that there is no possibility of ranking them as differentially important or separable save in a purely analytical context. Therefore, a commodity is, in the first instance, "something" that satisfies certain stipulations set down about those four dimensions.[4]

In his discussion, Marx frequently illustrates the meaning he attaches to *commodity* by reference to cotton or linen cloth or thread, iron, (shoe) blacking, coffee, tea, gold and silver, wheat, and only a few other products. In honor of its primary place in the industry of mid-nineteenth-century Britain, the time of the writing of the first volume of *Capital,* we might focus on cotton or linen cloth or thread as our illustrative commodity of choice. To make the exposition simpler, at this beginning stage I will omit the analysis of commodities that take the form of services; their peculiarities can be brought in later.

The four dimensions? In the first instance, commodities are produced in order to be sold, to be exchanged. Here he differs from the neoclassicals in that he understands the forms of exchange to have changed in important ways over historical time; they continuously evolve. In this he treats them under the rubric of what he calls "value forms," which we will discuss in the next section. Second, the physical or physical-social properties of commodities are relatively uniform among themselves. This, of course, is the meaning of *commodity* that has best survived in current usage. Third, each is the product of a distinctive, more or less uniform labor process, and, finally, each has socially codified uses. We can take the points up in this order.

Value Forms in the Sphere of Exchange

For goods to qualify as commodities there must exist social mechanisms to circulate them from producers to consumers. In Marx's time commodities were circulated in the "market," that is, a social space containing mechanisms of exchange essentially similar to the modern neoclassical meaning of the word. It is imagined, as at present, that the competition between different would-be suppliers and purchasers establishes the price and that the price then influences the production process with the effect of decreasing it to some apt minimum.

For Marx, unlike the members of the neoclassical school, exchange or "the market" is not imagined to have a merely abstract, timeless, fixed form, like the neoclassical auction, for example. It has historically evolving stages with markedly different characteristics. It is here that we run into the problems particularly associated with the coquetry already mentioned. The following is a somewhat simplified account of a famously difficult and obscure part of the text of *Capital,* that is, volume 1, chapter 1, section 3.

He discusses, in order, four different value forms, that is, analytic characterizations of distinctly different stages in the evolution of markets or exchange. He does not provide an empirical-historical narrative of the evolution of exchange, but his heavily schematic rendering of that evolution directly suggests that he believes it could be so narrated. The characterization is cast in terms of changes in forms of value. For Marx, the value of a commodity refers to the necessary labor expended in its production, with the quantity of expended labor ultimately controlling the terms of exchange. Accordingly, *value* and *exchange value* are synonyms.

The historical phases comprise what he calls (1) the Elementary or Accidental form of value, (2) the Total or Expanded form of value, (3) the General form of value, and (4) the Money form of value. Thus, the first, the Elementary or Accidental form of value, describes a historic situation in which goods are produced and then exchanged against each other but so occasionally and erratically that their exchange value begins to approach but does not fully reflect the quantities of labor embodied in them, that is, their "true" value.

He writes,

> Every product of labor is, in all states of society, a use-value; but it is only at a definite historical epoch in a society's development that such a product becomes a commodity, viz., at the epoch when the labor spent on the production of a useful article becomes expressed as one of the objective qualities of that article, i.e., as its value. It therefore follows that the elementary value-form is also the primitive form under which a product of labor appears historically as a commodity, and the gradual transformation of such products into commodities proceeds *ceteris paribus* with the development of the value-form. ([1867] 1967: 67)

The Total or Expanded value form reflects a second, further phase in the evolution of exchange. Rather than erratic and occasional exchanges, the making and consequent trading of a wide range of goods has become regular and orderly. That of course means that different items now regularly compete against each other for the buyer's favor. Producers vie with one another, among other reasons, to sell profitably but at a lower price. Buyers can make choices not only between similar items but about the different sorts of things they might choose to buy. As in the familiar renditions of "the market" in the textbooks, this dynamic creates powerful pressure for the ratios of value governing the exchange of any two commodities to become less arbitrary and begin to stabilize. The ease or difficulty of producing different goods affects those exchange ratios more and more. As Marx writes,

> The accidental relation between two individual commodity owners disappears. It becomes plain, that it is not the exchange of commodities which regulates the magnitude of their value; but, on the contrary, that is the magnitude of their value which controls their exchange proportions. (69)

As the development of exchange continues, it

> becomes evident that, since the existence of commodities as values is purely social, this social existence, can be expressed by the totality of their social relations alone, and consequently that the form of their value must be a socially recognized form. (71)

Here we are at the phase of the General form of value as, for example, in societies where cattle, or perhaps tobacco, is singled out in everyday practice as a socially recognized and acceptable embodiment of the value contained in commodities in general and can therefore function as a kind of primitive "money."[5]

Fourth, we come to the Money form of value in which a single, special commodity is set aside, as it were, and its other use-values are subordinated (in the practices of the period) to its usage as a medium of exchange and a measure and store of value. Historically speaking,

> there is no difference between [the General form and the Money form], except that in the latter, gold has assumed the equivalent form in the place of [other possible commodities]. . . . The progress consists in this alone, that the character of direct and universal exchangeability . . . has now, by social custom, become finally identified with the substance, gold. (75)

For Marx, therefore, in its first dimension a commodity is a commodity only insofar as it appears in the sphere of exchange whose bidding processes will directly discipline its price. His concept underlines the view that, at least in the dimension of marketing, commodities are exchanged under changing historical forms, with the latter concretely expressing the evolving relations between producers and consumers. It is in this respect that his views are more amenable to the historically changing exchange practices expressed in contemporary sale/purchase relationships.

Aristotelian Marxism

The dynamic character of Marx's view of the exchange dimension is obscured in some influential contemporary accounts, having the effect of fixing in theoretical form what are often merely the peculiar features of the Victorian economy or even of some abstract capitalist economy in general. Since the issue is central to the present study, we might pause before considering the other dimensions of commodities to give an account of it.

In Paul Sweezy's widely read and (in so many respects) estimable *The Theory of Capitalist Development* (1942), an account is given of Marx's commodity theory that is distorted by the author's reliance on a conception of mental "abstraction" that is at considerable variance with Marx's expressed views. I want to devote some special attention to this issue not only because of Sweezy's influence on current Marxist theorizing but because my critique of Sweezy bears equally on the abstraction, the "ideal type," that we've already seen in some neoclassical theorizing.

The main point of similarity is that Sweezy views fundamental concepts in economics, such as the Marxist "commodity," primarily as the product of a process of ratiocination, namely, "abstraction," rather than as the temporary terminus of a continuing process of evolution in human social-economic behavior. In a subtle sense, he overemphasizes the abstract "thingness" of commodities at the expense of the social practices in which they are embedded.

It is my contention that Sweezy badly distorts Marxist commodity theory into a (social) metaphysics through his reliance on an Aristotelian conception of abstraction. Understanding this distortion will free us to recover and then further develop a modern commodity theory of a historical-materialist character.

Of course, abstraction is part of any intellectual activity, as when we abstract, that is, more or less ignore, the differences in several actual bits of fabric to form the abstraction "cotton cloth." One can abstract further from the differences among various specific commodities to form higher levels of generality, such as cotton cloth, then abstracting to cloth of natural fibers, then to cloth, then to woven material, and so forth, resulting in the term *commodity*, which indifferently incorporates every possible good or service that is exchanged. In Sweezy, the path toward understanding the concept of "commodity" is essentially based on such a procedure. He devotes the better part of his first chapter to describing what he takes to be Marx's use of abstraction. Starting with a quote from Marx's *Communist Manifesto* ("Society as a whole is more and more splitting up into two great hostile camps, into two great classes facing each other—bourgeoisie and proletariat"), he writes:

> This relation must form the center of investigation; the power of abstraction must be employed to isolate it, to reduce it to its purest form, to enable it to be subjected to the most painstaking analysis, free of all unrelated disturbances.
>
> The adoption of this position requires a procedure involving at least two fairly distinct steps.
>
> First, all social relations between capital and labor must be provisionally assumed away, to be reintroduced, one at a time, only at a later stage of the analysis.
>
> Second, the capital-labor relation itself must be reduced to its most significant form or forms. . . . Significance, in this context, is a question of the structural characteristics and tendencies of the whole society. Marx, as is well known, selected the forms of the capital-labor relation which arise in the sphere of production as the most significant for modern capitalist society. . . .

What is the nature of this capital-labor relation? In form it is an exchange relation. The capitalist buys labor power from the worker; the worker receives money from the capitalist with which he acquires the necessaries of life.

Hence, he proceeds to his conclusion and definition, stating that "whatever is customarily intended for exchange rather than for direct use is a commodity" (1942: 16–17).

Note his procedure: first, a one-sided mentalist process of abstraction to something he calls "structural" characteristics; and then within that abstract account the analytical separation of the concept of a "commodity" replete with an appropriate definition. The neoclassical "exchange" is just such an analytical separation of buying/selling practices from more concrete historical narratives.

What is wrong with this account? For a start, Sweezy describes a mental procedure that defines *commodity* as an Aristotelian type-concept or "universal," or sometimes an "essence." For him, the term *commodity* refers indifferently to all those things, goods, services, and labor-power, because they share the common property that they have use-values that are produced for and enter the processes of exchange. As a shorthand for Marx, that's quite adequate. But as a theoretical representation of Marx's "commodity" it is fundamentally inadequate and indeed a source of endless problems.

Marx himself criticized just such a procedure of abstraction in the work of the German writer Feuerbach. In his *Theses on Feuerbach,* written as early as 1845, he argued:

> Feuerbach resolves the religious essence into the human essence. But the human essence is no abstraction inherent in each single individual. In its reality it is the ensemble of the social relations.
>
> Feuerbach, who does not enter upon a criticism of this real essence, is consequently compelled:
> 1. To abstract from the historical process . . .
> 2. The human essence, therefore, can with him be comprehended only as a "genus," as an internal dumb generality which merely naturally unites the many individuals. ([1845] 1968: 29)

In my view, neither a Marxist commodity nor a neoclassical exchange is an "essence," or a "purest form," a dumb generality. It can only be comprehended as the ensemble of definite sets of social relations; it is fully part of the ensemble of the social relations that produce and surround it, which, of course, is a another way of saying "human social practices."

If one accepts the Sweezy view, two objectionable consequences immediately follow. First, and most important, Marx's own account of capitalist commodity production and exchange is complete in itself and therefore unchangeable. If we've reached by abstraction a "purest" form of "commodity," that indeed must be its fixed and final form. There can be no evolution beyond that purest form. Sweezy, like Feuerbach, has abstracted from the historical process to the "essence." Everything that has happened in capitalist commodity production and exchange since Marx's death must represent, therefore, merely an "inessential" variation on an already fully developed theme. But to take this view (as Sweezy actually does), I would argue, is to substitute a timeless Aristotelian conceptual universe for Marx's historical materialism. The parallel to much neoclassical theorizing in elementary microeconomics hardly warrants mention.

By way of contrast an outlook based in historical materialism opens the possibility that capitalist commodity production may have changed importantly in the nearly 120 years since Marx's death or, equally, since the discovery of the marginal principle; a conceptual universe resting almost solely on a mental process of abstracting emphatically precludes the possibility. Or, to put it another way, by rejecting the Sweezy procedure and result we open the way to inquiring whether, among other things, there are commodity practices that go beyond those of Victorian capitalism and perhaps even forms of value that go beyond the Money form. In fact, modern capitalism has indeed evolved beyond the Money form of exchange and toward the capitalization of every value (see chapter 8). But we are running ahead of ourselves.

Second, Sweezy's position raises insoluble epistemological questions concerning "structural characteristics." What is the status of so-called structural characteristics with respect to historic and material reality? Is the structure something different in kind from the manifold relations of the things themselves? In other words, what is the nature of the genus we arrive at following our abstracting process? Does the concept itself represent something "real," that is, something "more," than the reality of the historical concrete commodities? Is there both an empirical, historical "level" of reality and another, distinct structural level? Many Marxists think so, as when they turn to the Marxist metaphor about "base" (or structure) and "superstructure" (Marx [1857] 1968: 182) into a fundamental "type" distinction. I think Sweezy's position must inevitably entail something like that.[6]

Most importantly, note that in the Sweezy account clarity and precision of meaning are provided by the mental process of abstracting, that is, by putting aside or ignoring aspects of the reality he studies. Can such a process ultimately result in anything more than a "dumb generality"? I think not.[7]

Marx's epistemological position, if I judge him correctly, is diametrically different: certain human practices, because they converge and crystallize, can be clearly discerned in their uniform generality by the observer. Our ability to generalize—to abstract—is here achieved not on the basis of a purely inward mental process but by means of our direct reading of the convergent tendency of the historical process itself. Structure reveals itself not to the abstracting philosopher but to the social investigator reading the tendency of events. Structure = the tendency of events, not a phenomenon different from and acting on events. What the investigator discovers is that different practices influence one another over time, converging into crystallized social institutions such as the Money form. The abstractness of the Money form or of labor-power does not result from the philosopher's mental processes; it is the actual historical precipitate of convergent changes in social relationships. Thus, Marx avoids the unfortunate philosophical dualism that in my view has become part of Marxism today and, if I am right, of much other economics theorizing.

Commodities, I would argue, have an ineluctable historical character in all their dimensions, not just in their manner of exchange. They emerge in the evolution of human productive, distributive, and consuming practices. "Things" that weren't commodities become commodities at certain periods of time, and commodities themselves change in each of their dimensions. One hundred and fifty years ago cotton and linen dominated the commodity group "cloth and thread." They play a much smaller role now, since the advent of artificial fibers, which, not unexpectedly, rely on different raw materials, are differently produced within a radically different institutional/commercial setting, and have vastly different use-values. That is, petroleum, not the cotton plant, is our main source of fabric for, say, human clothing. Such cloth is produced not by firms specializing in textiles such as then dominated British industry but often now by great international firms in which textiles represent only one line of business, perhaps not even the most important one. Formerly produced by means of immense amounts of hand labor and mainly in only a few regions of Europe, they are produced now by relatively sophisticated, somewhat less labor intensive techniques all over the world. And, of course, the quite small range of different textiles produced for mostly cheaper, relatively standardized cloth for clothing has given way to an immense variety of textile commodities, with that phenomenon closely related to the rise of mass fashions in clothing and furnishings, with the associated desire for variety in texture, durability, warmth or coolness, dyeing, finishing, and styling. In one sense, modern fabrics occupy the place in "the market" formerly occupied by cotton and linen cloth; but to concentrate on that crude similarity would be to ignore the vast and importantly different role played by modern fabrics today in the demands we place on nature, on our workers and engineers, on the enormous changes in international marketing practices, and, not least, in the very different role that textile commodities play not merely in our society but in our culture.

The Second, Third, and Fourth Dimensions of the Commodity Form

The concept of a "commodity" as representing ensembles of human social practices with respect to the material social world is also central to our understanding of, and is confirmed by, the other dimensions of the analysis.

The second dimension of commodity form is that commodities are relatively uniform among themselves.[8] As indicated, the modern usage of the word suggests this still. The cotton or linen cloth and thread that were manufactured and distributed by Victorian firms ranged within a certain fairly narrow range of uniform characteristics, such as the fineness of the thread, the density of the weave, and the nature of the finish applied to the cloth. Essentially we are talking about the isolation and heightening by human action of certain purely physical features of natural fibers into a relatively uniform product. Thus—again—it would be incorrect to speak of the cloth as a purely physical thing; it is more adequately described as a physical-social or material-social thing. Indeed, we should emphasize the possible arbitrariness of the physical characteristics of the natural substance that are heightened in a commodity. There is no implication that the most naturally useful features of the linen or cotton fiber are heightened in the cloth. Marx is quite clear on this; the physical features that are seized upon and emphasized in the process of changing natural substances into commodities have a deeply social, not "natural," character.[9]

As to the third dimension, at any given time for any given commodity there will be a distinct social labor process, incorporating a certain historical level of human effort, machinery (or tools), and techniques for its production. About one-third of the first volume of *Capital* consists of industrial history as Marx traces the changes in machinery and other technologies, the human skills and organization involved, and even the legislative/social setting in which commodity production in cotton and other commodities was carried out in the nineteenth century. Theoretically speaking, Marx was most interested in showing that because of the historical development of productive and mercantile relations the production of a commodity, whether of a unit or an aggregate, tends to require a uniform effort within convergent productive practices on the part of the workers. Different commodities require different quanta of human effort (different amounts of labor-power, to use his idiom), but the production of different examples of the same commodity tends over time to require the expenditure of more or less the same amount of human effort measured in either the time expended by the worker or the proportion of the total human effort exerted within the economy. Analyses of these different exertions of human effort are referred to by Marx under the rubric "value." Much of his economic theory is devoted to showing how value is produced and then distributed within an economy and to what effect (i.e., how the labor effort exerted within an economy is distributed and with what effect on various classes of persons).[10]

In their fourth and final dimension, commodities have utility or use-value; they are useful things. It is very important to note here that for Marx the utility of things is not abstract, in the sense of Sweezy, and it departs as well from modern neoclassical usage. That is, to say "cloth is for wearing," "bread is for nourishment," "brick is for shelter," or "commodities have utility" is far too abstract, even metaphysical, to accurately render Marx's very concrete conception of use-values. Marx is careful to point out that the use-values of a given sort of commodity must have an actual social and historical character and not merely be useful to me or you "in general." The use-values of commodities are not ultimately "natural" but socially codified. It may have been "natural" to use linen for crude clothing before the widespread introduction of cotton. In some early period in Europe, then, the use-values of linen included clothing nakedness and retaining a degree of body heat. But because we no longer devote linen to such crude uses its ability to clothe nakedness or conserve body heat is not strictly part of its social use-value today. In more modern parlance, commodities are produced and circulated within contexts that socially codify their uses or their services or, in Marx's terminology, their use-values.[11]

Thus, the cotton cloth produced in Manchester in the 1850s was understood to have and be directed toward an identifiable range of socially codified uses such as supplying human clothing and meeting a few other household needs. That you or I might idiosyncratically use cotton cloth to insulate our attic or clothe a terrier is a phenomenon somewhat apart from the socially dominant and intended use-values of such cloth as a commodity at that time and in that locale.

It is when we consider together the four dimensions of a commodity, when we consider each, to use a Marxist-Hegelian term, as a reflex of the others, that Marx's essential conception emerges. A commodity is any social-material object with relatively uniform characteristics, produced in a truly social way (i.e., with widely used techniques, skills, and technologies), and circulated through an extensive market in a social setting in which its use-values (or services, to use the modern term) are to a dominant degree socially codified. And in each of these related dimensions a commodity reflects a definite phase of the evolution of human social-material practices and relationships.

Clearly, the cotton cloth commodity familiar to Marx did not emerge full-blown in the first half of the nineteenth century. Each of its dimensions was part of a relatively long evolution in the four dimensions that converge to crystallize into a commodity. We know, for example, that the species of cotton plants grown for commodity production were modified over time so as to make for a more uniform, easily worked product, which was more easily evaluated in the market and more suitable for the sort of combing, spinning, weaving, sewing, dyeing, and styling then customary. In a parallel evolution, machines were developed and modified to fit them to working with cotton of such quality as could be made cheaply abundant. Marx himself devotes much of the first volume of *Capital* to the changing technologies and work routines of, especially, the cotton textile industry. His second volume gives similar primacy to the development of forms and modalities of exchange. Thus, to keep in mind that we are talking of a multidimensional social form in which social-material objects appear, rather than about the "thingness" of commodities, I will often substitute the term *commodity form* for *commodity*.

This concept of a converging evolution along the four interacting dimensions is central to the concept of a commodity. Each dimension—physical-material, productive process, market assessment and exchange, and social use-values—acts on all the others, so to speak, and is acted upon in turn in an evolution that over a historical period altered cotton cloth from a sometime human artifact of greatly varying characteristics used by only a few into a uniform material, the uniformly produced, uniformly marketed, and uniformly used cotton commodity that Marx observed in his time.

I think the best way to characterize a Marxist commodity is to say that the term refers always and centrally to convergent dimensions of human social practices with respect to certain physical substances, changing the physical-social characteristics of those objects and propelling them toward historical intersections at which those practices crystallize.[12]

Commodities in Marx are never purely physical objects, with purely physical characteristics, produced by purely physical technologies for purely physical uses. They are socially modified physical substances around which human social practices converge to such a degree that they crystallize into nests of relatively stable social relations of production, circulation/distribution, and consumption. In studying commodities we are studying the socially patterned ways in which we—society—produce ourselves and our material-social life. In the last instance, the word *commodity* must connote for us not "physical thing" but "social practice," not freestanding materiality but a material locus of socially productive and kindred relations.

The Victorian Adolescence of Capitalism

Marx opens volume I of *Capital* with the observation that the capitalist world reveals itself as "an immense accumulation of commodities." Actually, this is far less a description of the world Marx lived in than a quite prescient extrapolation from the world he knew to the world that was already growing within it. In fact, in his time very few social-material substances rated as commodities for final consumers' consumption—cotton cloth and thread, yes, but not items of clothing! Other commodities included coal, coffee, tea, and sugar, a mere handful of products! If we estimate that he ceased writing around 1880, only then was fresh and cured meat evolving into full commodity form, particularly in the United States. Prior to that animals were slaughtered and processed for the most part only locally, so their value, their quality, and even their use-values (as exemplified by the great variation in local sausage types) varied greatly from one country to another, one region to another, and even one city neighborhood to another. In the United States, which led other industrializing countries in these matters, the pre–World War I period still featured pre- or incomplete commodity forms of dairy products, beer, produce, poultry, and most other items of final consumption. In my parent's youth in New York City in the early twentieth century, store-bought bread was the exception, although already one might have home-prepared loaves baked at the local bakery. That was also true of pies, cakes, and pastry. One might use locally procured wood or charcoal to provide what little heating was used in the household and, of course, to cook and to boil water for the laundry. All of these things—home fuel, poultry and eggs, dairy goods, produce, and bread—were on the way to becoming commodities. This wasn't a matter of occasional, and therefore erratic, barter between farmers and city people, but neither was there a smooth flow of relatively standardized items produced in standardized ways and distributed or circulated through standardized channels. That wouldn't occur in the United States until the interwar period and in many parts of Europe until the end of World War II.[13]

In Marx's day, I think it would be true to say that commodities occupied an important and visibly increasing role in social-material life but that most goods and services still took pre- or undeveloped commodity form. In our day, commodities entirely fill the screen of our social-material life. So many things have been commodified, they play such an intimate role in our public and private lives, and they bear so heavily on our social and cultural mores that the situation can barely be compared to that which Marx observed. I want to stress that Marx's preoccupation with commodity production and exchange is testimony to his prescience in reading "the laws of motion" of his society, not in reading what was actually present. Insofar as we understand the profoundly historical character of commodities we must be led to suspect that, almost in principle, the analysis Marx made of them must be at best primitive and sketchy and often out of focus. The problem, therefore, is to put commodities back into focus by examining the salient changes in the social practices that surround them in today's advanced capitalist economies.

A Note on Terminology

One of the aims of this study has been to bring together, with a view toward synthesis, elements of the two main disparate streams of theorizing about economic phenomena: the neoclassical tradition stemming from the late-nineteenth-century discoveries of, most prominently, Jevons, Walras, Marshall, Clark, and Menger; and the older, classical tradition represented by the work of Adam Smith, David Ricardo, and especially Marx. Briefly, the effort here has the double aim of recasting the neoclassical "micro" into historical-materialist terms while simultaneously furnishing Marxist theory with an adequate theory of final or consumer demand. Such an effort can easily provide an opportunity for confusion in the meanings of different terms. Lest such terminological confusion slip in, I want to reiterate three especially important usages. I have opted to replace the neoclassical and Marxist term *exchange* with the term *sale/purchase*. For these older traditions the simple and symmetrical term *exchange* is adequate since a sale from the standpoint of the seller is a purchase from that of the buyer, hence a single transaction. My preference for the term *sale/purchase* is meant to emphasize that over time, as we've seen, the relationship between the seller and the purchaser may change, that the relationship is normally nonsymmetrical and may have—often does have—a many-to-one character.

The term *commodity*, synonymous with *commodity form*, is used in this volume to refer to the material locus of an ensemble of social practices of at least four dimensions. Obviously, in modern usage *commodity* refers to only one of those dimensions. Finally, from the point of view of economics, commodities are comprised of ensembles of "services" (not to be confused with service commodities) or, almost equivalent, Marxist use-values. My use of both *services* and *use-values* is much closer to the modern meaning of the former but with one major proviso. As the analysis of sale/purchase-in-time makes clear, the services of a commodity are often transferred from buyer to seller only seriatim and not, as more familiarly, en bloc. Moreover, it appears to be a major feature of the modern commodity form that certain services, for example, the adaptability of a PC to add-ons, are socially bifurcated. As was explained in chapter 1, one may fully pay for such a service and yet only partially receive it in the initial sale/purchase. The full service is not transferred until later, when on payment of further monies one buys the, say, laser printer and thus finally obtains and can enjoy the actual use of the desired service. We will take up this discussion again in chapter 4, defining such bifurcated services as "quasi" or "potential" services. They will be shown to furnish the analytical element for the revised micro presented in this study.

On that understanding, we can summarize what has been discussed to this point by saying simply that we have been developing the microeconomics of the sale/purchase-in-time of the services that comprise modern commodities. We are now in a position to examine the further social relationships within which commodities are distributed and, especially, actually consumed.

3 | On the Social Relations of Distribution and Consumption

In the Victorian era economy, which Jevons and Marx, for example, actually observed, there was only a small to nil public sector providing "social welfare" and related services and only a relatively small amount of private and church-related "charity." Market exchange of commodities was undoubtedly the most important way in which goods and services were distributed for "final" or consumer's consumption.[1]

In our own day individuals and families purchase and consume private sector goods and services within a wider social context of higher or semi-guaranteed earnings that are the product of the modern welfare state. Moreover, the social and cultural effect of the welfare state, most notably in education and health services, has fundamentally altered the kind and the quantity of private sector commodities purchased and consumed and, of course, how we consume them. Naturally, we don't live in two economic universes, as our private purchases and state provided services tend to complement and otherwise condition one another. Accordingly, this change poses an analytical problem that we must address if we are to give a useful account of modern consumption issues. Obviously, we need an analytical scheme that incorporates equally the so-called final consumption of both private sector commodities and the goods and especially services provided by the public authority. We will treat these matters under the category "social relations of consumption."[2]

What I want to show in this chapter is that the different social relations of consumption normally occur as constituent parts of wider ensembles of social relationships with producer institutions, both the public authority and the private firm, to such an extent and in such a manner that we find not "final" or "terminal" consumption but forms of productive consumption. What one is really arguing is that consumption in a modern economy is normally linked to and conditioned by its further productive effects on the consumer as producer. It has a feedback effect and, as we shall see, something more as well.

In a modern or advanced economy the two most important kinds of social relations of consumption are exhibited in the (public sector) administrative relationship and through the (private) sale/purchase state or sale/purchase-in-time. Typically, the first is thought to impose a degree of constraint on the citizen-consumer because, as with elementary schooling or fire services, all of us are compelled to pay for them through the tax system, thus hindering our ability to provide alternatives to the services via the private sector. However, there are further, equally significant kinds of constraints on the consumption of public sector goods and services, and these are not dissimilar to those we find in sale/purchase-in-time.

Social Relations of Consumption I: Administrative Relations

Schooling, for example, and public health measures such as vaccination are often directly "administered" to the client by a government office or functionary, that is, across an administrative relationship, the terms of which are an administrator or functionary on one side and the client on the other. That peculiar relationship has not to my knowledge been sufficiently analyzed as a social relation of consumption, that is, an ongoing relationship in which the client receives and then consumes services and goods under the aegis of the administrator and/or his or her office. The following characterization of the modal administrative relationship is severely condensed but adequate to the present inquiry.

Imagine someone of no unusual social influence, perhaps yourself, dealing with some large, public-service-providing government institution, say, dealing with a school official over your desire for your primary school daughter to do something just a little bit out of the ordinary, perhaps to enroll in a French class. Imagine yourself entering and sitting down in the office of the teacher, departmental chairperson, or other official. How do we characterize the relationships between the two people in that encounter?

1. Your relationship with the official, nominally one-on-one, is in fact a one-to-many relationship since he or she represents a significant institution and its rules, procedures, and so forth. The client—in this case, you—represents merely you and your family.

2. The official will normally have more than a little information

about you "from the files"; in this respect, although he or she is anonymous to you, the files provide a good indication of your social, economic, cultural, and perhaps even personal characteristics.

3. The official is a specialist on the particular rules and regulations, procedures, and priorities of the institution with which you are coping; often you can be put off with the flat declaration, "It can't be done!" and it is then up to you to divine whether it can be done, how, and by whom. In short, the official operates in a relatively knowing way in the relationship, and you function in a relatively unknowing way.

4. The official has a menu of organizational assets with which to act should he or she choose to; you have only your personal persuasiveness and, of course, your potential power as part of the group "parents."

5. The official's attention to the problem is relatively enduring; his or her memory of the matter can operate after you have left the building. He or she has, so to speak, "institutional memory." To the point, most administrative decisions affecting your child are made when you are not present. That is, however important an effect you might have on this or that issue, the overall pattern of effects operating on your child lies in the first instance at the school's, here the official's, disposal.

6. The initiative to act on the matter at hand rests entirely with the official; you mostly react. His or her decision, say, to refuse admission to a French class, made in a moment, can often be undone, but that reversal is likely to take up considerable amounts of your time.

7. The official probably has personally and directly the power to satisfy or deny you, for example, by signing a form; your sanctions are more extended in time and normally will involve the cooperation of others, as in a petition or a motion made at a parents meeting.

8. You need to persuade the official to act favorably; the official needs to keep his or her job, that is, your need is immediate while the official's, though ultimate, is distant from your present encounter and therefore its influence is normally weaker.

One can see how the term *bureaucracy,* as it is used in either the negatively polemical or Weberian senses, is inadequate to grasp a relationship so frequently found between an individual and the various public "bureaucracies" that provide essential services for consumption. In fact, my choice of a school example underestimates the possible one-sidedness of functionary-client relationships. Had we chosen, say, the sort of relationship found in an unemployment or tax office, the odds would be more against you. At any rate, the concept of an eight-dimensional "administrative relationship" gets much closer to the truth, especially to the roots of the power of the administrator to constrain the client's access to certain services and perhaps, as with the child's education, to exercise a degree of constraint over the very process of the consumption of the service. Taking one thing with another, government-administered services, even when they are not compulsory on the client, have a degree of constraint in the mode of their delivery and final consumption. It goes without saying that this constraint reflects wider government and social policies about, among other things, the characteristics of today's and tomorrow's labor force.[3]

It seems equally the case that those administrative relations we enter into with the private sector, as with warranties, auto and health insurance, or union-administered pension schemes, and so on, don't really differ. Their constraint may even be more powerful over time, for there we have only a contractual standing whereas in the public sector we are citizens. In both cases the phenomenon of constrained consumption is not by any means a minor one.

This eight-dimensional analysis of administrative relationships is representative of the normal case when we deal with an institution over a service we need or want it to provide. There is a ninth dimension as well, namely, our own skill and social status. If the client is also an administrator or manager, he or she will normally be more skillful and/or experienced in institutional lore than, say, a bus driver, clerk, or housewife. Similarly, if the client is a professor of French at the university or some other celebrity or specialist in the subject at hand, he or she may overwhelm the other eight dimensions and win easily. If, however, the administrator is highly placed in the organization while the client is just an ordinary "consumer," then this ninth dimension tilts the relationship even further against the client.

Administrative relationships are normally tilted relationships, and that tilting occurs to some significant degree in one, some, or all of the cited dimensions. For the client, this is among the most important forms of constrained consumption of some of the critical services through which the work force is produced. Administrative relationships also provide the historical and social context within which we carry out the purchase and subsequent consumption from the private sector of contemporary goods and services.

Social Relations of Consumption II: The Sale/Purchase State

I want to turn now to the main kind of social relations of consumption, those that are present in modern commodity form. Here we pick up again the microeconomic thread that is central to this study. These relations occur within or directly as a result of the sale/purchase of many, almost surely most of the private sector consumption commodities. We want to uncover how they, no less than government-administered social services, are distributed and consumed in socially constraining ways. And we want to see how these, too, generally comprise a "productive" and not merely terminal or final consumption.

As we have seen, a characteristic of commodity form analysis is that commodity forms manifest themselves socially. They take the form of dominant social practices that can be readily observed. As was argued earlier, commodities represent a convergence and crystallization of human social practices with respect to the social material world. By no means is the investigator looking to divine, as in Plato, the occult "Forms" that cast deceptive shadows on the wall of the cave. He or she is looking to see where and how social practices take on such codified form that they force themselves on the consciousness of the investigator. I do not claim that commodity analysis is simple, like reading a sports page, but the information from which one starts must be simple and observable and its patterns insistently discernible, the way radio music is distinguishable from background static. In Marx's still useful terminology, they must be "socially manifest."

In introducing sale/purchase-in-time we began with automobiles, electronic equipment, insurance and health plans, and semiprepared foods. These are all specifically "modern" commodities that play a significant role in the lives of modern consumers and the activities of modern producers. All have of themselves a notable quantitative significance in a developed economy; for example, prepared, semiprepared, and related foods now make up at least one-third the dollar volume of annual food sales in the United States (*Statistical Abstract* 1999: table 1279). Finally, their commodities characteristics seem to me to readily typify those of the great range of modern commodities and even the modern tendencies of many old and familiar commodities.

Several findings that emerged from the earlier microanalysis can be summarized here. First, the actual consumption of the services of the commodities in question incorporates a temporal social relationship with the producer, which typically endures throughout the life span of that commodity. By way of contrast, in the old bidding market, the producer/seller of a commodity is imagined to have only a fleeting, immediately terminated relationship with the consumer/buyer. Here, instead, there is a finite duration of time, a span of time in which the buyer and the seller continue to have active, definite, and significant economic/ social relationships built around purchase and consumption.

Second, within that time interval or state, the actual consumption of the services of the commodity by the consumer/purchaser is normally dependent on the continuing cooperation of the producer/seller. That is, the consuming relationship is normally an unequal one wherein the purchaser/consumer comes in some material way to depend on the future actions of a seller/producer for the duration of the sale/purchase state. Again we meet a form of constrained rather than free "final" consumption.

Third, consumption within that interval also involves the consumer/buyer in equally potent and dependent relationships with institutions that are not party to the original sale/purchase. Again, by way of contrast, the market is imagined to erase all relationships between the consumer and the earlier owners or producers of the commodity in question; in fact, this erasure is what Marx had in mind in his lengthy discussion of the "fetishism of commodities" in *Capital* ([1867] 1967: chap. 1). The modern sale/purchase relationship is not, as imagined in the classic market, a symmetrical one-to-one relationship but a nonsymmetrical, many-to-one relationship, that is, a typically somewhat one-sided social relationship of consumption between multiple producer/sellers and one person or family. This characteristic of modern commodities, like the distinction between the actual and potential services of the car at point of sale, underlines for us the increasingly social character of the inner processes of modern consumption and further emphasizes the normally unequal character of the sale/purchase relationship.

Further Observations on Modern Sale/Purchase

The distinction between the actual and potential services of a commodity became a manifestly social characteristic of vehicle sales only in the twentieth century. In this the auto industry was the pioneer, particularly General Motors. Prior to the rise of GM to automotive prominence in the 1920s, cars were simply sold by the manufacturer like any other classic commodity so that the dichotomy between actual and potential services was only a natural phenomenon and not of particular importance in social material practices. At that earlier time, the further maintenance and repair of the vehicle was left to whatever arrangements the owner might choose to make with others. Ford, the industry giant before the rise of GM, offered its famous Models T and A, but they were technologically primitive even for the time. This was deliberate on Ford's part. They were designed primarily for farmers, who, it was imagined, were as capable of rewelding a broken axle on a car as on a farm wagon—or had ready access to the same sort of primitive repair services as would fix a hay rake or a plowshare (Jardim 1970: 118ff.; Lacey 1986: 102ff.).

General Motors' cars were different, and that difference has set the standard for cars even since. They were overtly designed for city dwellers.[4] There were two related, dominant factors in the change. First and most obvious, as the 1920 U.S. Census had revealed, the urban population of the country had exceeded the rural for the first time. If one was to find an expanding market for the auto-manufacturing business, it had to be keyed to city dwellers. Moreover, the GM people realized that whole new classes of auto users would become important, most notably women, who would presumably want a more user friendly vehicle, and those who "motored," that is, drove primarily for pleasure.[5]

Accordingly, GM sold cars within a system of "forward satellites" (dealerships), which would continue to service the vehicle, provide spare parts, offer major repair services, and even stock optional items such as radios. That way of doing business soon became a modal feature of the modern auto industry, and I think this point establishes the disjunction between the actual and potential services of the car as a commodity feature, not merely an accident of modern selling or a "natural" feature of the car. Practically speaking, the buyer/consumer was thereby made dependent on GM or its licensees for spare parts and typically at least some of the services performed on the car. Even if one goes to an independent auto mechanic, the latter is dependent on GM for service manuals and on GM or one of its licensees for replacement parts. If, as is usually the case, the buyer/consumer will sell the car before "running it into the ground," the price he or she receives for it will be importantly influenced by GM's engineering and sales behavior during the span of the relationship, that is, through the time subsequent to the initial sale. In short, sale/purchase creates not only a significant continuing relationship between GM and the consumer but one in which the consumer is in an essentially dependent mode. I don't claim that this is a dire dependency; the facts won't bear that interpretation. But it is clear that in the time period in which the consumer owns and uses a GM car, his or her fortunes are significantly affected by GM's behavior. And yet the consumer has little power to affect that behavior.[6]

To buy a car today also creates a set of continuing relationships with agencies and groups that are not parties to the original sale. The car owner must license the vehicle, insure it, and fill it from time to time with gasoline, oil, wiper fluid, glycol, brake fluid, and so forth. Here the acquisition of the car, which of itself initiates a relationship with GM, also initiates for the purchaser/consumer a set of not dissimilar relationships with a state licensing bureau, the auto insurance industry, the petroleum industry, at some point perhaps the tourist industry, and possibly others. These relationships, which were more or less absent in Victorian selling, are now modal and as such should be entertained as part of modern commodity form.[7]

For analytical purposes, we can say that as it is sold the car as a whole comprises only quasi services, that is, services that can be brought out and enjoyed only when they are complemented with other quasi services within the sale/purchase state. This, of course, is literally true. To enjoy integral services, to consume them, requires that roads have already been built and are maintained by others, that others are ready to provide gasoline and other road services, that such services are widely available, that someone has created a backup system for maintenance and repairs, and so forth. These, too, only represent quasi services until they are combined with the car to create integral services, services that can actually be consumed by the owner/driver.[8]

The continuing, dependent relationships established between the auto maker and auto consumer are in a sense technologically driven, as is that which the auto consumer enters into with the petroleum industry. The situation is somewhat altered when we look at the markets that have been constructed for refrigerators, home heating units, cooking stoves (both conventional and microwave), air conditioners, and such. In each case, the manufacturer tries, through the warranty as well as such technological devices as continuing design changes, to maintain the relationship with the buyer, and there is an important degree of continuing support and repair services offered and used. But here the situation is not as dramatic as in the case of automobiles, although, insofar as a home appliance, for example, needs replacement parts and electricity to run and food to put into it, it has only quasi services as sold.

For some appliances the sale/purchase relationship is typically directed not toward services, repair, or the sale of add-on equipment but toward persuading the refrigerator buyer to purchase another appliance—an air conditioner, home freezer, or cooking stove—with the same brand name or to make a follow-on purchase when it is time to replace the original item. Companies such as General Electric and GM, which pioneered the home refrigerator business, also pioneered many related lines of business, especially the production of air conditioners, home freezers (now typically included in the refrigerator), and more recently home humidifiers and dehumidifiers.

The relation-creating and relation-extending character of modern commodity form is even more pronounced when we look at the patterns found in the area of electronics for home consumption. One buys the television so that one can watch programs, the compact disc player so that one can enjoy music on CDs that will be separately (and subsequently) purchased, the videocassette recorder (VCR) so that one can rent or record films. The appliance itself plays a much smaller role in the overall relations between consumer and the several producers than does a refrigerator or air-conditioning unit. Basically, it is a ticket to commodities such as CDs or digital video discs (DVDs). The pattern is somewhat more mixed in home sales of personal computers, since the latter often require extensive add-ons—a mouse, a modem, an ergonomic keyboard, a special desk or stand, a printer, an eye-saving screen, disks, and so forth. At the same time, additional services are common—an Internet connection, a Web page, software that is continuously upgraded—so that PC distribution combines the features of both goods and services in a single commodity.[9]

Looking at the same phenomenon from the side of the prepared and semiprepared food industry shows the complementarity of modern marketing strategies. The modern food industry now provides not only frozen, canned, or dried semiprepared foods but also fresh but incompletely prepared foods such as typically need only to be heated or parboiled, additionally spiced, and so on by the home food preparer. We can consider this form of consumption to be a sort of second wave, that is, a mode of consuming that assumes a population already used to purchasing foods that are semiprepared. From frozen dinners and cake mixes, it is only a small step—though a huge commercial one—to making available to home preparers such foods as ready-mixed and washed salads, fresh cuts of meat that are already marinated, fresh pasta in need of only brief cooking, and so forth. Again we see the phenomenon of quasi services, which embody and then require combination with the quasi services provided by the microwave seller or the maker of bottled salad dressing, in order to become integral services at the family dinner table. When this occurs, the purchaser/consumer becomes a coproducer of the services of the commodity.

It does appear that in a wide range of contemporary goods and services their relation-creating and relation-expanding character is prominent, constraining the consumer to remain in a tilted relationship with an institution, or more likely a network of institutions, as a condition for the normal use of one's car, air conditioner, microwave, video recorder, CD player, or PC.[10]

I have deliberately refrained from discussing the role of advertising primarily because I want to emphasize the importance of the real and one-sided social relationships represented in sale/purchase and not just the symbolic phenomena of advertising. It is undoubtedly true that advertising plays a major role in those relationships, with the emphasis on *in*. Advertising does not constitute the relationships, a point not at all clear in the consumerist literature pro and con. Purely symbolic transactions and relations between producer and consumer are but one element in the constellation of such preeminently social relationships and often not the most important. For example, advertising is deeply influential in, say, our choosing an sport utility vehicle over a compact or a Ford over a Chevy, but the need to make such a choice comes from the fact that a transportation system built around private ownership of a vehicle is now socially imposed on the potential buyer, as is the subsequent need to keep it serviced, insured, inspected, and so forth. For most adults most of the time, one must own a car and thus enter the systems that maintain it. It is mostly within that real social imperative that advertisers work their magic.

To continue, even when the one-sidedness of the sale/purchase-in-time is disguised, it too often emerges when the commodity as sold is what is called in the auto business a "lemon." To get a faulty VCR or PC replaced or avail oneself of the medical services a health maintenance organization (HMO) seemed to promise is often a lesson in the essential inequality of modern sale/purchase relations and of our inability to avoid entering into them.[11]

Medical, insurance, retirement, and investment plans each overtly establish a continuing relationship between the producer and the consumer. Each in the nature of the case entails an expansion of the relationship beyond the original parties: the medical plan creates definite networks of relations between the potential patient and the actual providers of medical services and insurance and retirement plans involve one in relationships with the firms the insurance or retirement plan in which the carrier invests. Here, as earlier, the social relationship of consumption on one side involves an individual or family and on the other involves a typically large producing institution with links to the other producing institutions brought into the sale/purchase relation by that initial relation. The degree of dependence this brings to the consuming relationship always varies and its intensity in each case must be individually investigated, but it is always present and almost always significant.

"Engineered" Markets and Commodity Form

One could, of course, methodologically treat a car sale much as Jevons/Walras microeconomics treats any other purchase, that is, as a set of transactions no more related to one another in the economic sense than the choice, say, to divide one's income between food and clothing. Or one might aggregate the various choices involved in buying and maintaining the car. Then all the utilities the purchaser gained from the purchase could be interpreted in part as a set of anticipations operative at the instant of a sale/purchase and the future costs of operating and maintaining the vehicle as "disutilities" that the purchaser/consumer thoroughly considers in the showroom at the moment of the sale. From a purely intellectual, even analytical standpoint, the way in which we analyze the sale/purchase of a car is not, in the last analysis, forced on us. While the greater realism and naturalism of the analysis of the sale/purchase-in-time is clear enough, "realism" and "naturalism" don't always provide the final, decisive, scientific word in choosing between competing analyses.

Even the conundrums found (in chapter 1) to accompany the Jevons/Walras micro need not be fatal; no scientific analysis worth its salt is ever complete, final, or static. Often it is precisely the problem areas of a theory or analysis that eventually open up the way to future understanding, future breakthroughs.

It is in commodity form analysis per se that I find the superiority of the proposed microeconomics manifest. It is clear that the various features that were found within the sale/purchase state were not in any sense accidental. They are all integrally connected to the evolution of modern business methods in the production and marketing of goods and services, methods that have swept the older practices from the field; even Ford was quickly forced to copy the GM way of doing business. In short, it is when we realize that the features of the sale/purchase do in fact represent hard won evolutionary changes in codified economic and business practices as well as in the most important modes of consumer's consumption that we have sufficient reason to displace modern day variations of the Jevons/Walras microeconomics, adopting instead the microeconomics of sale/purchase-in-time, which better grasps the salient features that make a twenty-first century capitalist economy different from a mid-nineteenth-century one.[12]

The concept of commodity form incorporates, in the first instance, the fact that the production and marketing of "privately" produced goods and services is distorted when we characterize them as a form of exchange. We saw most prominently in the auto example that the services of the car were not entirely transferred from the seller to the buyer at the point of sale but rather were serially alienated across a period of time. This aspect of modern sale/purchase was central to the new relationship that GM was consciously trying to forge with its customers. It was a relationship that would carry with it further capitalistic advantages that could not be garnered if cars continued to be made and sold in the older, Ford way.

By shifting to the design and production of a car that retained links to the seller several important new lines of business opened up for GM and in fact enabled it to rapidly surpass Ford as the world's leading car manufacturer. For a start, GM, through its franchised dealers, gained a very large and profitable business in repairs and auto parts. Second, this extended repairs and services empire of itself enabled GM to add an innovative technological dimension to cars that the old Ford system had prohibited. New features such as self-starters, high-compression engines, and later automatic transmissions both required technical backup from the company and encouraged car buyers to rely more on GM services and parts. The company further encouraged a continuing relationship with its customers by introducing the annual model changeover and attempted to produce more aesthetically pleasing cars in different colors and so on. Naturally, this placed GM and its dealers at the center of an additional and very profitable automobile market, the market for used cars. Finally, GM pioneered the consumer loan to would-be car buyers, literally financing its own sales. In short, a Ford sale was a one-off. No capitalistically advantageous relationship between producer and consumer was established. The new GM way of doing business used the initial sale of a car to a customer to try to establish a number of concrete, continuing relationships with that consumer, and in practice it frequently succeeded.[13]

One can fruitfully sum up these changes by saying that with the GM way of marketing, eventually adopted by virtually all major U.S., later international firms, modern capitalism ceased to treat markets are neutral and "natural" social spaces in which bidders and takers merely call out the prices they desire.[14]

This phenomenon has been misidentified, misnamed, thus misanalyzed by calling it monopoly. Recall that a monopoly is a phenomenon of the classic market. It assumes, for example, that the various sellers are selling essentially substitutable goods in a situation in which demand is more or less fixed, that is, a definite demand schedule is assumed in the analysis. But modern corporate selling doesn't occur in classic markets, the various sellers normally avoid direct head-to-head price competition by varying their product lines by means of unique features—style, color, imputed panache, and so forth—and, more important, they try to expand demand in both the qualitative and quantitative dimensions. Finally, modern firms are diversified producers that can and will subsidize some of their product divisions in order to gain a stable market share; they simply can't be priced out of a "market" in which they wish to participate, and any attempt to do so would be ruinous for the competition.

A big firm really cannot retain a monopoly even on technological grounds against its competitors. For example, SONY tried to retain such a monopoly with its Beta system of video recording, which was vastly superior to the alternate VHS system. But by restricting and overpricing licenses for the Beta system, it merely encouraged other electronics firms to use, proliferate, and improve the rival system to such an extent that Beta has lost all its markets in the English-speaking world. All in all, modern firms are not fragile, as monopoly theory assumes; they are robust enough to force their rivals to coexist with them.

It was a truly historic change in marketing when firms such as GM, Sears, and General Electric learned to engineer the size, shape, and processes of markets, even to the extent of infusing them with credit so as to assure that they would have the high (volume) absorbency, the steady rhythm, and the adaptability over time that was needed at the sales end to absorb as systematically as possible the high volume of mass and large batch production of ever new kinds and classes of goods and services (Averitt 1968). These are the crystalline social practices of the modern commodity form.

Other characteristically modern social-commercial practices complement and extend this concept of engineered markets. These include the brand name, manufacturer-extended credit (culminating in the credit card), franchises and other forward satellites, advertising, provision of support and upkeep services, product tie-ins, discount cards, and so forth. In a modern economy I think it fair to say, markets for the different commodities are designed with as much care as their productive processes and equivalently weighty amounts of capital are invested to create "marketing channels" through which those commodities will smoothly and massively flow from ultimate producer to final consumer. The sale/purchase state-in-time is the element that, aggregated and combined, constitutes the marketing channel.[15]

The government has also contributed to the reshaping of markets from "natural" to engineered institutions. Through Keynesian and welfare state policies, governments have both raised and stabilized consumer incomes, pumped monies into underdeveloped regions, provided for more stable currencies and surer sources of credit for both producers and consumers, and, most important of all, altered the productive characteristics of the work force. At both the national and international levels, governments have striven to standardize such commodity components as screws, washers, voltages, weights and measures, dosages, nutritional requirements for vitamins, and standards of purity and freshness.[16]

In a second coordinate dimension of commodity form, there has been a vast proliferation of not uniform but families of commodities. Part of this has come from the private attempts of the various firms to create and/or find and then fill each niche in the "market." Thus, automobiles come in many sizes, models, prices, and colors and with varying options. Music is available in the record shops to fit the infinite varieties of taste, as are PCs, TVs, and other appliances. A modern supermarket is a veritable cornucopia of foods and other goods, so much so that, as I directly remember, travelers from poorer countries coming to the United States a half century ago regularly included supermarkets among the tourist sites they wanted to visit. As a rule the modern word *goods* has replaced the older *commodities,* and conventionally the latter is now reserved for such items as wheat, steel, raw coffee, sugar, and so forth. Today, the point of mass production is not merely to turn out masses of relatively standardized, relatively interchangeable products and consumer goods but to make sure that there is also massive, exhaustive variation in what is marketed.

Perhaps the major point about the proliferating production of commodities is how that production has become so intimately tied to the sales effort. Modern production processes cannot really be conceived as separate in any way save analytically from the distribution of the things they produce. Production and distribution are reflexes of one another, not, as in Marx, distinct "spheres" organized on different principles. Whether a mass production run can be considered in the first place is obviously tied to the anticipation that the run can be disposed of in a timely and profitable way. Thus, the choice of productive method is in part a function of the sales effort, as are the engineering and design characteristics of the items in question. Even the packaging is considered from a unitary sales/manufacturing standpoint. Reflexively, one cannot consider a mass marketing campaign unless the good or service in question lends itself to a process of mass or large batch production.[17]

I will not belabor the point that the processes of both production and consumption in a modern economy have evolved in tune with the other dimensions of commodity form. To draw an example from the realm of consumption, the introduction of home refrigeration to general social use made possible and encouraged a new codified social pattern of food consumption and use. From a situation in which consumers at, say, the turn of the century purchased and used a narrow range of staples, often of local origin, such as flour; salted, smoked, or canned meat; winter vegetables for storage; and fresh fruit and vegetables but only locally grown and in season, the combination of the refrigerator rail car and the home refrigerator helped to create a much more varied diet and the national, now international, market in foods of all sorts to supply it. In short, home refrigeration, later the home freezer, and even later the microwave oven helped to create for consumers a wider net of relations of consumption with a wider, more intricate network of food producing and distributing institutions. Here the dependent relationship between the consumer and the producer is not as marked as in the auto area, a matter more of changed social custom and practice than, as with autos, a sometimes dire technological dependency.

It is very difficult at present to conceive of the processes of final consumption, even within the home, as occurring independently of the larger, modern economy. One can investigate one's own daily pattern of consumption, and there it is indeed difficult to find a product or service that was available in the precorporate era or can be consumed without continuing assistance from one or more corporations. In many cases, we have even had to be taught by "the" economy" how to consume these new things: how to drive, thaw and prepare frozen food, use a PC, or operate a video recorder. Alternately, "the economy" has also "untaught" us, so to speak, the skills of the previous generation, for example, how to bank a coal fire, strop a razor, shell peas, or care for a horse.

There is a story that used to make the rounds of advertising agencies and may or may not be true. It does, however, make a point. It is said that when firms such as General Mills first introduced prepared cake mixes to the supermarket shelves, all one had to do was to add water and throw it in the oven. The product didn't sell well until producer and advertiser learned that the housewife was being asked to do too little. If she wasn't really "to bake a cake," why not just buy one already made? Sales took off only after the recipe and the instructions were altered so as to require that the housewife add eggs. In short, the housewife had to be an active partner with the manufacturer in the production of that "home-baked" cake. It's an appealing story, but, more the point, it is now modal that even in the home we work in partnership with the producers, distributors, and sellers of commodities to coproduce their and our desired services. This coproduction may be as trivial as checking the oil in the car, as elaborate as programming the VCR, or as intricate as using a word-processing program to write a novel or purchasing whole sets of power tools and how-to manuals to remodel the basement.

"Final" Consumption as Productive

Earlier I interrupted the microeconomic narrative to discuss the state-citizen administrative relationship mainly with a view toward establishing the idea that the development of the consumption of school, health, and other publicly administered benefits was to a significant degree a form of both dependent and productive consumption. It was dependent within the administrative relationship and productive in that the consumption of the benefits had a definite historical relationship to the evolution and production of a modern labor force. Granted that the "final" or consumer consumption of modern commodities occurs within sale/purchase-in-time in one-sided, somewhat dependent relationships; it can also be shown to be a form of productive consumption.

First, and most obviously, is the sense that some consumption of consumer goods directly contributes to, and makes possible, productive activity on the part of the work force. This is trivially true of the food the worker consumes, of work clothing, of any tools he or she may be required to own. In still another sense, the car that takes the worker to work, transports his or her groceries, or takes the children to school serves to support or alter the productive characteristics of the work force and in that sense is a form of productive consumption.[18]

In the general case, insofar as the services of a car, semiprepared food, a PC, or a medical plan materially abet or enhance any of the productive characteristics of the purchaser/consumer, its consumption is obviously productive as well. Of course, if, unlike "those brutal South Americans" Marx referred to, we left individuals to consume things entirely by and according to their own personal lights, we could still speak of a "private" and "final" consumption. But our practices of consumption are codified in such definite social modes and processes that they directly and with discrimination result in the production of different productive characteristics in different parts of the work force. To overlook this would be to overlook the evolution of business and social change during the past full century.

There is a second, more subtle dimension in which the consumption of, say, the car's services by the new owner/consumer is also a form of productive consumption. This feature turns on the many-to-one character of sale/purchase, already commented on, and from the constraint on the purchaser/consumer to maintain the car in good repair and operating order. Basically, the sale/purchase state is socially embedded in different nests of social relations of production. Of course, looked at from the side of the purchaser/consumer, the sale/purchase relationship appears to be consumption, pure and simple. But from the side of the seller/producer that sale/purchase state is a constituent, complementary element in its business strategy. As the early history of GM's innovations reveals, sale/purchase-in-time has institutionally evolved as a complement to the productive activities of the producing/selling firm. Because modern markets are engineered, the so-called final consumption of the consumer of the several quasi services of the car is an intrinsic part of a larger, dominant productive relation that is socially coordinated with the production of the complementary quasi services by the producer. In other words, it is an element of modern commodity form.

In this sense, the sale/purchase state, which we have heretofore conceived to begin at the point of sale, is actually prefigured in the linked engineering and marketing strategies of the industry. For a car of a certain model and year, the firm can anticipate for any definite time period a more or less definite quantum of demand for this or that replacement part or optional feature. That's at one end of the spectrum. In addition, the vacation and tourist industries, like the petroleum industry, make their calculations of demand for their services or products based on the numbers and kinds of cars sold (or leased) in a given year—corrected by other, statistically generated trend data. Sale/purchase relationships, from the standpoint of the producers/sellers, range across the spectrum of definiteness from those two poles, from direct, concrete relationships with definite groups of consumers in some instances to essentially statistically generated relationships. But, in terms of the time dimension, they typically precede the actual sale/purchase engaged in by the eventual consumers.

There is a third dimension to the productive character of consumers' final consumption as well, that is, where the consumption of the commodity serves to produce or coproduce further services. For some industries this is a central feature of their business. In the case of semiprepared foods, stereo equipment, or PCs, the consumer/seller must cooperate in, respectively, finishing the preparation of the food, in choosing and purchasing discs, and in purchasing and then using services such as the Internet. These new services are manifestly coproduced. This coproduction is also of especial economic and commercial importance in medical and dental insurance schemes. There the services are offered passively by the provider while the strategy and initiative of one's own health or dental care are left to the consumer/purchaser. In that sense, the coproduction of the actual services is intrinsic (not merely complementary) to the insurer's productive process. Often, of course, this coproduction takes place within an administrative relationship.[19]

There is a fourth and particularly striking way in which the consumption of the consumer/purchaser has a productive character. Recall that in purchasing the car one pays for a number of potential services, which will have to be complemented later in the sale/purchase state with the purchase of further quasi services. One pays for better engineering, but its higher quality won't be manifest until later in one's ownership. Here one advances monies to the manufacturer for services not yet fully available, and moreover to avail oneself of them one will have to make further payments in the future; the superior engineering of a premium car requires the owner to pay extra and longer for the maintenance necessary to make use of it.

The key point here, however, is that the extra money paid for the car at the point of sale, that is, the money advanced to pay for services that are as yet only potential, makes the consumer/purchaser a coparticipant in the investment process undergirding the manufacture of the automobile; the purchaser/consumer quite literally advances part of the investment. Modern sale/purchase typically involves the purchaser/consumer in making such advances for what only later will become integral services, and that fact makes the purchaser/consumer a direct participant in the investment process itself. Note particularly the time dimension here. The firm's investment flow comes not only from the commodity services it has transferred at the point of sale, as in the conventional account. The purchaser has, in addition, made an advance for services still under the disposition of the firm, and in that sense the customer partially underwrites the firm's investment. Basically, we are dealing with payment flows that precede in time the transfer of the services.

This coinvestment in the services of the car also validates our earlier assertion that sale/purchase states act backward in time. From your standpoint as consumer, or mine, our money advance for potential services is significant only from the point of sale forward, but for our partner, the producer/seller, the stream of those advances from us and others is, has been, and will be intrinsic to its investment, producing, and selling strategies and to an appreciable extent actually underwrites them.

The importance of this phenomenon is easier to understand if we look at the dimension of the sale/purchase state that involved the purchaser/consumer in those wider relationships with the insurance, petroleum, and licensing institutions. To buy a car is already to initiate a set of statistically significant purchases that in an anticipatory way will fund investments in larger production runs. This phenomenon goes beyond the conventional concept of "consumer demand generating growth" in two precise senses. First, and most importantly, in that some of the monies paid for the car are advances against future services, not purchases of existing services. Second, the link between the consumer's purchase of a car and the petroleum companies' increased output is not interrupted by a bidding market in which the would-be consumer has an institutional right to buy or not to buy; the sale/purchase state bridges the purchase of the car with the requirement to buy gasoline and oil. One may shop around for a better gasoline price, but one must buy gasoline in any case.

Fifth, and finally, these advances initiate a system of operative but future liens against one's future income. Even if we paid for a car "in cash," out of savings perhaps, its use will require that we make further payments for fuel and maintenance in the future, which constitutes a lien against the exercise of our labor-power at a future date. Looked at from a broad social standpoint, from looking at the labor force as a social ensemble, in consuming modern commodities that ensemble is at the same time and by the same token creating a system of liens against its productive powers in the future, which will require payments that have to be earned in the future. In our terms, the sale/purchase state incorporates a series of continuing liens over its duration. These liens are a call against our productive powers, against the consumer today as producer tomorrow. It is the fifth dimension in which so-called final consumption is now set within productive relationships, and in that sense it is fairly called productive.

Here it is important to stress again that in examining the system of liens attendant upon sale/purchase-in-time we are dealing not with a natural but with a social phenomenon. As we recognize, it is always possible for this or that person to work, buy, and consume in ways that are deeply idiosyncratic, perhaps to "beat the system," to be a "deadbeat" or a pure parasite, to consume but never produce. But looking to the labor force as a whole, to the labor-power of a society, it is clear that the system of liens so briefly described bear against that labor force and that, in the social dimension, the system of liens is more or less seamless with the production and consumption of modern commodities. Again the social relations of consumption, especially when looked at from the temporal dimension, are significantly incorporated within wider social relations of production.

In a very real sense, in a modern economy genuinely "final" consumption is not a particularly important phenomenon. Even our private, spontaneous decision to buy an attractive purse, have an espresso, or see a film places us within wider ensembles of productive and distributive relations of a deeply social character. It is simply an illusion, a fetish if you will, to conceive, as is so often the case still, of consumption as a private and personal sort of thing. In a modern economy, consumption normally occurs within wider, many-to-one social relationships emanating from the productive firms and tilted by them to a significant degree with a view toward their own interests.

These things will become even clearer when we go beyond viewing consumption in society as merely the aggregate of individual and firm behaviors and raise the analysis to the true social level (in chapters 5 and 6), that is, when we examine the social processes of consumption that characterize the production, reproduction, and alteration of the social labor-power as an organic whole, not merely the individuals within it, as a producer commodity.

4 | Critical Commodity Theory

In Marx, the word *critical* and its cognates refer to the desired transparency of a theory. The term echoes Kant in that to be critical a theory must justify its own methodology, that is, in contemporary terms one is aware of the security and scope of the deep assumptions of the theory one is using, sometimes called the "metatheory," and one takes explicit cognizance of the initial and boundary conditions for employing the theory.[1]

Marx's use of *critical* includes the Kantian meaning but adds to it an "ideological" dimension, namely, that one ought to be aware of the social-material and historical conditions within which the theory has emerged, of the limits of its claims to universality or historical transcendence, and of the social-material interests that the theory may variously highlight or obscure, advance or retard. At this point, we should adopt such a critical attitude to the differences between old and modern commodity form.

"Quasi Service" as Analytical Element

The microtheory of modern commodity form is built up from the analytical element "quasi service," that is, a service incomplete in itself, which must be complemented with other quasi services. It is "the primitive element of the system" and plays an appreciable role throughout the findings of this study. As a theoretical element it is intended to supersede both the neoclassical, unmodified "service" and Marx's similarly unqualified "use-value," and to that extent it has the effect of revising and updating the logic of both traditions. In my view, an unqualified service (or use-value) is inadequate in principle to the description and analysis of modern commodity form. In Marx, for example, commodities often seem to be depicted as things that provide use-values, and it is the things that come to be exchanged, with the use-values following along as if on a leash.[2]

But this locution—or, better, this analytical construction—does not allow for the possibility that the different services of a commodity can be transferred over time rather than being alienated all at once or that they may require complements. As I'll explain in the following section, this didn't make much difference in Marx's lifetime because of the very primitive state of capitalist production and exchange. Altering our conceptual apparatus to quasi services, including especially "potential services," that is, quasi services as modified by time, provides a much more supple, realistic, and socially warranted instrument for analyzing modern commodity practices. The change in terminology also serves to underline the fact that in modern practice—and modern usage—it is the services per se that are subject to exchange and distribution and we have already signaled this meaning in preferring the term *commodity form* to *commodity*.

The unqualified use-value also points up the oft-cited weakness of the Marxist theory of "final" or consumer demand (e.g., Arrow and Hahn 1971: 2). Admittedly, one must be cautious in speaking of Marx's "theory of demand" for consumer goods since there is no systematic, unified treatment of the subject in *Capital*. But its elements and the way he puts them together are clear enough.

There are two closely related inadequacies. As was suggested by our earlier citation of those "cruel South Americans," in Marx's view final consumption is left to the laborer's own "instincts" and accordingly occurs outside the economy per se or, as he would put it, outside the continuous circulation and recirculation of capital.[3]

I think that the best way to understand the second point is to observe that Marx treats all of the working class's consumption *as if* it were a single, undifferentiated service. Basically, his notion is that there is a mass of commodities falling to the lot of the workers, the very limited size and variety of which "springs from" the actions of the economy, but that mass is normally only just large enough to reproduce the working class more or less as it is, that is, as a proletariat. How that limited mass of commodities is consumed, what sort of services it is comprised of, and its further effect on the economy, especially on the productive characteristics of the work force, are not really subject to analysis in Marx's scheme of things. All in all, the use-value of workers' consumption commodities is to make sure that more or less the same working population that worked yesterday will return regularly to work tomorrow and the next day. The following elaboration will make his view of consumer demand clearer and in passing will illustrate the limited contemporary value of the unqualified concept of use-value.

In passages drawn from the second and third volumes of *Capital,* an economy can be modeled as consisting of three distinct Departments (Marx's term) in equilibrium. Department I produces means of production, Department II produces consumption goods for workers, and Department III produces means of consumption for capitalists.[4] In the Marxist scheme, the net of the output—roughly, his surplus value—goes to the capitalists either to invest for current maintenance and future growth (Department I) or to devote to their own private, final consumption. (Department III). In a nongrowth model, Department II (workers' consumption) is treated strictly as a recurring cost and no part of the surplus is devoted to it. The workers' share is determined by the level of income necessary to maintain and reproduce the working class at the level determined by what Marx calls the General Law of Capitalist Accumulation.[5]

Thus, from the wording of the law it is evident that Marx had in mind that the mass and quality of consumer goods going to the workers would normally be pressed down toward the minimum necessary to sustain the working class at a quite primitive physical and social level.[6]

He does allow, however, that the operations of the General Law are also modified by custom and the political power and influence of the working class and its social allies. In fact, the very long chapters of volume 1 of *Capital*, "The Working Day" (about 70 pages in the standard English-language translation) and the even longer chapter 15 on "Machinery and Modern Industry" (about 120 pages) are mostly devoted to the conflict over the length (and conditions) of the working day in England from the fourteenth to the nineteenth centuries with special attention paid to the political/legislative struggles to enact protections for the workers, that is, the various factory acts. Thus, while workers' consumption may from time to time rise a bit it is continually being dragged back down by the operation of the General Law.

As one can see, it is not unfair to say of Marx's theory of demand, as it applies to the workers, that the entire mass of consumer goods going to them can be treated as providing a single, generic service, namely, to maintain a working class of relatively static social-productive characteristics. The different kinds and qualities of consumer goods are of no great concern to the General Law, and the manner of their consumption lies outside the circuit of capital, that is, outside of the economy. The General Law is the central point of the conclusion of volume 1 of *Capital*, and if it is true one doesn't really need a more differentiated concept of use-values or services. The unqualified variant is more than sufficient to describe what he wants to describe, that is, the condition of a laboring population being maintained at a relatively primitive economic and social level, hence with relatively static productive qualities.

Of course, to maintain this "theory of demand" today, when substantial numbers and kinds of commodities are consumed by a working population, the effect of which, partially a matter of deliberate capitalist policy, alters its productive characteristics, is simply to elide the differences between a modern and a primitive capitalist economy. If we are to go beyond this primitive theory of demand and in particular relate workers' consumption and changes in worker productivity, then the shift to an analytic of quasi services will be indispensable.[7]

The shift to the element "quasi service" also enables us to merge, as they ought to be, microeconomics and marketing and thus avoid the paradoxical "deep" assumption of the mainstream theory that there aren't any fundamental differences between the Victorian and modern sales efforts. Then, too, the unqualified "service" is itself too closely linked to the abstract "utility" of the older, classical tradition in political economy, which, following Smith and Ricardo, treats markets as more or less "natural," or at least unchanging, phenomena.

The concept of quasi service also allows a more adequate account than much current thinking about "the mass market," "advertising," "consumerism," and such like. In the latter, one employs a paradigm of quite impressionable consumers succumbing to a mind-bending ruling class ideology or purely symbolic commands, perhaps even acting on their subliminal hopes, fears, and fantasies. Undoubtedly, some advertising is successful precisely because of this, but the analysis depicts the social relations of consumption as only operating within almost wholly symbolic modes. It does not further articulate the ensembles of actual social-material relations through which consumption is directly constrained under wider, more powerful productive and distributing relationships and the implications of this regarding the influence of capitalism on the construction of general social relations per se.

As we saw in analyzing sale/purchase-in-time, the element quasi service brings out the very existence and force of these wider productive relations, enabling us directly to develop a unified theory of capitalist production, distribution, and consumption without add-ons and without recourse to one-sided, essentially Feuerbachian schemes of abstract "commodification," "the mass media," the crude, ahistoric materialism of assuming a human propensity to herd psychology, and such.[8]

Relatedly, the unqualified service or use-value too often comes to be depicted in economics writing as either natural or generic in character. Is it simply "natural" for a hammer to serve to drive nails or for (leavened) bread to assuage hunger or are these two services not the product of a lengthy coordinate social evolution in the four dimensions of their commodity form? By treating services as generic one erases the historicity built into commodity form. The element, quasi service helps to keep that historical dimension in the foreground.

Neither does the unqualified service sufficiently bring out a main, emergent feature of modern commodity form, namely, that goods and services, (i.e., service commodities such as laundering or hairdressing) don't represent two quite separate species of commodity but, more typically, that modern commodities per se are comprised of both goods and services mingled in ever more complex ways in their reflex dimensions. Here the unqualified service or use-value again creates an unnecessary analytical and descriptive hurdle when we trace the development of commodity form from Victorian to contemporary times.[9]

Finally, as will be shown in chapters 7 and 8, the unqualified service thoroughly distorts value theory, raising theoretical paradoxes that are as unnecessary as they are unresolvable, burdening economics with the unfortunate doctrine of price determinacy or what I have called "price realism."

A Historical-Materialist Account

The concept of quasi services also helps us to better understand the primitiveness of the capitalist context that faced Jevons, Marx, and their contemporaries and unfortunately shaped the logic of their analyses. What I want to show is that these writers mistakenly thought that they lived within a capitalism that was already well enough developed that they could experience and thus analyze its mature, stable features. In fact, the capitalism of their time was in a distinctly transitory stage, a stage that was passing away almost at the point in time when these authors legislated its features into their basic microeconomics.

Marx may serve as a prime example here. He opens the first volume of *Capital* with the observation, "The wealth of those societies in which the capitalist mode of production prevails presents itself as 'an immense accumulation of commodities,' its unit being a single commodity."[10]

But as we've already seen, there were relatively few true commodities, in the Marxist sense, in that Victorian economy, that is, commodities embedded within production/exchange relations characterized by the General or Money form of value. This was especially true outside Great

Britain itself. But even there only corn (wheat), coffee, sugar, tea, and a handful of other semiprocessed agricultural goods along with manufacturing coal, wrought and cast iron, gold, silver, and a few other minerals had achieved commodity form, as had cotton, woolen, linen, and perhaps silk thread and cloth, leather and blacking, and a small handful of other manufactured items. Such transportation services as were afforded by stage lines, railroads, canal and river barges, and ocean steamers had also reached commodity form. As one reads *Capital* or any other historical account of the middle years of the Victorian era, it soon becomes apparent that few other goods or services appear in those accounts as illustrations or examples of commodities. Most foodstuffs, for example, such as fresh and cured meat, milk and cheese, beer, fruit and vegetables, were produced and sold only locally, hence with the expected nonuniformity in product, manner of production and distribution, and manner of final consumption we would associate with the Extended form of value. Coal for home heating was only beginning to assume commodity form. Cloth came as a commodity but not garments, nor household tools or furniture, nor drugs and medicines such as they were, nor candles and tapers, nor seed and fertilizer.[11]

Marx's assertion about a "huge accumulation" of commodities represents prescient insight, not a literal description of the commercial and industrial world of his time. Most goods and services that were made and offered for sale, especially for the final consumer, had not yet been sufficiently amplified in the four dimensions of commodity form to qualify as such. Their physical/social characteristics varied too much from region to region; they were produced under significantly different productive conditions; their distribution, including their prices, was only local or otherwise erratic; and/or the consumption of their services had not yet converged into familiar, widespread, crystallized social practices. In this sense, Marx and Jevons lived and wrote during the very infancy—childhood is probably more accurate—of modern commodity production and thus gave an account of commodity production in its childhood. This serves even today to mislead readers as to the stage of development reached by commodity form in the England of 1850–80.

Recall that economists of the time were experiencing and writing about a capitalism that had only recently shifted from handicraft production to the factory system or, in analytical terms, from the Expanded to the General form of value. In the former, we would expect that, say, batches of iron produced under the handicraft system would vary widely in their technical and commercial characteristics. As early railroaders or bridge builders would discover to their dismay, different batches of iron differed so much in their technical qualities that rails would crack, boilers would burst, or the bridge would collapse. Unless one had previous experience with the producer, the iron one purchased would have essentially unpredictable services or, more or less the same thing, one would discover its real usable qualities only after the fact. Socially speaking, utility or use-value at this stage of capitalism and of exchange is highly specific, as fits the Extended form of value, not the generic, as is required for the later, more developed General or Money forms of value.

Factory production introduced a greater uniformity in commodities but in a period in which both distribution channels and metallurgy itself were undeveloped. The situation was not like that of the present, in which the producer/seller enters into enduring relationships with the metal's user and as a result can more or less customize the technical qualities of iron and steel to the user's needs. In the still emerging Victorian factory system, however, the combination of an elementary distribution system based on "the market" and an underdeveloped metals technology meant that the producer could provide only an iron whose qualities lay within a range or band of technological reliability. That represented an advance over handicraft iron since that range or band of technological qualities made the iron more or less equally useful and reliable to the cutler, the boilermaker, the bridge builder, the rail layer, the naval architect, and so forth. Not ideal for any of those uses, it nevertheless was predictably serviceable for all of them.

Analytically and socially, however, this means that the services of that iron now had a generic rather than specific character, and it is this that is reflected in both Marx's treatment in *Capital* and in the writings of Stanley Jevons. In that sense it was apt to the real historical situation to say that the commodity has use-value or utility, the singular term referring to the genus or band of the specific services adaptable by the different end users.

Interestingly, in its youth the U.S. auto industry exhibited an analogous history. First, a multiplicity of very diverse vehicles were made in small workshops, often by bicycle and carriage makers trying to extend their techniques. Thus, they produced very diverse products with very diverse intended uses and reliability. Then came the Ford Models T and A, designed with simple features and a simple but very reliable technology for use by the farmer but adaptable for the same reason by hosts of others.[12]

Then, as we saw, came the true modern commodity auto in which the dimensions of its commodity form are much further developed. Hilferding's account of the adulteration of higher quality coffee to qualify it as a commodity coffee for the Hamburg Exchange lends itself to the same interpretation. One has first to create coffee as a single, predictably reliable, familiar commodity, not as many puzzling coffees. On that basis the coffee commodity can later develop into many differentiated coffee commodities. The progression, in this reading, is anarchy, simplification, standardization, and finally articulation within a system of producer/distributor/user integration.

In nineteenth-century accounts such as *Capital* we are still in the simplification phase of commodity production and consumption in which there is a band of uses of commodities indifferently useful to different purchaser/consumers. This phenomenon can mislead the unwary reader into taking the uses of commodities as "naturally" generic. It is only later in the history of commodity form, when the intervention of producers into the relations of consumption becomes socially manifest, that we are forced to break down the broad category of utility (or use-value) into such subtypes as potential, quasi, and integral services. To have done so in Victorian times would have added an inexactness directly into the logical structure of economic theory, an essentially speculative component. For us not to do so now is to ignore the real world development of commodity form in the ensuing century and a quarter.[13]

As suggested, "the Market" is the abstraction that best reflects a situation in which a producer, limited by his or her productive abilities and the primitiveness of distribution conduits and relatively ignorant of the precise services needed by the eventual customer, simply sends goods out into the "void," there to be taken up by anyone who finds the band of their services acceptable and comes to prefer them because of their predictable uniformity. In an economic world still preoccupied with moving away from precommodity economic "anarchy" a relatively unadministered, unspecialized market seems most apt. Looked at in that way one can see that this market abstraction, still the foundation abstraction of so much economic writing, is profoundly inadequate when we have to analyze today's infinitely more articulated relationships between modern products, their producers, their distribution modes, and their final uses.

Analytically speaking, the classic market, or more specifically the whole genera of utility theories of "natural" demand operating in a market, represents an extrapolation of these bands of historically rooted generic services into a single abstract, generic, socially and culturally transcendent service or utility function. In that sense, those theories do injustice to the workings of a modern economy.

It is this willy-nilly extrapolation that, I suspect, has given rise to the plethora of narratives purporting to make empirical sense of the Jevons/Walras microeconomics of demand. There are obvious differences cited in the narratives built around, say, Marshall's "wants and their satisfaction," Jevon's "final degree of utility," Bentham's "felicific tone," the textbook's "marginal utility," Pareto's "ophelimity," and Walras's "maximization of satisfaction," but these are stories trying to make sense of a deeply paradoxical theory of demand, combining a particularly demanding logic of utility with a spectacularly inarticulate conception of that same utility. In retrospect, it is clear that the very abstractness of the desired utility logic must cause every apparent tale to run into the sort of philosophic tangles we find in such Anselmian narrative devices as "perfect knowledge," "perfect market," "perfect equilibrium," and "full" opportunity cost.[14]

In our contemporary phase of commodity form, the historical evolution of commodities has led to articulated quasi services. These are typically complemented by the producing firm, which offers the needed quasi services at a later time and requiring new payments. Or this complementarity may be provided by other firms, by distributors (as in the credit system), or by the government. The point, of course, is that as a historical materialist Marx himself would have been forced to recharacterize use-value in some equivalent analytical way to take account of the historical evolution of commodity form.

Implications for the Theory of Property

Both the neoclassical pioneers and Marx wrote during the historical time period in which modern private property came to full development, and their formulation of microeconomics is very much connected to this and limited by it. The economic universe we live in today does not fit that private property template, although we contemporaries tend to think and act as if it did, in spite of the fact that quite fundamental property relations have been changing not in spite of but because of the exigencies of contemporary capitalism. In truth, modern capitalism rejects private property, except at the rhetorical level, and actually requires and operates within a system of already socialized or quasi-collective property.

What we call modern private property appears to have developed only very slowly from perhaps the fifteeenth century on, but it did not come into full social and legal flower until the first quarter of the nineteenth century in Britain and France, perhaps a generation later in the United States, and with analogous lags elsewhere. When we speak of a society and economy organized around private property we normally understand certain features to be thoroughly embodied in the law, business practices, and related social activities as they bear on land and other productive (and personal) goods. To wit: (A) the land, money, or goods, that is, the property in question, is fully in the possession of the owner and/or on his or her authority is in the delegated possession of another. The decisive shift toward so-called modern private property comes with (B), under which, subject to only minimal restrictions, the owner may alienate the property or any of its services as he or she solely chooses. Sale, gift, bequest, rental, lease, and other forms of the transfer of property or its services fall within this rubric. (C) Any and all yields from the property, or liabilities, fall to the owner, as with the fruit from one's tree or the output from one's machinery or the damage inflicted by one's dog. Finally, (D) there is a title to the property, that is, there is a legally and customarily recognized procedure by means of which the property attributes A, B and C are guaranteed and protected by the reigning political authority. Obviously, there are variations in the property features if the property is owned by a partnership or even a (premodern) corporation, but these don't radically modify A,B,C,D.

As indicated, it is according to point B that we generally characterize "modern" private property, and it is this feature that the neoclassical and classical economists seized upon in their conception of the exchange of commodities. It was really only in the nineteenth century that the alienability of private property became fully developed. The social form of this is the "free market," wherein all manner and types of property may be fully "sold," that is, all property and its services may at the discretion of the old owner and new purchaser be exchanged and all claims to the property are transferred without restriction from the seller to the purchaser.

This, of course, represents an enormous change in social practices from the previous periods of human history. As Marx so bitterly puts it in the *Manifesto,* all human bonds formerly held sacred and inviolable were replaced by "the cash nexus." Before the Jacksonian era in the United States, before the Revolution in France, and somewhat earlier in Britain, the uses to which owners could put some important kinds of private property were severely restricted, and those restrictions remained in force even when the property in question was sold or bequeathed. Until the French Revolution shopkeepers were normally compelled to sell staples such as bread at "fair prices"; some employers were socially required to pay "fair wages." Even as late as the 1870s in the United States, there was a widespread public expectation that an employer "owed" some sort of guaranteed tenure of employment at "fair wages" to his employees; it was precisely the threat to this custom that led to the great U.S. railroad workers' uprising of 1877 (Yellen [1936] 1974 : 3ff., especially 12). Certain classes of rural dwellers retained residual rights in the land of others for firewood gathering, winter grazing or browsing, pond or lake fishing, and ice cutting. Naturally, this evidence of an earlier property system declined very slowly, retaining some importance well into the nineteenth century.

Analogously, point C was often hedged; others might lay claim to part of a crop (gleaning the residue left after the harvest perhaps), the game found on the land, and so forth. It was again only in the nineteenth century that the last important remnants of others' claims to the fruits or products of ostensibly private property fell away and that all four property attributes became fully and socially enacted.[15]

If we have this paradigm in mind, the transfer of a car from manufacturer to purchaser doesn't fit. The new owner of the car, as expected under a private property system, now enjoys A and D, but B doesn't quite hold and neither does C. As we saw in a different context, not all of the services of the car have been fully alienated to the new "owner." They are not now his or her property to freely and exclusively enjoy; to enjoy those that stretch beyond the ten to twenty thousand mile mark will require the assistance of the company at some future time (e.g., for tune-ups or spare parts). And, even more significant, the owner will require the assistance and cooperation, and the money to pay for them, of petroleum, tire, insurance, and other institutions. Similarly, the auto manufacturer may be held liable for injuries caused by the vehicle.

In these two important senses, the sale or transfer of the integral services of the car occurs over a period of time, and until that period has elapsed the new owner has only partial "ownership" of the services of his or her property. Analytically, the transformation of some of the quasi services of the car into integral services is not under the exclusive control and disposition of the owner of the car. In short, by shifting our perspective from the unqualified or integral service, we see that the nature of ownership has been altered in an obviously significant way both in law and in economics.

It may be that continuing liability is less important outside, say, the automobile and pharmaceutical industries. But whenever sale/purchase transfers only quasi services stipulation B is not satisfied and we are therefore not confronting classic private property but something importantly different. The practices surrounding quasi services indicate a sort of collective, collectivized, or partially socialized property. Obviously, a whole new meaning must be attached to those otherwise familiar words. During the sale/purchase state the car manufacturer does not "own the car," but does clearly continue to "own" at least some of its potential services.

Thus, when we pass from the car as simple physical object and look to see the sort of social-material relations in which it is embedded, it is evident that some of the key property features of the car, some of its services, are shared in a quite familiar way between producer/seller and consumer/purchaser—even though they've ostensibly been sold.

The concept of quasi services also lends us some insight into a subtle but powerful tendency for the provision of investment capital to become deeply socialized even as its earnings remain definitively private and exclusive.[16]

We have already discussed the phenomenon of consumer advances within the sale/purchase relationship, but the subject will repay the effort of further analysis. Here, the advent of quasi-socialized or quasi-collectivized property fundamentally alters the very logic of investment.

As pointed out earlier, one normally pays more for a modern commodity than its actual integral services would warrant. One pays for quasi services that remain under the effective control of the seller. And then one pays a second time to bring about their transfer to the buyer. The potential services will not be transferred to the purchaser until he or she lays out further monies to purchase the keyboard, get on the Internet, or acquire additional software. Note that the difference in price between the integral services actually transferred and the potential services that will become available later is not unfounded, at least insofar as the more powerful PC represents more extensive engineering and higher manufacturing costs. But at the same time further expenditures must be made to acquire those potential services. Here one both advances monies to the manufacturer/seller and incurs an effective lien to pay further monies later.

One wants to say that the purchaser/consumer "invests" that particular part of the purchase price, and in one precise respect that is just what one does. One advances a sum of money, which leads to a return at a later time. But, just as in modern property, where we saw the traditional ensemble of its four attributes split apart, something like the same thing occurs here vis-à-vis the normal progression we expect of an investment, namely, that X invests and normally gets a return. Here X invests but Y also gets a return.[17]

In this sense, the PC itself, though sold, still functions like classic Marxist constant capital. That is, it is the material subject that will be altered by the producing actions of the producer/seller.[18]

In each case "our" consumer product and at least a portion of the money tied up in it provide the material subject for the further profitable producing activities of the producer/seller. Given these quite significant economic and other productive relationships it would appear warranted to say that some of the investment expenditures made for the commodity in question are not fully "private"; by virtue of the consumer/purchaser's advances they are partially socialized. From the advance of monies by others, the producer/seller reaps a return.

Of course, the purchaser/consumer is not legally constrained to make those additional outlays, but in the normal, usual case he or she must make them so as not to lose the value of the initial advance. Thereby the purchase/state also comprises, as we have seen, liens upon the future income of the purchaser/consumer. It is the combination of the advance of value to the producer/seller and the fact that those liens fall to the latter's advantage that leads us to say that the investment process has been partially socialized. Obviously, the conventional connotation we attach to the term *socialized* (fully social), which sharply contrasts with *privatized* (fully private), has to be rethought. Here *socialized* simply means that the processes that provide investment funds and the processes that will yield a further profit to the producer/seller have both "burst the integument" of a purely private property.

The producer/seller gets returns without making advances, and the purchaser/consumer gets liens against his or her future income instead of returns on the investment. This is doubly interesting, even paradoxical, when we consider how "the morality of investing" is treated in the history of economic thought. There is a whole tradition of theorizing, which includes writers as varied as Nassau Senior, J. S. Mill, and Alfred Marshall, that links investment to the "denial of satisfaction" or "waiting" attendant upon "saving" and thus provides what is argued to be an ethical basis for a return on investment. This position cannot be sustained in a modern economy in which the provision of investment has taken on a process character involving advances and saving from a populace whose claims to the return on that investment are subordinated to advantageously placed "free riders" both individual and institutional. Thus, we see here an extension and deepening of the private and exclusive right of the producer/seller to a return on someone else's investment that we would not otherwise expect on the basis of a classic private property system.

Commodity Fetishism and "False Experience"

The present analysis underlines what I think is a key feature of our modern society, the phenomenon of "false experience." The term seems to be a contradiction; one can falsely judge an experience or falsely identify the source of an experience, but how can there be, purely and simply, a false experience?

This subject is actually an extension and deepening of a phenomenon pointed out by Marx under the rubric of commodity fetishism and can perhaps be best approached by recapping his views. In the first volume of *Capital* he devotes a lengthy exposition to what he calls the fetishism of commodities. He argues that the while commodities are the product of dense nets of social relationships those relationships are pushed to the background of our perceptions and tend to be replaced by the things themselves. We say that "the factory" produces the goods when it is the people who work there who do so. Or conceive that "technology is irresistible" in such a way that we block out the fact that the imperative to alter technology has social, political, and economic roots that are at least as powerful as the technological ones and often more so. Here we come to see the world as furnished with objectified but fictive relationships between things instead of, as we should, a world made up of the social relationships of the producers and users of those things.[19]

If I read him correctly, Marx does not lay any particular stress on the fact that social relationships themselves can be fetishized into false ones. He appears to limit himself to the point that some social relationships tend to be erased by relations between things. But our expanded analytical apparatus, which stresses the greater social character of modern commodity form, indicates that commodity fetishism now has both a greater amplitude and a finer grain.

Under modern commodity form social relations are sometimes directly distorted into fictive social relations or even sometimes created out of whole cloth. Thus, the fetish character of modern commodity form takes on more than symbolic or communicative reality, enacting new, ongoing, and causally significant ensembles of social relationships. These distortions and creations do not occur independent of the sort of fetishism described by Marx but extend far beyond it.

Modern producers/sellers often seize upon existing aspects of our culture and social relationships and distort them to suit their purposes. For example, and as previously described, modern marketing typically seizes upon the preexisting inclination of some part of the consuming public to identify itself with some favorable characteristic or other, such as being "adult," youthful, avant-garde, sexy, exotic, or affluent. This advertising does not rest on generalized or universal human propensities, as its theorists often claim. As we now know so vividly from the public controversies over tobacco, selective advertising is directed at what are imagined to be especially volatile potential consumers—in that case adolescents. In short, the producer/advertiser's strategy is to create new social behavior within an especially susceptible target group whose example will encourage others to emulate them and thus yield material advantages to the firm, especially to the degree that the greater profits generated through this process can be subsequently used to expand the market.[20]

If the commodities so advertised achieve the level of a mass market, they create further industrial, financial, and symbolic social relationships in the form of a major industry, its wealth, its influence, and so forth, which then underwrites the continued social behavior on the part of "consumers" that was the goal. Here fetishism becomes self-creating and self-expanding. Thus, we do not merely (and falsely) imagine that smoking is a consumer-led phenomenon; we actually experience it. The tobacco industry can claim that it is only serving the desires of part of the public and antismoking and related ordinances and campaigns are negative, puritanical, and at their limit anti–civil libertarian.

One must stress here that the dynamic of the fetish is only triggered by symbolic means, by advertising. The hoped for aim is to create a body of social-material relationships that will "take off" well beyond the direct effects of the advertising and then maintain themselves long after the advertising campaign is terminated. Something of this nature is involved in all brand name marketing, but the point is that the tobacco industry has created an enduring demand for its products, an actual sector of society that behaviorally and in other ways materially reproduces itself and influences others' behavior, not merely their ideas.

A less frequently discussed but equally important fetish is enacted by the automobile industry. In public policy discussions about transportation, mass transit is typically contrasted with the automobile as the social versus the private. We understand the first to have a (good) social character while the second is only "private" and "individualistic." But the truth, brought out in the features of the modal sale/purchase states for autos, is that a transport system based on autos is no more private than one based on buses or trains. One's use of a car is deeply conditioned by its immersion in a system of *social* expenses and dependencies. Ironically, what is really "private" about an auto-based system is that the bulk of the investment necessary to bring private profit to the auto companies is provided by the public, both in the expense of building and maintaining roads and in the costs incurred to change the vehicle's potential services into actual ones. Thus, the privateness or individualism socially associated with the auto represents a false or fetish relationship between the driving public and the industry. Here the fetish is wrongly imagined to be keyed to the vehicle itself. Of course, there are undoubtedly those who are infatuated with the fetish perception that their car is "manly" or "sporty." That's the sort of thing discussed in Marx. But at the level of transportation policy discussion, either by the professionals or the public, the fetish lies in the distortion of the social relationship between public and industry, not individual and car.

In both of these examples we find false or fetishized social relationships, "false" not because they don't exist but because their origin, growth, and character are fundamentally manipulated into existence and then become socially/materially self-sustaining. Here a purely commercial phenomenon manages to create a social "fact" that will depict itself as "natural." Thus, "we"—society—come to experience a humanly engineered and managed phenomenon as a spontaneous, entirely natural sort of thing.

This raises a most interesting area of discussion, namely, the way in which in a modern society our very experience can be falsified. Note that I differ from postmodern views here and also from an intellectual strain traditional in Marxism. It is not false ideology that is at the center here, nor "false consciousness," but experiences that are genuinely bogus. That we falsely render these experiences in fictive or ideological symbols is consequence not cause. The fact creates the idea not the other way around. Because of the burdens it imposes on our private purse, we falsely experience a socially organized, auto-based transport system as private. This falsification of experience obviously goes beyond purely commercial sorts of things; it is a societywide feature, a system property, I would argue, of a society whose contours are more and more socially fabricated and less and less of spontaneous origin.

In a parallel case in the United States, for example, many white people actually experience their own social superiority to nonwhites. They experience—not "imagine" or "ideologize"—nonwhites as possessing the indubitable marks of social inferiority, as less educated, less healthy, and less wealthy, with higher levels of social pathology and with "less educated" customs and speech patterns. This experience is confirmed and deepened by the police, who treat nonwhites like inferiors; by the municipality, which undercollects trash in nonwhite districts; by employers, who typically hire nonwhites for menial tasks, and even by the media, which treat nonwhites as exotic—commendably exotic, perhaps, but exotic and therefore "other" all the same. Accordingly, to think that nonwhites are inferior is not ultimately and effectively rooted in false ideas or via ideologies of advantage such as "whiteness"; it comes of reading and reacting to the content of our social experience. One requires critical, independent-minded reflection to reject the racialism taught by one's own experience.

Insofar as society evolves from the spontaneous sort of thing celebrated by Popper and Hayek toward being made up more and more of ensembles of mutually supportive social relationships enacted by business, the media, the mass political parties, and other institutions interested in fabricating what C. Wright Mills used to call "official versions of reality," we have less and less reason to believe that "experience," "common sense,","public opinion," and even "expert advice" stand outside fetishized reality. This involves more than just rejecting the older progress myths. It is not merely that society is failing to get better and better but that we cannot rely on the claim that society is self-correcting or self-equilibrating. In short, a trajectory of human regress is just as likely, and perhaps more so, than any of the alternatives.

With the rise and spread of modern commodity form, false experience itself becomes a major, often dominant social phenomenon. If, as I believe, the modern labor force—the labor-power of society—is produced within commodity form, then the phenomenon of fetishized or fictive social experience already represents a major, obviously dangerous conundrum, namely, of the shrinking of the spontaneous dimensions of society and the expansion of an importantly engineered society and with it the widespread phenomenon of experience itself, which is false.

5 | The Commodity Form of Labor-Power

The Concept of the Social Labor-Power

In a modern society virtually every person at every stage of life exerts productive effort either directly in the economy or ultimately helping to shape that economy. This is true even of the preschool child, at least insofar as those exertions prepare the child to go on to school and then to play some productive role in society. So, too, we have to count among modern producers those who parent, mentor, and teach them. This is the case regardless of whether the mentoring and teaching is or is not paid labor within the labor force. If, of course, the child and its parents lived in an isolated region, with only a subsistence economy and few or no economic relations with the larger world, and culturally isolated as well, we could view parenting, mentoring, learning, and socialization as substantially irrelevant to that larger economy. But surely such cases are rare in a modern society and growing even rarer. In a very palpable sense, a modern society seizes hold of the whole process of child rearing and the training of young persons and directs them into what it conceives to be channels that are particularly desirable from the standpoint of the existing and prospective economy—through the school system, through the medical and pharmaceutical industries, through the continual acculturation of parents into "up-to-date" thinking about child rearing, through the media, and even through the industries that produce children's clothing, toys, and games. The mesh of this net of institutional activities is not so fine that children are as a rule directed into this or that specific skill, knowledge, or vocation, but neither is it so coarse that children and young people have no constraints in choosing their futures.

This near universality of productive effect of the people in a modern society is, of course, the reflex of the different forms of constrained productive consumption we explored in chapter 3.

These reflections immediately raise an analytical challenge. We really don't have a concept that comprehends the universal productive effort and effect so characteristic of a modern economy and society. As I'll shortly explain, neither of the terms drawn from the dominant economics traditions, the neoclassical "labor force" and Marxist "labor-power," are broad enough because both formally conceive of "work" as something that goes on within "the economy." The sort of work that preordains what sort of work the economy will and can exert tends to be analytically excluded. Accordingly, I want to define the *social labor-power* as comprised of all those persons, and particularly their exertions, both potential and actual, that either directly or indirectly affect the economy.[1]

The definition of the *social labor-power* is very broad and in fact makes it almost coterminous with the population itself. That's both deliberate and necessary, if for no other reason than the fact that few persons and efforts in a modern society stand entirely outside its overall productive apparatus; whether as consumers or workers, parents or mentors, tots or graduate students, most of our efforts most of the time are part of wider ensembles of relations of production, that is, of the economy. More simply, we produce things, and we produce the people who produce things, which of course affects the sort of people who will be produced in the next round. A modern labor force is continuously being altered by social action, often as a matter of deliberate government or industry policy. Thus, we need a somewhat wider concept than "manpower," the "labor force," the "working class," "labor," "labor-power," "workers," "producers," "the producing class," and other, analogous locutions. All these terms express the static result but not the constitutive processes of that altering. The concept of the social labor-power is the fundamental unit for study if we wish to investigate the commodity form of modern labor-power in all its dimensions, including its production.

The meaning of the *social labor-power* will be clearer if we contrast it with the two other, familiar ways of talking about our subject, the statistical labor force and Marx's (unqualified) labor-power.

Rethinking "the Labor Force"

The expression, "the labor force" includes only the employed and those who are (estimated to be) unemployed. That reservation—"estimated to be"—is very substantial. Many would-be workers simply disappear from the official count. In the United States statistics number as unemployed only those who are, in the argot of the Labor Department, "ready, willing, and able to work." Technically speaking, that means that the person has actively sought employment in the prior ten-day period. The Labor Department makes additional estimates of those who, working only part time, would like to work full time and of those who have temporarily given up the search for work either because their work is normally seasonal (as in agriculture and tourism) or because local prospects are very poor (as in "the Rust Belt"), or for other pressing reasons, such as a lack of affordable transportation or child care. But even these additional estimates of the unemployed fail to reflect the fact that the concept of the labor force has a false ring of definiteness to it. For example, the number of people who are "ready, willing, and able" to work varies with the wages that can be earned. If, for example, the costs of gasoline, work clothes, and/or child care eat up too much of one's potential wages, that will block a person otherwise desirous of working from taking a low-wage job. A rise in the level of wages will accordingly expand the labor force. Or a wife may want to work but is not permitted to do so by her husband; hence a decline in sexist practices will also expand the labor force. Or one may have to move to a new region or city to find work but cannot make the move for economic, family, or other reasons; again, a higher level of wages or a change in family practices may make the move possible, with the result that the labor force will be larger than it now appears.

There are even more varied cases that restrict admission to the labor force and, it should be added, serve to hide the real level of unemployment. One may be very keen to work but have no skills or abilities that employers will recognize. Or one may have an erratic employment history because of fluctuating local economic conditions, which diminishes the willingness of would-be employers to hire. Further, a person may be one of those millions who have served time in jail and want to start over again—in an economy deeply mistrustful of "convicted felons." One may have been forced into what one feels is premature retirement or have a health condition that would periodically—but only that—interrupt one's attendance on the job.[2]

Still another inadequacy in the concept of the labor force is that the force has been growing over time in virtually every industrialized country, notably in proportion to the relevant age cohort that participates in the labor force; this is mostly due to the increased participation of women in paid employment and to the increase in part-time jobs (see *Statistical Abstract* 1999: table 1377). All in all, as a measure of the numbers of people who are in some sense available to work for wages at any given point in time the concept of the labor force is an extremely narrow, often arbitrary device. Clearly, if we are to be able to understand the phenomenon of work in our society we need a subject concept that, unlike labor force, doesn't analytically exclude the factors that govern its size and changes. In this context, the concept of the social labor-power prominently includes in the first instance all those persons in a society who might under appropriate circumstances seek and take a job. Technically speaking, the social labor-power is the independent variable in manpower discussions and the labor force is the resultant of factors acting on that social labor-power.

But this expansion of the meaning of the social labor-power is still not sufficient for our inquiry. We want to include in our subject concept all the changing productive services exerted by workers, hence all the persons who aid or participate in the production of workers. The fact that income in a capitalist economy is directly steered toward those who are in the labor force—though indirectly via such tax classifications as "dependents"—seems somewhat arbitrary to those deemed not to be part of it. We should include the labors of parenting, community or other volunteer service, and so forth. Here the criterion is not "does he or she have or can he or she take a job?" but "does his or her labor produce enhanced productive abilities in others?" If the answer is "Yes!" then that person is part of the social labor-power.

There is a third category of persons to be included under the concept of the social labor-power. The labor of trainees, students, apprentices, and so forth adds to their later productive capacity, that is, it contributes to the production of tomorrow's labor force. It, too, is included in the concept. This subject will receive particular attention in chapter 6.

The concept of the social labor-power is—to this point—only that, a concept, and one whose worth must be justified within commodity form analysis. By employing the concept we as yet suppose nothing about any empirical outcomes. But we must start with a concept that appears to be adequate to the scope of our inquiry or, equivalently, offers the possibility of expressive completeness.

Labor and Labor-Power

The social labor-power comprises a modification of the concept of the labor force into a more inclusive group of persons. Further, however, this concept of a social labor-power also embodies the Marxist distinction between labor and labor-power but with a crucial difference.

Conventional economics generally speaks of the labor of workers, not their labor-power. In that usage, the labor of workers is analytically constituted by the quanta of the physical product from the labor expended or, more commonly, from the money value of that product in relation to their wages; this is the familiar "marginal net product" analysis. For our purposes, what is significant here is that the workers' productive qualities are taken as given in a particular analysis; as I pointed out in chapter 1, by aggregating this assumption, as one does in conventional "micro," one is left with only a static view of the productive characteristics of the productive populace. Thus, it is said that some persons are in principle unemployable because their skill levels, or reliability, or stamina don't exceed some threshold of employability, that is, their marginal product is or would be too low (unless, as in the 1940s, their labor is needed badly enough). Alternately, workers, it is said, may put themselves out of a job if they price themselves too high because the marginal product needed to pay them would exceed industry, regional, or some other standards.

On either supposition, the limits, indeed the inadequacy, of the static concept of labor as used in mainstream economics is apparent. It is also wrong-headed. The physical output of a worker or the money value of his or her output may vary enormously depending on factors other than skills, attitude, energy, and health. Obviously, the sort of tools, equipment, and systems he or she is given to work with will be of capital—pardon the cheap pun—importance. Just as significant, one of the most important economic developments of the past century has been the massive expansion of the ranks of managers and cognate professional and technical employees in industry. The rates vary in the different advanced economies, but basically such managerial and technological cadres have grown from less than 1 percent of the late-nineteenth-century labor force to a figure on the order of 15 to 25 percent of all those employed in such economies today, often with radically higher rates found in manufacturing. Industry believes, as apparently economics does not, that labor productivity varies with the number of managers and technological specialists. This division of labor between managers and production workers has been central to the development of the corporate form of business organization.[3]

Almost from their "invention" in the latter decades of the nineteenth century, modern corporate firms have tended to replace the earlier forms of organization of the productive population, the familiar "division of labor," with a single, universal model based on the relationship between manager and worker. Earlier writers, of course, noted at least three historical forms of the division of labor. Adam Smith in his famous chapter 2 of *The Wealth of Nations* ([1776] 1970: 117ff.) emphasized the social division of labor, that is, a division between fisherman, farmer, trapper, merchant, artisan, shepherd, swineherd, and so forth. Marx, writing roughly three-quarters of a century later, found it necessary to distinguish between the division of labor in society, as in Smith, and that which holds in manufacturing. In the former, he pointed out, each producer produces a commodity that can be exchanged with others. In the latter, several workmen combine to produce a single product, which under the factory system is sold as a commodity by the capitalist owner. The workers receive their income through the wage system rather than through a direct exchange of products ([1867] 1967: 331ff.).

With the rise of different, specialized technologies, often science based or science dependent, in the latter part of the nineteenth century one might want to add to this list a technical division of labor. This would appear to overlap but perhaps not replace both the other species.

What is most striking about the division of labor in a modern society is that the relationship between manager and worker has absorbed all three of these species. In this—often called the "industrial"—model the major division is between the manager, who (crudely) monopolizes the directing or brain functions of work, and the worker, whose effort is limited to physically carrying out tasks defined by and under the direction of the manager.[4]

In farming no less than manufacturing, in the research laboratory as in the school or university, in retailing as in fisheries, the organization of modern work features a sharp division between the manager and the managed, and the tendency is for that distinction to deepen. For example, in mass production manufacturing to date, the modal worker has been a machine operative, that is, someone who operates a machine of greater or lesser complexity, under a regimen presided over by a manager, while the machine itself carries out a task designed into it by the manager's associated technical and engineering colleagues. In the post–World War II years and especially as abetted by later computer and electronic communications developments, the modern office worker, retail clerk, hospital employee, and even library worker has also become in good part a machine operative too. Or, to put the matter another way, the older hard and fast distinction between blue collar and white collar (or pink collar) workers has been rapidly eroding, the evident tendency of this erosion being to homogenize the work regimen of every sort of productive activity into the industrial model.

When we compare the potential productive services of workers with those they actually accomplish, the role of managers stands out. Even if we assume for the sake of the argument that managers engage in no direct production of a product it is still true that their effect on the workers' efforts is as a multiplier of the workers' efficiency (within the terms of the management system) and output. But, however we interpret the productive effect of managers, this difference between the workers' "labor" and the workers' "labor-power" has been the fulcrum of a major, perhaps *the* major, change in the composition of the employed population in the past hundred years.[5]

Given this reality, Marx's concept of labor-power is more fundamental to studies of work organization and productivity than the current concept of labor because it makes explicit the point that the potential of workers is one thing, how much the workers produce is another, and that capacity may be well or poorly utilized in a given situation or an economy as a whole.

Marx appears to have understood that management and work organization deeply affect the productivity of workers; that very subject forms the substance of volume 1, part 4, of *Capital*. On the other hand, management systems in his time were relatively primitive and meagerly staffed. In the small, family-owned firms characteristic of the era, the owner carried out management functions along with a foreman or two, while back in the office a humble clerk scratched away at the accounts and the correspondence with a quill pen. More to the point, in Marx's "equilibrium model" of a capitalist economy, the distinct work of managing is analytically collapsed into that of the workers. He devotes little explicit analysis to the distinction between managers, who even then would have been relatively well off, and workers subject to the General Law of Capitalist Accumulation. This lacuna is partially explained by the fact that it was only in the decades just after Marx's death that the radical expansion of the management echelon began, most notably in the United States, during the "trustification" era.

Marx, however, did understand and stress that the wages paid to workers and the effort they expended (hence the location of their marginal net product) were affected by several factors: child labor, the length of the workday, the capital intensity of the productive system, and so forth. His discussions of labor-power also invariably take account of the effects of the unemployed, the hidden ones as well as the ones trekking about in search of work. This is essentially the meaning of his notion of "the reserve army of the unemployed" who influence wages, productivity, and working conditions because of their threat to take the employed person's job for less pay and under less favorable conditions.

Thus, Marx's "labor-power" is simultaneously a more useful, analytically acute concept than either the conventional macroeconomic "labor force" or the microeconomic "labor." The latter two concepts can be analytically developed within "labor-power," as species of the genus or subsets of the set, whereupon their limits are more readily apparent than when they stand alone as fundamental concepts of analysis.

The Social Labor-Power

However, today there is a problem with Marx's "labor-power," for his conception comprises simply the sum of the uniform labor-powers of individual workers ([1867] 1967: 45–47; for the quotation, see chap. 2, n. 10). This was perhaps apt to his times. Analogous to the way in which other commodities were being standardized in his time, he saw that the modal form of labor-power in capitalism then took—or was taking—the form of the proletarian, that is, a person who is forced into the capitalist labor force under such dire conditions that his or her other social and socially productive characteristics are milled into a relatively uniform labor-power of minimal skill. As Marx puts it with telling accuracy in *The Communist Manifesto,* the man and the woman and the child, the skilled worker and the novice, the urban dweller and the newly arrived migrant from the agrarian districts, the Scot, the Briton, the German, the Frenchman, and even the Chinese and the "Hindu," are stripped by "the cash nexus" of their formerly differentiating social and other characteristics to become, in the argot of manufacturing, mere "hands" in the satanic mills.

But, as I suggested in speaking of other commodities of the time, Marx's extrapolation of the processes of commodification of labor-power has not been borne out. In short, those processes acting to simplify and iron out the capitalist labor force that were anticipated in, say, the 1850s and 1860s and are reflected in the analyses and description of volume 1 of *Capital,* more or less reversed themselves in the latter part of the nineteenth century and throughout the twentieth. Taken as a whole, the labor-power of society could no longer be accurately depicted as made up of or tending to an additive aggregate of uniform labor-powers. Instead there developed a multiplication of the sorts and kinds of labor-powers within the manager-worker relationship.[6]

The concept of a "proletariat" still lurks in some Marxist discussions of labor-power issues, referring particularly to workers who have been "deskilled" by the development of modern management and technical productive systems.[7] But, looking at labor-power developments as a whole, whatever skills have been lost by the workers, it is evident that they have been more than made up for by the expansion of technical knowledge and ability among the managerial ranks. That is, in the social labor-power taken as a whole there has been a dramatic amplification, not simplification, of its productive services and potential productive services. This comes of the explosion, still continuing, in the number and variety of professional specialties, technological specialists, types of line managers, types of specialized staff experts, and so forth. What the popular press calls "the knowledge explosion" of the twentieth century is actually a disembodied shorthand for this extraordinary proliferation of what the French call the "cadre" of modern society and industry. It is precisely that sort of phenomenon that requires a change in our concept of labor-power.

Analytically, the contemporary social labor-power cannot be well depicted as a sum of uniform productive services; it is an ensemble offering varied but complementary quasi services. That is, in a modern economy the work of no one person, of no individual kind of labor-power, constitutes of itself an integral productive service, just as in the world of commodities goods what we find among workers and producers of various kinds are quasi services that must be combined with the efforts of other workers to produce usable commodities. That is what I had in mind earlier in saying that the social labor-power was the proper unit of study for manpower, producer, and related issues. The social labor-power must be viewed as an aggregate of individual and even group labor-powers, which, taken together in various combinations and as a whole, are complements to one another, not merely replicas, with the ensemble forming more or less a single organic productive unit. These complements most prominently include the relationship between cadre and workers and, equally, the complementary activities of workers who today work in organized institutional productive systems in which the product is of the team and not of any individual worker. And, of course, they include the relationships between mentors and those they mentor.

Courses/Channels and the Commodity Form of Labor-Power

There has been an evident change in the forms of sale/purchase of labor-power throughout the evolution of capitalism. For example, in the period just preceding Marx's lifetime, there was, properly speaking, no employer-employee relationship; there one finds basically a master-servant world. This was as true in the workshop as in the home. The major difference was that between master and servant there were nets of mutual obligations that not only dealt with wages and tenure of employment but might obligate the servant to seek the master's permission to marry and to whom, to leave the employment, and perhaps even to frequent a tavern. Typically, the servant would have at least some tenure of employment, perhaps the right to receive special foods at different times of the year, a new suit and shoes, and so forth. Toward the end of the eighteenth century, at least in England, within the development of the private property system, the net of mutual obligations between master and servant gave way to the "cash nexus" or, in labor system terms, "free labor." It was only then that there evolved what we see today as employer-employee relations, that is, a narrowing of the relations between master and servant to a few economic dimensions, with all other traditional obligations being effectively nullified. The change, of course, did not occur overnight. Even in the earlier decades of the twentieth century the system of free labor was not quite fully developed.[8]

Under free labor the laboring relation is stripped of every dimension save the fact that there is a contract "freely arrived at" between employer and employee. Accordingly, the employment is "at will', that is, it can be terminated by either party. Wages and conditions of employment cease to be set by custom and precedent and instead are arrived at by means of bargaining in "the Market." The development of this new free labor system in Britain during the Napoleonic era, and in France shortly afterward, also lurks behind the concept of a "proletarian" when, it seemed, the social, economic, and legal conditions of the proletarian would simply sweep away all other labor arrangements.

Sale/purchase of labor-power in an advanced economy shows a mixture of free labor and a variety of limitations on it. In spite of their current travails, unions remain important in many areas of economic activity and have won contractual rights limiting employers' "free" scope of action. But even when there is no union, professional contract, or civil service, employment is, at least legally, still "at will," though not cleanly or thoroughly. Virtually every employer in private industry effectively "tenures" (i.e., gives semiguaranteed employment to) a core work force, notably in middle management and among especially skilled or scarce categories of workers. Many also practice the layoff/recall system whereby workers are released from employment but retain an effective right to be called back to work, by order of seniority, at some later, often predictable time. On the other hand, employers still reserve the right to dismiss employees when and as they see fit.

Modern legislation forbidding discrimination against minorities, women, the handicapped, and older persons also materially restricts the scope of "at will" employment. As the system works in the United States, these categories of workers are specially protected in the law and employers are positively regulated in their dealings with them. Such protected persons have presumptive rights in the hiring queue; in their treatment when hired with respect to promotion, pay, and so forth; and in the manner in which they may be dismissed. In addition, they may bring complaints to special courtlike regulatory bodies in which the burden of proof may rest on the employer not the complainant. Minimum wage laws also restrict the operations of a pure system of free labor. Thus, at least in the private sector, free labor or at will employment is vastly hedged, perhaps even covering only a minority of the labor force. On the other hand, of course, all those historical measures limiting the free labor system have come only after epic labor-management or electoral battles, and most efforts to extend the system of modifications are resisted by employers and their elected representatives.

When we try to sum up a contemporary, modern employment system, we see an apparently limitless number of different kinds of jobs and employment conditions. Yet the industrial division of labor does tend to sort this mass of employment situations into a small number of types, and these bear the marks of modern commodity form.

I have adopted the terms *course* (from *life course*) and *channel* to characterize these types. It is my contention that, under analysis, each type of course and/or channel can be shown to possess the coordinate characteristics of commodity form and in fact that they constitute that form. Basically, I'm making three claims here. On the one hand, the most significant division of the social labor-power at present in the developed world is into the seven courses/channels shortly to be described. Second, those courses/channels together constitute the commodity form of contemporary labor-power. And, third, each consists of a distinct ensemble or family of related sale/purchase states more or less uniquely linked in time and keyed to the person's eventual place in the productive system.

A course should be understood in the first instance as the genus of the term *career*. We customarily use *career* to trace the course of a person's working life from their entry into the job world—in some cases nowadays from their entry into preschool—up to and perhaps beyond their retirement. The idea of a career is that one's work history, and the preparation for it, is "of a piece," so to speak, that someone who will become a bookkeeper will follow a different educational path, acquire different knowledge, learn different skills, earn more or less money, have different prospects for promotion, and consequently enter into a different set of social relationships and experiences extending over time than, say, someone who becomes a physicist or a laborer or a salesperson.

Unfortunately, the term *career* is normally class bound. It expresses the fact that only some members of the working population require special, longer preparation; can confidently expect to greatly increase their incomes, authority, esteem, and job perquisites; and are likely to enjoy all the opportunities that a high and rising income affords for travel, hobbies, socially rich entertainments, and such. And of course they will pass some of these advantages on to their children when they embark on their life courses.

It is useful to strip the word *career* of its connotation of privilege and adopt in its place a cognate term that can be employed to talk about the life course of every sort of person with respect to the economy and the social labor-power. We can do that by generalizing the concept of a "career" into that of a "course," whereby we can as easily speak of the life course of a factory hand as of a lawyer, of a homemaker as of a journalist. Because most of what we do and consume in every stage of life involves sale/purchase, those commodity transactions, including the sale/purchase of our labor-power, will, through the course of a lifetime, group themselves into distinct ensembles with a "family" similarity within the same course/channel and marked differences from those outside that course/channel. These family differences mark off the different commodity forms of the social labor-power.

The term *course* has some affinity with the concept of "roles" in contemporary sociology, although it is here intended to have a political-economic, not a sociological, meaning. Yet the sociological term suggests that the "roles" one plays out in life are to a degree crystallized for us ahead of time; we do not create them so much as step into them. I think it unexceptional to say that people's courses tend for the most part to be mapped out for them; a course is normally a kind of prefigured channel for the different roles that one successively adopts over the period leading up to and throughout one's working life. Thus, the concepts of course and, with subtly different emphasis, channel can serve as counterweights to the normal connotation of the word *career,* which is that a career is an individual's unique creation and achievement.

I will use the terms *course* and *channel* more or less interchangeably. To speak of the course a person follows emphasizes the activity of that person; to speak of the same phenomenon as a channel emphasizes the social prestructuring that has already laid out the alternate paths that course may lead to, underlines the presence of key turning points, and in general looks at the person's work as an element not solely of his or her individual life but as a constitutive element in the social labor-power. As a rule, when we employ either term we should understand that the other is implied.[9]

Modal Courses

It is, I think, not accidental that as the number of discrete jobs, professions, and specialties has increased they all tend to be organized into only a few distinct courses. One can identify seven as by far the most significant. These are: (I) elite corporate employments or occupations at the top rungs of other major institutions or professions, henceforth abbreviated simply as "Elite"; (II) nonelite managerial, professional, and technical work, henceforth abbreviated "Managers"; (III) entrepreneurship and/or the individual operation of a entrepreneurial profession, as for many lawyers, henceforth abbreviated "Entrepreneurs"; (IV) nonmanagerial workers, normally full time and with a modicum of, if not job permanency, then regular employment, henceforth abbreviated "Regulars"; (V) workers whose occupational courses are irregular or typically only part time or characterized by moves from industry to industry, sometimes called contingent workers, henceforth abbreviated "Marginal Workers" or "Marginals"; (VI) workers generally excluded from paid work over their whole course, henceforth abbreviated "Excludeds." There are, finally, (VII) homemakers and others whose kindred contributions lie outside the labor force but whose labors help to produce that labor force, henceforth abbreviated "L(abor)-P(ower) Producers." Some employed persons, of course, help to produce labor-power—teachers, for example. But I want to include among the courses those labor-power producers outside the paid economy. By definition these people aren't directly paid for their work, but socially patterned ways and amounts of resources are directed toward them, and to that degree they represent a commodity form of labor-power. I have not included students and trainees as a distinct course because Courses I–VII tend to comprise a different sort of education/training/acculturation within themselves. This last point, in fact, seems to be emerging more and more as a feature of the modern commodity form for labor-power.[10]

Terms such as *Elite* and *Marginals* function as commodity forms, not "ideal types." They assert a complex empirical claim that can only be illustrated here, not "proven." On the other hand, if in fact each of the seven courses/channels represents a distinct commodity form, then it should be socially manifest that this is so, a question more of our recognizing an unusually prominent pattern than divining a secret meaning. Courses comprise integral life paths in preparation for, entry into, and activity within an "Americanist" world. Under examination each should embody a distinct process of production of recognizable, relatively standardized, productive services, a distinct path into or into relation with the occupational world, typically a distinct job tenure, a pay and rewards system also unique to itself, and each should have a recognizable social evolution into its present form.

Taking a critical standpoint, we know that individuals can change course within a lifetime and also that there are course changes between generations. One way of dealing with this theoretically would be to allow the courses to shade into one another. Thus, we could postulate a course continuum with, in this case, seven nodal points. That formulation would in no wise falsify the reality and significance of the different courses but it is analytically more fruitful, I believe, to conceive of each course as an integral phenomenon marked off from the others but to conceive of there being especially important switching points between the courses. In this formulation, the schooling system functions not only as a labor-power producer but also as one of the main switching points wherein young people may change course, either to rise—as our national myths emphasize—or to fall—a less studied phenomenon, although the two are obviously related.

A course does not represent a genus of a group of jobs, a "dumb generality" reached through a process of abstracting. A claim is being made here, in principle empirically verifiable, that there exists a multidimensional pattern to the seven courses that corresponds to commodity form.

The Higher Courses

At present a university or equivalent education constitutes the most important economic/vocational frontier in a modern economy. Not to have one is normally to be relegated to the ranks of Regulars, Marginals, or the Excluded, while to have completed a bachelor's degree, and now perhaps a master's or its equivalent, is to have acquired one's ticket to the two higher courses.

In virtually any significant-sized corporate firm, a nongovernmental organization, other mainstream institutions, and the government itself the educational frontier is mirrored in the sharp distinction that is maintained between the managerial echelon and the production work force. While industrial practices have long distinguished between the generic manager and the generic worker the modern distinction was historically crystallized through the work of Taylor and other "efficiency experts" around the turn of the nineteenth century, most notably within the organization practices of the then new multisite, multiproduct firms being organized in the "trustification" movement. So universal has been the distinction between manager and worker that it is routinely coded in the "rights of management" clause in virtually every labor contract and has been enshrined in law through a number of Supreme Court readings of the Taft-Hartley Act of 1947. It is also reflected in the statistical categories of the main data-collecting agencies, public as well as private. Like so much "Americanism" the distinction has become almost equally important in all the main capitalist countries.

Intuitively, we all appear to recognize the difference between a worker and a manager, and in this case that intuitive understanding is largely correct. Less intuitively clear, and less widely understood perhaps, is the strong modal difference between the Elite and Managers courses, as both are a kind of manager. Basically, modern firms and other organizations that copy corporate organizational form mark off a small group of upper managers as tending toward the strategic or "entrepreneurial" side of the business who—accordingly—will choose the lines of business in which the firm will be active and how it will pursue them. The firm's strategic relations with its organized workers, government officials, and some of its main customers, suppliers, and rival firms will also tend to come within the purview of this upper or inner management group. Once these strategic directions are determined and decisions made, it is "middle and lower" management, or some such locution, that will be tasked with the details of carrying them out, both directly by supervising workers and indirectly by providing the staff services (legal research, accountancy, laboratory testing, etc.) that are ancillary to the firm's various lines of activity. This prominent difference between the two management groups provides the analytical basis for the separation into two different courses/channels. (For more on this point, see Chandler 1962; and McDermott 1991.) When we conceive a course as an ensemble of closely linked, often overlapping sale/purchase states, the differences between Elites and Managers are readily clarified.

The significant elements of the course that will normally lead to and then constitute Elite employments in the United States today begin with the identity of one's family, comprising most importantly its social standing, wealth, race/ethnic identity, and educational level or level of (high) culture. That will of itself skew the family to seek a prestigious preschool and elementary school for its Elite child following in the family's footsteps. Here the privileges and economic advantages accruing to a well-off family enable it to make an integrated, patterned series of sale/purchases in tuition, camps, after-school activities, and so forth, which will assist the child to take the next step into either a prestigious private high school and/or an equally prestigious track within a highly esteemed public high school. Obviously, in our highly commercial society most of the details of preparing for and passing through high school are carried out through patterned sale/purchase arrangements.[11]

There is of course no assurance that however affluent and well connected the parents their offspring will gain a privileged post at the next or university level, but the probabilities are heavily in their favor. In fact, we should methodologically conceive of a course as made up of probabilities related in time. Thus, the social associations one engages in come to be reflected in differential probable patterns of expenditure for clothes, travel, cultural pursuits, and so on, both prior to university and during the undergraduate years. Skipping ahead, if all goes well there will eventually be a degree from an elite postgraduate institution normally followed by direct entry into the "fast track" of an elite corporation, law firm, or other institution. This often promises relatively rapid promotion into the lower ranks of the institution's "strategic" posts, and with this comes widening access to substantial proprietary income and/or perquisites from one's institution; this represents the beginning of the net return from the considerable costs of the previous stages of this Elite course. Now there is some positive likelihood of eventual candidacy for upper management, the upper levels of one's profession, or some equivalent post that will also be associated with greater access to proprietary income and/or perquisites in the form of stock options, large bonuses, partnerships, travel, conference invitations, and so forth.

The course/channel for non-Elite managerial, professional, and technical workers, what the French refer to as "cadre," bears many formal similarities to the course/channel for Elite employment. There is the same progression through preschool and either a "good" elementary school and/or its higher "tracks." There would normally be an academic degree in high school, itself in a higher track, then a bachelor's degree, perhaps even begun at a community college, then either direct entry into the managerial echelon of some business or professional institution or the same but following the completion of a graduate program.

In this country at least, this Course/Channel II may at points overlap and intermingle with Course/Channel I. Even the most exclusive private schools and the most prestigious public ones, such as New Trier High School in Winnetka, Illinois, or Brookline High School in Massachusetts, mix boys and girls with vastly different prospects, but over time the courses will likely diverge. Even at the most prestigious institutions, for example, one can often identify those who are more likely to go on to high-flying careers because they come from the right social background, often including a particularly prestigious secondary school, or, just as important, have been taken up by Elite mentors and are being groomed for a preferred future.

The secondary school and university are, I estimate, the points where one may switch from a course otherwise destined for modest success in business or the professions to the Elite channel. As above, this channel jumping, usually described under the rubrics of "social mobility" or "meritocracy," is an important reality in a modern society and economy and, to repeat, an even more important myth.

In the posteducation world, most—nearly all—important mainstream U.S. institutions have different entry points for employment. The ordinary personnel office will normally suffice to hire and then place regular production workers who present themselves, while a different section of the Personnel Department will actively seek out and evaluate those with specialized degrees in management, science and technology, or some other university-created area of specialization and expertise. But there are special recruitment programs (e.g., "headhunters") and special entry points for those who come from elite social and educational backgrounds, and their subsequent careers are not managed by the personnel specialists of middle management. Instead, as we colloquially put it, they are "groomed" by a "senior person" for eventual candidature for the highest levels of management.

The "Worker" Courses

Course/channel differences are even more marked when one steps to the other side of the university-education frontier. Here we may most usefully shift the focus of our discussion from the production of labor-power to the modal differences in conditions of employment. One of the main dimensional differences between the three "worker" courses and the higher courses, respectively, and between the different kinds of workers, has to do with the degree of change one experiences, or is led to experience, within one's course/channel.

While Managers and Elites have careers that are channeled by institutionalized promotion steps, this is not so for employees in the three worker courses. Occupational immobility is the rule there. In the same vein, while the two managerial courses feature relatively strong job tenure, job fragility is more often the rule for the worker courses. These differences are not only rooted in the industrial practices of the developed countries but often have, as in the United States, explicit legal backing. Thus, much of the point of employer efforts to keep unions out or weaken them is aimed at preserving an "at will" employment relationship with Regulars. And, for all but the most fortunate Regulars in private industry, the best one can say of a worker's job tenure is that seniority places the older worker farther up the list whose bottom rungs are surely destined for the layoff or even permanent separation. On the other hand, compared to the employment security of Marginals and the Excluded, Regulars often do enjoy the benefits of unions, with their seniority lists and other forms of job and task protections.[12]

Reality is always more messy than any law can prescribe, but the manager/worker division is exceptionally well maintained in the United States, not least because whenever the division weakens to the detriment of managerial authority both management and the labor regulatory system have been prompt to reseal it.[13]

For a Regular the band of opportunity for "rising on the job" is very narrow. One is condemned to be a "hand" not a "brain" worker. Basically, it is the case that one doesn't normally go from high school into management; one would lack both "qualifications" and credentials. And one doesn't normally go from college into the production ranks, for then one would be "overqualified." Further, there is no continuous path to promotion in industry. One does not normally gain management experience in the ranks of the workers, and that fact, like the lack of the proper educational credentials, tends to minimize "promotion from within the ranks." The two different courses of labor-power, Managers and Regulars, are produced differently, and that productive difference carries over and is coordinated with their later utilization.[14]

The restriction of "brain work" to the management echelon has also served to make more homogeneous the productive qualities of workers, at least those in the Regulars. I don't mean that the workers, as men and women, personalities, and so on, can thus be reduced to a type. One must not imagine that managers need or indeed employ more brainpower than production workers and that production work is therefore brainless. This common prejudice, like so many others, is rooted in a mélange of ignorance and class snobbery. The distinction between the two sorts of labor-power rests not on the personal productive qualities of the two sorts of employees but on the course/channel they occupy. Most managerial work consists essentially of supervising the work routines of production workers (or of designing new ones in which technology will do the supervising and pacing). From the nature of the case, the social role of the one emphasizes using one's brain, while the role of the other is to obey someone else's brain.

The most numerous category of the Regulars in mass production industry are those occupationally described as "machine operatives." While the absolute number of machine operatives would appear to have fallen with the decline in manufacturing, the introduction of industrial techniques and technologies to office work—computers, printers, fax machines, photocopiers, and so on—has in fact increased their number. Many members of the work force in sales also operate machines. Modally, such operatives feed and/or operate a machine that carries out one or a series of routinized operations and then route the product to the next step or stage of production. Paradoxically, this homogenization of their modal course role deceives the unwary as to their productive qualities, which must be rather high.[15]

A Note on the Other Courses

I will not devote space and attention here to Course/Channel III, that for entrepreneurial pursuits either in business or as a freestanding professional, such as a lawyer practicing on his or her own. Very often persons who take this course come from backgrounds similar to those for Courses I and especially II, and their divergence from those courses is often a matter of personal choice, luck, family tradition, and so forth. Also the failure rates of modest-sized firms, professional or otherwise, are such that there is always much interchange between Courses/Channels II and III (i.e., Managers and Entrepreneurs). Primarily, however, the persons who run the most important and numerous entrepreneurial businesses or practice their professions through their firms are really part of Course II. Because of the rapid expansion of franchising and licensing, more and more small businesses, typically the most profitable and long-lived, are backward or forward satellites of larger firms, so their business systems—accounting, labor relations, technology, production processes, and distribution systems—are typically closely prescribed and monitored by the larger firm, as in the fast food industry. In these cases, the Entrepreneur is only partly that. He or she is also a quasi employee of the larger firm, almost as subject to its management system and relative success as are its employees.

As was suggested earlier, what is significant about Marginals is that they do not have the opportunities and job security of either of the managerial courses or the Regulars. Marginal workers include those who are part timers or work only when employers need them. Normally paid the minimum wage, and often less, without benefits, and with few seniority lists and no promotion path, they are often subject to the whims of foremen and other supervisors or to poor treatment because of their age, gender, race, or ethnic background or because they are immigrants. Below them are only the Excluded, those who can find work rarely, if at all, and then only of the poorest kind.

The brevity of my remarks on Marginals and Excludeds should not belie their vast numbers or their economic importance. Further, I have not made a calculation, but the narrative evidence seems overwhelming that business firms have succeeded in using Marginals in many jobs that used to require higher paid, semitenured Regulars. A business friend once described to me the latest office system for processing credit card payments. The office in question was then located in Lower Manhattan where a large college student population guaranteed a regular and ample supply of educated, relatively reliable labor-power. As my friend explained, the managers expected to be able to replace any worker on half an hour's notice, that is, not only to place a new worker at a vacated station but to have completed his or her training to the acceptable productivity and reliability standard within that time period. At present, this sort of office production system is as likely to be found in Bombay or Dublin as in Lower Manhattan for the same reasons and to similar effect.

Course VII, L(abor)-P(ower) Producers will be taken up in chapter 6.

Course, Commodity, and Conditions of Employment

To summarize, my argument is that the commodity form of labor-power within a modern economy per se is distinguished into subvariants by the several courses. This occurs in several coordinate dimensions, most significantly (1) in the juridical and customary employment relationship, which differs for each course; (2) in the actual differences in the ensembles of productive quasi services used and work routines carried out by different course participants; (3) in the form, quantity, and regularity of remuneration; (4) in the distribution of labor-power by course/channel across the economy or, equivalently, the dominant division of labor; and (5) in the manner of its differential production.

The Formal Employment Relationship

In a modern economy the position of every person can be analyzed as an element in a five-termed relationship of both a juridical and practical nature whose other elements are (b) his or her employer, (c) profession or union (even when empirically absent), (d) government both de facto and de jure, and (e) the institutional network of L-P Producers, including, for example, the university credentialling system. In these dimensions each of the courses importantly differs from the others as, to take an example, in the nature of job tenure or, more technically, in the way in which they have modified the doctrine of "at will" employment as it applies to the different categories and courses of employees.[16]

I earlier commented on the at will character of modern employment in the private sector. Yet each of the other four players in the employment relationship have seen fit to modify it with respect to the different courses

The private firms themselves cling to the doctrine of at will mainly for tactical reasons, but they have historically and unilaterally modified it, as we saw in their practice of maintaining a core group of employees. In their management echelons in particular, they have socially enacted the category "career" by unilaterally adopting regular promotion systems that lead some of their employees through a calculable number of steps from beginner to retiree. Then, too, it was the private firms that more or less unilaterally instituted the seniority governed layoff/callback system, thereby conferring a sort of limited and modified tenure on their workers.[17]

Unions, even when absent, have played an enormous role in modifying the employment relationship. The current reduced size and influence of the trade unions are in fact almost irrelevant here. Historically speaking, unions contributed to making socially manifest the distinction between, on the one hand, Managers and workers and on the other hand Regulars and Marginals. The historic introduction and maintenance of the relative privileges of the Regular course was probably as much due to the threat (or reality) of unionization as anything else. And it has been in part through union disinterest in organizing part-time and seasonal workers that the Marginal course has come to be socially enacted as a major mode within the labor force. It has been predominately through union cooperation that distribution of the narrow perquisites and rewards that are available to mere "hands" has been rationalized and systematized through the adoption of seniority provisions in the contract and/or just in routinized practice. Even today business firms typically try to treat their employees just well enough to keep a union out or to be adequately placed to defeat it if one turns up.

The professions have thrust themselves into the employment relationship both through the institution of credentialling, often accompanied by legal sanction, and, with the aid of the universities, by inducing employers to place their members within the privileged managerial echelon. In fact, the Managerial course can be seen as a joint creation, in the first instance, of employer and university.

Government enactment and influence have differentially altered the employment relationship through the (earlier) support of trade unionism and its later action in the labor regulatory system to restrict managerial tasks to management, more or less forbidding their performance by members of trade unions. More important at present have been government programs such as antidiscrimination law for several classes of employees—women, minorities, the handicapped, the older worker. In all of these cases, discretionary government authority is interposed between the contractual "at will" relationship of employer and employee and modifies it quite substantially. But by and large, the main weight of these antidiscrimination programs has been directed at and successful in the managerial echelon. One gains the distinct impression that, save a few dramatic cases mostly in the building trades, discriminatory practices in the worker courses are not viewed as of very great importance in U.S. public policy.

Seen as a labor-power-producing institution, the university system has importantly deepened course differences in employment relationships through its own promulgation of the roles and authority of the several professions and its joining with them to make sure that industry and government recognize those professional prerogatives. Government frequently assists them in this, for example, when the licensing of the professional is tied to his or her university-provided credentials, as in the law, medicine, civil engineering, and so on. Obviously, the Elite course is reciprocally enhanced by the continuing prestige of certain elite institutions.

Productive Services

It would be belaboring the point to comment extensively on the productive services deployed in the different courses. If any overall tendency is to be marked here it is that the managerial capacities of management have been increasing in tandem with the growing adaptability of the various worker courses to be managed. Relatedly, the increasing capacity of the managerial profession to train and direct workers and the increasing scope of formal education have been shifting the borders between Regulars, Marginals, and even Excludeds. At one time, for example, industry often preferred to keep on the payroll workers who were temporarily not needed because it was too expensive to train their successors at a later time and because it was, probably with reason, assumed that inexperienced and very young workers were too irregular in quality. But the growth of the fast food industry in particular and of industrialized office work challenges those older truths. The very large pool of educated women and high school and college students offers potential workers who are prescreened to some significant degree, and new management systems and techniques have enabled first the fast food industry and now many others to hire and train such workers as needed on a temporary or a part-time basis. The point I would make here is that the borders between Regulars and Marginals, once relatively fixed, are becoming more fluid and may become less important. Against this, the manager-worker divide seems to be becoming even more crystallized.

Pay Systems

Payment and other rewards systems for different classes of employees are dominantly arranged by course. Here it is not simply a question of more or less; payments to members of the different courses may overlap at various points in the course. Equally important are the security of the wage or salary, whether it is programmed to rise and by how much, and the scale and surety of benefits and perquisites. On the other hand, the prices found in the sale/purchase of labor-power are differentiated considerably by course. Essentially, Elites receive some multiple of Manager pay primarily because their regular (higher) salaries are regularly augmented by special access to proprietary gains such as stock options, profit-related bonuses, or other indexing of their income to profits. Thus, over time they typically come to "earn" a much higher multiple of their starting salaries than ordinary managers, and of course the increase in their status and authority over the course of their careers is equally dramatic.

The pay of ordinary Managers, while not in the stratosphere, is conventionally set by taking a multiple of the wage of the workers they supervise. For all Managers, there are also modest opportunities for increases in pay, authority, and professional esteem over time, that is, over the course of their careers. Their benefit systems also tend to be calculated at some multiple of those accorded to workers in the same firm or industry.[18]

Regulars can normally count on some tenure of employment, hence regular wages over the course, and in addition they typically have their (higher) wage scales augmented with various benefit schemes such as sick or vacation pay. Pay is often increased simply due to length of service. There is also the opportunity for advancement, thus higher pay, though admittedly within only a very narrow band of increased pay and authority. On the other hand, workers still normally receive wages that are calculated in terms of hours worked or units produced; Managers classically receive salaries not for the number of time units they work but for the entire period they remain on the payroll.

The Marginal course is a relatively recent arrival in the employment picture. Until very recently it made sense to distinguish a corporate from a peripheral sector of the economy (see Averitt 1968). These two modal forms of business differed in firm size, product lines, pricing behaviors, the geographical size of their markets, their rates of technological change, and several other key business dimensions. Among other things, the employees of the peripheral sector of the economy had much in common with today's Marginals, earning a great deal less than those of the central economy and enjoying much less security of employment.

One of the most striking changes in U.S. business in recent years has been the invasion of firms from the central economy into the old periphery, for example, in fast food, apparel, real estate services, cinemas, poultry production, and a veritable host of other areas. The economic significance of truly entrepreneurial firms has radically declined as they have been replaced with franchises and other forms of satellite business (they have not, of course, lost their ideological significance in the "free enterprise system"). By and large this invasion—too carelessly grouped under the rubric services—while drawing these lines of business ostensibly into the central economy have not raised their workers to Regular status. Thus, the Marginal course, which at one time existed at a distance from the center, is now as often a course within the central economy. Its employees, though now clearly integrated into the national economy, still generally earn close to the minimum wage, even when they're performing the same tasks as Regulars and are almost universally excluded from benefit packages. Insofar as they remain in the Marginal course, there is little opportunity for advancement with pay raises, and, as their job tenure is almost nil, so is the security of their income.[19]

As I argued earlier, it has been due to advances in management techniques and the systems of production that Marginals are now able to carry out many of the same tasks, utilize the same quasi services, and staff the same productive systems as Regulars. While this implies a shift in the borders of these adjacent courses, the industrial/practical reasons why firms retain some core employees, even among their "hands," seem to be pressing enough that the Regular course cannot be entirely dispensed with, although it may continue to be radically reduced in scope.

In brief, then, the wage and rewards structure of a modern economy is organized in the first instance by course/channel. The empirical differences in amount of pay or other opportunities within each course/channel may be significant, but in general the kind, amount, regularity, and duration of an employee's income and other rewards are dominantly conditioned by his or her course.

Division of Labor

As pointed out throughout this chapter, the division of labor by course, a major fragment of which is the industrial division of labor, has become dominant in every calling, in every area of productive activity, in town and country, and so forth. It is in fact especially striking that divisions within the work force as seemingly ancient and profound as those between town and country or fisheries and husbandry are now almost entirely encompassed within the different courses.[20]

The Production of Labor-Power

We have yet to deal in a sufficiently systematic way with the modern production of the social labor-power, but, as I argue in the next chapter, that analysis also tends to confirm that courses/channels exemplify the modern commodity form of labor-power.

6 | Producing the Social Labor-Power

Human Capital Revisited

As we have been stressing, the dominant neoclassical microeconomics assumes a labor force whose productive characteristics are not altered by the goods and services it consumes, that is, that its size and other productive qualities are "exogenous" to the microanalysis of ultimate consumer demand. Naturally, this assumption is dropped in many exercises in applied economics, as in development theory or productivity studies, but it is retained in fundamental "micro." There appeared to be a breakthrough on this particular point in the late 1950s and early 1960s when human capital theory aroused a certain amount of interest, and that interest has since entered the economics mainstream. But here, too, the theory was policy oriented and has not challenged the foundation principle that the nature of final demand is not itself altered by the workings of the economy, not even, paradoxically enough, by investments in human capital. Nevertheless, the subject is not without interest to our present task.

The professional legitimacy of human capital theory was crowned with the publication in 1965 of Gary Becker's *Human Capital: A Theoretical and Empirical Analysis with Special Reference to Education.* Becker was primarily interested in investments in human capital that took the form of discretionary investments made by private persons and/or families, primarily for education.

In his pioneering undertaking, Becker analyzed the relationship between prospective increases in an individual's wages and prior investments in further education. The investment is analyzed in equations expressing in the general case how a greater net return will come later to the educational "investor" as a result of present education and/or training. The analysis is extremely theoretical, even to the extent that the equations relate not the costs but instead years of schooling to the promised higher returns from investment. Becker applied his analysis to a range of postulated situations, including most prominently the age of the worker; the level, duration, and vocational specificity of the education; and sociological categories such as race and gender. The analysis and results are quite straightforward; there are no surprises. In the general case—"all things holding equal"—further years of education will lead to an increase in net earnings over time. The microeconomic individual acts rationally in deferring earnings or paying out of pocket educational costs with a view toward earning a net higher income over time.

As indicated, Becker's methodology links economic rewards to years of schooling, not its costs. His relative lack of interest in costs undoubtedly reflected the time in which his book was composed. Through the mid-1960s, dramatically increasing numbers of students sought higher education, their job and pay prospects were to remain unusually good (at least until the early 1970s), and apparently educational costs had not yet begun to inflate (as they would subsequently do), so there seemed to be a wealth of corroborating evidence, which didn't need citing, that years of education correlated with multiplied income. At the present writing, however, one would need a more nuanced approach, almost surely requiring price modeling, to take account of the various costs and opportunities associated with the different courses/channels.[1]

It is much to Becker's credit that he provided an interesting and powerful start in modifying wage theory toward greater realism by going beyond the idea that the differential productivity of workers was based on natural endowments rather than phenomena subject to further economic investigation. Becker's simplifications, however wrong some of them may appear now, were, I think, a factor in the rapid acceptance of human capital theory in mainstream economics. He seemed to show that no real alteration was needed in the neoclassical paradigm to bring social services such as education, which have an ostensible nonmarket character, into market analysis. As already suggested, his work has had an important effect on policy questions and virtually none on fundamental micro. Oddly enough, this paradox has helped rather than hindered the acceptance of his work, the normal intellectual conservatism of the economics discipline thus being led to view his contribution in a favorable light.[2]

More important for our purposes, Becker's work assumes a conventional analysis in which wages equal marginal product. Capital investment will bring higher wages and that implies increased marginal product. This is a most elegant analysis for it fits well with the idea that an increase in the educational attainments of the work force will correlate with a more productive economy.[3]

The tension between the modified workforce of human capital theory and the static one of the Jevons/Walras micro is obviously unsatisfactory. A more useful, less paradoxical theoretical result can be found if we approach human capital questions by analyzing the production of the social labor-power along the same lines as the production of commodities generally.

To (Re)produce Labor-Power

To produce or, alternatively, to reproduce labor-power is simply to increase productive services in some part of the social labor-power, that is, to increase its capacity to produce further services in persons or "things" or, indeed, itself.

These are historically conditioned quasi services, not integral ones. In a modern economy a worker's or potential worker's skill, technique, knowledge, and so on are effectively social, not individual acquisitions. They require as complements a measure of physical and energy resources, a stock of goods and equipment, and an organization or institutional setting that the worker cannot provide independently. Also included are the level of technology and science, the peculiarities of the economic system, the prospective distribution of income and work, and the character and function of various mentoring institutions such as schools, institutes, family, "peer culture," apprenticeship, and so forth. Thus, whatever training, teaching, or acculturating the potential worker receives he or she receives it in a context already more or less fully defined in its several social-material dimensions. Young people have to find their way through ready-made channels in a ready-made social-material world.

One must accordingly stress the fact that modern production routines are social in nature, which is to say that no single worker is likely to be able to take in hand the production of significant commodity services from primitive start to final completion. Training, learning, and so on are normally directed toward the trainee/learner working as a complementary producer within some part of that setting.

In short, producing or reproducing productive services in workers of all kinds, including Managers, is a phenomenon itself located within the social labor-power. It comprises, essentially, a modification and often an expansion of that the social labor-power in terms of the number, variety, potency, and novelty of the services located within it. From the terms of discussion, the social labor-power has the unique quality that it is self-altering and can be self-expanding.

With this prefatory material in mind, we can examine the elements of the productive relationship within which labor-power is produced. The elements of this productive relationship include (1) the commodities consumed in the process by the learner/trainee; and (2) the characteristics of the institution, usually a family, educational institution, and/or "apprenticeship," as for on the job learning, within which the learning or training takes place. For a modern economy, the university is the central institution around which most of the others pivot, so we have (3) the labor of a mentor or mentors and, of course, (4) the labor expended by the trainee or student. Under this point I would stress that the labor of the student is qualitatively different from that of the worker and that the labor of the worker is in at least one highly significant respect best understood as a sharply constricted, even distorted form of studentlike labor.

Varieties of Constrained Consumption

About point 1, all one really need add to our earlier discussion is that most of the commodities are consumed most of the time under some form of constraint imposed upon the consumer.

There are a few commodities that are bought from the private sector and then consumed by consumer/purchasers, which instance the free choice celebrated in the doctrine of consumer sovereignty. At the other extreme, elementary schooling is nearly universally compulsory. It is possible to distinguish several other consumption modes between these extremes that are only partially constrained—not free, not compulsory—and materially enter into the production of the social labor-power. Around a typology of constraint, we can thus observe the following varieties.

Unconstrained Choice

As indicated, the Jevons/Walras micro assumes consumer sovereignty, a claim that comprises the further claims that (a) all consumer spending is essentially discretionary and (b) that for every consumer the marginal utility of money is equal, that is, differences of income are irrelevant in the analysis.[4]

Obviously, some consumer consumption takes this form, as when we spontaneously buy an ice cream cone on a summer day. The purchase is readily imagined as (a) fully discretionary as to choice and (b) inexpensive enough that both the wealthy person and the poor one can more or less ignore the cost. On the other hand, even under this rubric of unconstrained choice, as we move from cheaper to dearer commodities, the differences in the marginal utility of different consumers' money begins to exert its effect. Thus, even within the category of nominally free choice, we are dealing with a range of constraint values moving from "zero" to "appreciable." Obviously, the different courses would tend to occupy overlapping but different segments along the axis.

Legal Compulsion

We are so accustomed to conceiving of consumption as a free choice phenomenon that we overlook just how much consumption is de facto compulsory. The most obvious candidate is public elementary and secondary education, which is compulsory for the age group six to sixteen in most cases. As with Social Security, even those who forego the consumption of the public service are obliged by law to contribute to its costs. Less dramatic but no less important from the point of view of labor-power production are public fire and health services; police and roads; in most cases water, sanitation, and sewage services; and so forth. In dollar terms these are not small numbers, and in fact in a modern economy they may encumber a third to half of all private income.

In addition, most of these services are consumed within administrative relationships, which add a further dimension of constraint to the processes of consumption. As was argued earlier, their constraining power normally lessens as we go from the lower to the higher courses.

One could argue that the historical evolution of this constrained consumption in developed countries was guided by the desire on the part of capitalist Elites to assure the production of a better work force—better, that is, because its altered social-productive characteristics would better lend themselves to the capitalist use and be accompanied by sociocultural attitudes supporting a relatively cooperative relationship between capital and labor. By and large that is a supportable thesis, but we need not rely on it here.[5] It is enough to say that without these kinds of highly constrained consumption we would be dealing not with developed economies but with the "underdeveloped" kind. Thus, the category of legally compulsive consumption exists within a complementary productive and social-productive relationship with modern capitalism. Without it we do not have modern capitalism; we have some earlier variety, that is, a variety that like the capitalism of Marx's time more or less took its workers as it found them. As a corollary to this last point, this is again one of those areas in which necessary productive investment, here in labor-power, has already been largely socialized, even though its product is often predominantly advantageous to the private sector.

Contractual Constraint

In a modern economy there are goods and especially services that employees are contractually constrained to accept and presumably use. Two of the most important of these are company- and union-sponsored medical and retirement plans. Here the constraint is often sweetened by the employer, who makes a contribution or matches one from the employee. (This is almost always only a cosmetic change in the form that the wage payment takes, not a net increment to the wage.) In many, probably most, cases the individual has no choice but to contribute to the plan—however cosmetically this may be disguised—and, of course, to make use of the benefits. Here, too, the benefit reaches the beneficiary through an administrative relationship, with the latter adding its extra degree of constraint to the situation. Historically speaking, plans such as these were introduced by employers in order to stabilize their work forces, and in some cases, such as Ford Motor Company's old Sociology Department, the intent was to improve employee productivity by improving employee "morals" (Lacey 1986: 131ff.).

Social Constraint

There are important and diverse areas of consumer spending and consumption that are socially constrained. One of the most obvious and important is the ownership of a private automobile. There are large sections of the country in which alternate transportation is simply not available for going to work, the store, school, and so on. This is clearly true of most rural areas. Again some of this social constraint "just happened." But there is also the notorious case of GM buying up Los Angeles' public transport system and then tearing it down so as to force the use of the private car. Modern marketing strategies aimed at sales to young people have a different twist; they exploit the desire of adolescents to "fit in." Marketers in music, clothing, and accessories try to establish norms for appearance and ownership that socially constrain children, young persons, and their families to spend money they might devote to other things. Educators, especially at the secondary level, often complain that these money pressures, translated into young persons working long hours at low-wage jobs, are a serious impediment to their education.

More widely and only a bit less successfully, marketers, by engineering markets, try to socially constrain consumer/purchasers to buy their wares. At the personal level, for the individual consumer/purchaser these skewed markets impose pressures to buy but they can be resisted. There is only mild constraint here, not outright compulsion. At the social level, these engineered markets have a differential impact on various consumers; it is, for example, an advertising industry "truism" that poorly educated consumers buy the more expensive name brands in the supermarket because they would be embarrassed to be seen buying house brands, which, they have been convinced, are of lower quality and carry less esteem.[6]

Conditional Constraint

One may buy a commodity in the free choice mode but then, as we showed in our initial analyses of sale/purchase, that choice may obligate the consumer/purchaser to engage in a whole series of further expenditures on such items as for repairs and insurance for the car, discs for the stereo, or maintenance of state of the art technology with one's PC and operating system. The choice to pursue higher education has much the same character, as once one has set out on that course changes in credentialing standards may obligate one to seek a higher degree at greater expense than one had originally intended.

There are three important implications of even this brief review of the range of constraint.

1. A not insignificant degree of constraint is the norm in consumers' consumption.

2. As a rule, this constrained consumption is a form of productive consumption under one or more of the rubrics described in chapter 3. This is true whether it is a legal compulsion to go to school, the social constraint to own a car and accept liens against future wages to keep it in repair, or the contractual obligation to accept the company medical plan. Sometimes the productive relationship has a dual nature, as when we buy a PC for use in school. On the one hand, the consumption of the PC is directly productive of labor-power of improved characteristics, and those new labor-power quasi services will in time normally enter into tomorrow's production of commodities. On the other, the PC itself is a commodity consumed, as we have seen, within a system of conditional constraints under the aegis of the producers/sellers, accompanied by wage liens, fructive of further purchases of commodities such as disks and printers, and so forth.

3. To the degree that the production of new labor-power services enters or will enter into the production of other commodities, including even the consumption of public services, it is socially manifest that it is ancillary to the commodity system and part of the circuit of productive capital. The point is not that, say, unemployment insurance was designed to complement commodity production (although it was). The point is that through the complementary effects it has in altering the productive characteristics of the social labor-power, unemployment insurance becomes a constitutive part of any wider producing relationships that the worker or family is a part of or will subsequently enter into. Thus, we should see compulsory public elementary and secondary education, much public health expenditure, expenditure on fire and sanitation services, and so on as ancillary to commodity production and to that extent subsumed within private sector commodity-producing relationships.

Further, because public sector services are socially universal, commodity producers in the so-called private sector can incorporate their distribution into their own marketing strategies. Banks, for example, now provide that one's Social Security check can be directly credited to one's account. On-line companies provide course aids, even term-paper "drafts," keyed to various high school curricula. In this sense we can designate such publicly funded and delivered services as commodity complements.[7]

The Institutional Production of Labor-Power

We can view the educational system of a modern economy from any number of perspectives, but here we should view it primarily as a labor-power (re)producing institution. Into it as raw material enter virtually the entire population of the country, whereby they are sorted, differentially trained, acculturated, and credentialed primarily into the different courses and occupations. Appropriate to such a mammoth productive undertaking, the system employs an equally mammoth labor force and is among the main consumers of producer goods as diverse as electricity and books, construction materials and luncheon foods, security personnel and yellow buses.

Seen in this economic light, and contrary to its self-image, especially at the university level, its production of knowledge, however important in itself, is an ancillary function, ancillary not to its immediate teaching functions but to the production and expansion of the productive powers of the social labor-power.

I grant that in the United States especially it sounds odd to so describe the educational system. We are more used to thinking of the system not as a system at all. At its lower levels, for example, the principle of local control results in an apparent crazy quilt of different programs, requirements, and standards, one extreme of which is marked by continuing controversies about not teaching evolution—either in the biology classroom or, in the sex education classes, where abstinence is the byword. Even at the level of higher education, there are Ivies in the picture side by side with the sort of junior colleges that specialize in filling job slots for the more influential local employers. Yet out of the apparent confusion—erratic "tracking," academic and commercial degrees, local control, state monitoring, public admonishment, and federal largesse, public versus private, secular versus religious, union versus management, competing textbook behemoths, elite institutions and degree mills, high-powered technical institutions and relaxed finishing schools for both sexes, meritocracy rewarded and privilege confirmed—the whole does behave as a system at least to the degree that it has been sensitively responsive over time to the changing needs of the wider productive mechanism.[8]

Four observations support the interpretation that we are dealing with a more or less coherent "productive system." One, as befits an economy that exhibits rapid technological and business institutional change, every level of the U.S. educational system tends to spend more per student on the high flyers than on the low. In a real sense, both technologically and even morally, lower performing students are a byproduct of a system that winnows them out in the process of identifying those who will gain the higher or more prestigious degrees and go on to staff the ranks of the cadre or the Elite.[9]

Second, as in other areas of (at least) the U.S. economy, a considerable amount of "coarse planning" is carried out. By this I mean that autonomous institutions cooperate with one another to produce not necessarily a single product but more commonly a coordinated production and distribution system for a group of complementary products. A similar example of this sort of institutional cooperation is provided by the airlines, aircraft suppliers such as Boeing, engine suppliers such as General Electric, the communications industry (electronic booking and flight control), the travel industry (marketing), and the electronics industries for various ancillary equipment.[10]

Probably the best way to describe the process of coarse planning in the world of education is to point out that many organized publics and institutions are normally consulted on virtually all educational decisions and departures. This may take the prosaic form of local business executives on the boards of community colleges or of chief executive officers (CEOs) of nationally and internationally famous firms serving in the same capacity on the boards of the most influential private and state universities. It may take the form of the great foundations funding educational or cultural initiatives. It may take the form of a diverse list of firms and organizations asked to participate in a prestigious presidential commission on technology or even just to testify before the legislature on educational bills. Or, equally important, it may take the form of the close links that as a rule are maintained between the university, the professional association, and the end user of a particular degree, whether it be in electrical engineering or law. The result of such multifaceted "planning" has been that the services of the social labor-power have been modified over time to produce the requisite skills and knowledge, in the requisite numbers and "more or less coherently," for the economy.

Third, we again meet the phenomenon that Gramsci called "Americanism." This provides a common frame of reference for all those voices under point 2. In this country at least, no educational program or institution can stand entirely outside the Americanist framework, that is, cannot take cognizance of the economic values and labor-power needs of the corporate productive framework. There can be different interpretations of the point in U.S. history when Gramscian Americanism became so dominant and of why it continues with unabated strength, but that it has such strength and influence is beyond doubt. I think it is a prime factor in supplementing coarse planning because it provides a directing rationale for every teaching institution to devise for itself some useful role within the Americanist framework. No government planning office is necessary here, no educational czar, merely a willingness to fit usefully into the "system." Maverick institutions exist, although they typically face the double scourge of state educational displeasure and a limited ability to raise money from the wealthy. It is, however, important to emphasize that a system feature of a modern economy is that institutional cooperation and integration, absent government compunction or common ownership, play a very big and necessary role. The United States is much more accurately called a cooperative than a competitive economy. What this means in practice is that Elites from the public and private sectors become commingled on the boards of the big firms as well as on those of research institutes, hospitals, nonprofits, educational institutions, foundations, and so forth. Many such Elite men and women move back and forth from executive posts or consultantships in the different institutions. This is one of the central phenomena that constitute the Elite course.

The fourth factor concerns the very direct links between educational institutions and the different courses/channels. As already argued, the different courses first take shape within the educational system. The key switching points occur there as well, and the more elaborate training of the higher courses preoccupies a system weighted empirically at the university level. Here I think we see further confirmation of the fact that the primary commodity form of labor-power is comprised of the several courses and not of the precise occupations and métiers. Let me put it this way: a university, for example, provides more than just the precise training needed to qualify a student for, say, electrical engineering. Many, perhaps even most engineering graduates, like lawyers, will not work throughout their lives as engineers or lawyers per se. One's technical specialty is often only an entry point to industry and may be used for just a short while before the employee is promoted to other, often managerial positions. This is especially, perhaps uniquely, true for persons with higher education. In a related vein, university training represents not only the acquisition of a body of knowledge or skill and its consequent credentialing; it also represents a process of acculturation to the higher courses. Thus, what is almost certain is that the graduate, no matter what his or her job, will spend his or her life within one of the two higher courses. Much of the university's actual training, certainly its credentialing, and even a good part of its acculturating prefigure this outcome.[11]

Mentors and Learners

Under the category of mentoring I include the actual work of care giving, teaching, counseling, socializing, training, and so forth, which enters into the production of some part of the social labor-power—from birthing classes through postgraduate training.

A modern economy draws virtually everyone into its web, no matter how seemingly isolated, and extracts from that person some work meaningful for the economy per se. This goes far beyond the statistician's category, the labor force participation rate. That index only gives the percentage of persons in the (paid) labor force for the significant employment years, normally ages sixteen to sixty-five. In a modern economy that rate has tended to climb, reflecting mainly the increased participation of adult women and now of teenagers generally. It is a useful figure, but it vastly underrepresents the work of adult women. What has most deeply changed and what is grasped in the concept of the social labor-power is not merely that women have, as it were, left the nursery for the office and mill, but that the office and mill have invaded the nursery, integrating its functions with their own and on their own terms. In an eminently practical way, today even the work of the mother of a very young infant is part of the social labor-power. Invariably, the style of mothering will be affected by norms promulgated in her course/channel by the wider society; she may make use of the medical profession and its institutions, and the birth may be assisted by socialized commodities in the form of the hospital, its support services, and especially its work force. Invariably, too, a host of commodities will be consumed even in the first weeks and months of the child's life. The earliest family or personal decisions about what sort of life the child is to have will be taken in light of an existing social and economic fabric and so on.

The work of mentoring, of every sort and of every kind, is nowadays deeply affected by the economy. That is why the mentor course does not in reality represent a single life course as does, for example, that of a Regular or even a Marginal. Insofar as there is course/channel continuity between the generations, each course supports and uses different kinds and durations of mentoring in different institutional settings. Aside from the dominant Americanist ethos, probably the most important point in common is that for all of the courses purely private labor in the home is being replaced everywhere by mentors whose mentoring is complementary to that of the labor-power-producing institutions and who productively consume commodities to prepare and shape tomorrow's labor-power. In short, the modern division of labor also incorporates all the different kinds of mentors in its ranks, including mothers.

When we turn to the productive labors of learners we can see right away that the contemporary concept of "human capital" can't really be taken literally; it has mostly metaphorical and ideological meanings. It is only a metaphor because, unlike the investor in securities, whose labors are perhaps limited to the rigors of depositing checks, the investor in human capital has to go out at some point and exercise that acquired capital for forty hours a week, fifty weeks a year, for at least a couple of decades. Ideologically speaking, the concept of a human "capital" expresses the fetish claim that we are all property owners and capitalists, thus marking the final end of the historical class conflict so wickedly championed by that scruffy German.[12]

Insofar as a young child is doing work that will even indirectly fit him or her into a life course, the child's efforts are a part of the social labor-power. Crudely, the modern division of labor by course that directly makes possible the mass production and distribution of modern commodities also indirectly enables capital to absorb into its reproductive circuits virtually the entire population of a country no matter at what a person's stage in life or even what he or she is doing at the moment. Marx's old charge that the "cash nexus" replaces every sort of human relationship is, in a modern economy, quite literally true.[13]

The productive relationship between the learner and the mentor has some similarity to that of the worker and the manager. Both, of course, are catalytic ones in which complementary services and efforts combine to create an entirely new commodity, in this case an altered, expanded labor-power in the learner.

But, the qualitative roles of the learner as learner and worker as worker are radically different, at least in the present organization of the economy. In learning, a quantum of knowledge or skill is passed from mentor to learner, which results in new or expanded abilities in the learner. We expect, indeed demand, not a modest net increment in the final commodity but a substantial multiple. The learner's effort should lead to a comprehension of the subject that goes well beyond what was directly imparted. To use an old-fashioned example, one wants the geometry student to not merely memorize some theorems and proofs from Euclid's *Elements* but to understand them, even to the extent of being able to produce corollaries or analogous theorems. The example is out-of-date, but the point is germane; learning normally (or at least hopefully) involves a quantum leap or multiplied result in the services of the learner beyond what is literally "given" to him or her by the mentor. Ideally, after learning the learner should be able entirely to dispense with the mentor. One could even say that learning is the quintessential characteristic of the social labor-power in that it occurs within every activity.

This aspect of the mentor/learner relationship is in sharp contrast to the manager/worker relationship under which other commodities are produced. There the manager imparts to the worker little more than the rote "elements" of the job. The worker certainly should not learn enough to be able to dispense with the services of the manager entirely, no matter how "cooperative," "team-oriented," or "decentralized" the work relationship. The knowledge and the skill to translate on-the-job knowledge, experience, and hence learning into a full competence on the part of the worker so as to be able to dispense with the manager to some greater or lesser degree—this of all things is to be avoided in the manager/worker productive relationship, but it is the distinct—or at least ideal—desideratum when we consider the producing relationship that we call learning. If we consider productive interchange with others and nature as intrinsically a learning experience, then it is a perversion of work to constrict learning within it and to prevent work from having a socially cumulative learning character.[14]

We treat learning in the general case as already explained, as an expansion of the potential productive services of the learner. Sometimes this is abetted by a mentor, but in research, also a form of learning, the key energy and direction may arise predominantly from the individual researcher or researchers alone. In both cases, from the standpoint of labor-power production we see a self-expansion of labor-power, an expansion that goes well beyond—in both the qualitative and quantitative senses—the aggregate sum of its social, social-material, and physical inputs. This is the true "surplus value" of a modern economy.

For the individual learner, this expansion consists only of quasi services, that is, productive services that will have to be combined with others to produce usable commodities. From the standpoint of the entire the social labor-power, however, it implies an expansion in the range and number of its own services and underlines the central idea that the social labor-power is itself a self-expanding phenomenon. This self-expansion will prove to be the key to unraveling the contradiction, preeminent in our capitalist economy, between value and price.

Labor-Power as Commodity

Four different kinds of commodities enter into the production process of non-labor-power commodities, to wit, the labor services performed by the prototypical manager and prototypical worker, producer commodities of various sorts that are consumed in the process, and the services of organization, coordination, and of course investment by the institution or institutions within which the particular production processes are carried out.

One can employ the same productivist schema for the commodity production of labor-power in the individual and of course of the social labor-power. There are the labor services exerted by mentor and the learner. That process is accompanied by the consumption of commodities, which from the nature of the case are producer commodities and in great part occur within and under the influence of the Americanist institutional network.

The same commodity production of labor-power can be viewed as an overlapping series of sale/purchase states in which the learner traverses a channel located within the network of Americanist institutions, some of which produce labor-power and some of which consume it in their own production processes. Obviously, there are differences, for example, between producing a lathe and a bachelor's degree and between using that lathe and that college graduate. Nevertheless, both are dominantly marked by commodity form.

One could argue that the positions of the learner and employee are different if for no other reason than that the learner is the payer while the worker is paid. But if we credit our morphology of constrained forms of consumption in this chapter and of the analysis of consumer goods in chapters 3 and 4, much of what we pay and/or are paid, in every setting, simply passes through us in ways prescribed by constraints promulgated by others, not by our untrammeled will. And of course they add further to the productive services of the social labor-power.

The course of a modern person's life is not simply a set of discrete events. The terms *course* and *channel* have been coined here to bring out the reality that a modern society and economy really do impose a channel on life that differs at many, many crucial points from the other courses followed. If there is "coarse planning" in the production of the social labor-power the degree of coarseness is not particularly set to make sure that I'll be an assembler in an electronics factory and you will teach at Harvard. There are many switching points between the different courses, and they are taken advantage of by legions of individuals. But for most people, whether socially mobile or immobile, it doesn't matter; most of the time our economy and society act to keep them within socially prescribed courses and channels. In a modern economy and society, we "coarse plan" courses, one's generic place in the economy.

In our discussion of the nullity of final consumption as a modern category of analysis we saw that non-labor-power commodities never, or only rarely, exit the circuit of productive capital. The latter has manifestly taken on a true process character no longer interrupted by "the Market." Insofar as the nurturing, socialization, education, and utilization of modern producers of all kinds occur within one of the several courses, a parallel conclusion may be drawn, namely, that the social labor-power is produced, used, and reproduced more or less entirely within the productive circuit of capital. This covers the production of the person as potential producer, the ways in which he or she is actually used within the productive apparatus, and, through the dual system of liens and courses, how he or she will continue to participate as a nominal "consumer." Here, too, we find a process phenomenon that is not significantly interrupted by either the Market or its sociological reflex, the "open or individualist society."

7 | Price and Value

The Value Subsystem

Debates about value theory occupy a much more prominent place at present in the Marxist tradition than in the neoclassical one. That undoubtedly comes of the fact that the analysis of final demand in Marx is widely considered to be inadequate, even among Marxists themselves; witness, for example, the "repairs" introduced by the influential book by Baran and Sweezy (1966) discussed in chapter 2. In addition, there is the famous "transformation problem" in Marx, that is, the difficulty of establishing a consistent relationship between values and prices, which we will shortly discuss. This is not to say that the neoclassical conception of value, as represented in the Jevons/Walras microeconomics, is problem free, but neoclassical dominance is so complete at present that critical voices are not often heeded.[1]

Notwithstanding the heralded differences between the two traditions, from the standpoint of value theory they are analytically quite similar and, of greater importance, both exhibit the same methodological flaws. To appreciate this we again have to draw a sharp distinction between the narratives they offer about their value theories and the logic of the value theory itself.

At the narrative level, Marxists and neoclassicals could not be more different, with the former casting theory in terms of units of labor exerted and the latter in quasi-psychological units, the one essentially supply oriented and the other demand oriented, and the one purporting to speak of objective, material sorts of things and the other speaking at the subjective level. It is when we move from narrative to analysis that their similarities emerge.

Analytically speaking, value theory minimally comprises two claims. The first we have met, namely, that broad classes of priced exchange behaviors by different people are in principle quantitatively comparable.

The second is that all economic propositions, no matter how complex, can be equivalently reformulated in the language of that elementary comparison. We can call these language elements "value primitives," consisting, respectively, of labor-power units in Marx or of units expressing desirability, satisfaction, or preferencing among the neoclassicals. Normally one does not rewrite propositions about empirical economic behavior into elementary value language but instead shows that such propositions can be inferentially transformed into their value terms.

The transformation itself rests on four claims that are shared by both traditions. These claims logically overlap and support each other, forming a distinct subsystem of analysis. The first is that each exchange price embodies a microcosm of the economic universe. Each price in an economy is simultaneously and uniquely determined by—their ratios precisely established by—every other price. There is a sense, of course, in which that statement is trivial. Any and every price, regardless of circumstance, is expressible in a definite mathematical ratio to every other price—thus, it is tautologically "codetermined." This comes merely from the fact that prices are expressed in the real number system of which the rationals are a subset. However, it is the nontrivial sense of this assertion that will concern us, namely, the idea that prices in aggregate "cause" each other, that the absolute magnitude and relative level of each price is precisely codetermined by each of the others in a simultaneous, interactive causation.

Second is the quantitative comparability principle just cited, the claim that a calculus of interpersonal "value" binds these prices into that interacting system. More simply, in their price behavior different people, acting at different times and in different markets, make maximizing choices that are fully and unambiguously comparable on an identical quantitative value scale and according to the same value calculus.

Third, in principle each commodity has at a given time one and only one price which corresponds to one and only one value.

Fourth, prices and price movements are in principle infallible clues, signs, and indicators of fundamental underlying processes (of effort and/or scarcity and preferences) bearing on that interactive causation, that is, "the economy." For "fundamental underlying processes" read "governed by the value dynamic." In other words, the subsystem is analytically closed. For ease of reference I will henceforth refer to this shared "value subsystem."

If one accepts the value subsystem then one adopts the doctrine of "price realism." The term is drawn in analogy to those older, familiar claims about "universals" in classic philosophic epistemology. There philosophical "realists" argue that names (i.e., concepts) grasp some "real" features of the things they name, hence that there is an inner logical connection between "names" (concepts) that can be explored and truly grasped by purely philosophic analysis and more or less absent any appeal to further, empirical information. In historical philosophy one would speak here of using apriorist methods; apriorist methods are prominent in both the Marxist and Jevons/Walras microeconomics.[2]

By virtue of this shared value subsystem the Marxist and neoclassical microeconomics, including now their narratives, are mirror images. In Marx, final or consumer consumption occurs under the laws of necessity, while in the neoclassical view there is only free choice. Here their point in common is that, at least in principle, no final consumption is ambiguous as to constraint. There is either utter constraint or utter lack of constraint; in either case the (claimed) phenomenon is so unambiguous that it is relatively easy to model it via the subsystem.[3]

Of course, both microeconomics introduce "escape" clauses. Marx allows that "an historical and moral element" modifies the working of the General Law ([1867] 1967:168). The neoclassicals allow that the poor are just as free to bid on baguettes flown in from Paris that morning as the rich should they choose to use their income in that way. Despite differences in income, all consumption choices are treated as if they are made in the free mode; this claim falls under the rubric that real world markets are "imperfect." However, if, as has been argued in these pages, virtually all sale/purchase has a one-sided character that introduces dependence or other kinds of constraint into the process of consumption itself, then it is theoretically unsatisfactory to leave this to be dealt with by "escape" clauses. One wants instead to bring the fact of differential degrees and kinds of constraint into fundamental microanalysis, that is, into value theory itself.

Rejecting the Subsystem

What I want to show is that the concept of "value" as it is employed in the subsystem is not sustainable. Introduced to make up for the theoretical deficiencies of actual prices, it turns out to be "price" under another name but as arbitrarily shorn of its deficiencies; in short, the value subsystem, put forward to explain price, is merely price in another guise, a disguised synonym.

It is fundamental at the outset to recognize that the term or concept of *price* represents an elided statement about human social behavior or, if one prefers, a "logic" of such behavior. In the first instance, the word *price* refers to a particular price, as in "the price of C"; the latter is the elided form of the four-termed proposition, "S(eller) exchanged C(ommodity) with B(uyer) for *p*." In economics, though not in commercial usage, the term *price* refers to a specific price in a specific exchange between a specific buyer and seller. Prices appended to classes of goods, as in "the price of a movie ticket," are derivative usages. *Price,* whatever other associations it may have, is ultimately a term designating particular behaviors, and many of the problems associated with its usage can be resolved by going back to the behaviors that are being indicated.

We tend to think of prices as the given, unanalyzed or primitive data for economics, the raw phenomena out of which one draws theory and to it that one returns to confirm or adjust that theory. That may be the pattern of other disciplines but not of economics. *Price* is not in fact a primitive term in economics; on the contrary, it comprises an elaborate analytical construct, that is, a construct that precedes and guides economics theorizing. For example, economic analysts have historically focused on sale/purchase prices at the point in time when the "deal" is made. But in an actual market different deals for the same items may be separated by a minute, an hour, or even a day or more in which prices may change. Conventionally, this time difference is ignored when economists consider prices as an economic category; whole classes of deals are treated as necessarily occurring at the same instantaneous time, while in general equilibrium theory all exchanges everywhere in the economy are conceived to occur at the same point in instantaneous time. But this is to extensively theorize microeconomics even before . . . one theorizes microeconomics. Much of the seeming unreality that laypeople ascribe to economics theory comes of this—I think illicit—procedure.

In the present study we postulate that modern sale/purchase normally takes place throughout a positive duration of time and that this obviates the need to substitute the analytic price for the empirical price, as if the substitution doesn't matter. Accepting a time framework as intrinsic and fundamental to microeconomic analysis, we open up the logical space to allow that even for the same commodity there will be rival prices claiming varying degrees of importance. Moreover, there is no need to assert a priori, as in the value subsystem, that one and only one price for the commodity has priority over the others, is *the* price. We accept that there are many different prices for a commodity, each of which has a different warrant and significance. There is, for example, still the sale/purchase price exchanged at the point of sale. That has some economic uses but more so does the sum of the prices spent for the commodity over the duration of the sale/purchase. Commodity purchases are not conventionally analyzed in terms of the latter price—unless of course one is doing some kind of cost/benefit/time study. Another price is constructed to overlook actual changes in the value of money. In comparing the price of food to the price of housing in the Jevons/Walras micro we assume that we are denominating both prices in the same price system—"constant dollars"—even though we know that the time frameworks for the two expenditures are different and hence that inflation or deflation will differentially affect them.

Another equally significant price is a percentage of one's income or, over time, one's income stream. That price doesn't normally come up in micro, but if one is in the position of underwriting credit to the would-be purchaser this is a much more important price than the others. In a modern economy, so reliant on consumer credit, this last price clearly has an enhanced significance.

There is no point in going on. It is clear that for any commodity the concept of the unique price is problematic. There are a number of different prices that are obviously of economic significance, their importance varying with the vantage point we select. That being so, there is no overwhelming, one-sided reason to describe the nominal purchase price of something as "the price." Or, as corollary to this, Marxist prices of production and Jevons/Walras equilibrium prices of, say, a new auto are just as much complex constructs of only conditional warrant as the cost-benefit price of the vehicle over its lifetime or the constant dollar price or the amount (the price) that a credit agency will be willing to lend you to purchase it. In short, to the different kinds of prices there correspond quite different microcosms.

A second objection is that few actual prices of any sort behave in readily comprehensible ways. Sometimes they are orderly, as when they obey what the TV pundits call "the Law of Supply and Demand." But equally as often the rise and fall of various prices are as mysterious as maritime weather—hence the attractions of the stock market to the adventurous. Even goods that bump up against each other in the same market, such as fruit and vegetables in a street market, don't always behave as those "laws" tell us they ought.

The value subsystem argues that prices should vary continuously in response to even subtle changes in the conditions of supply and/or demand; business practice tells us that it is very easy to lose customers by raising prices but harder to gain them by lowering prices.[4] The "laws" of supply and demand call for a lower price to be associated with greater sales, but there are whole classes of goods whose overpricing is intended to raise, not lower, sales (Stiglitz 1987). Taking one thing with another, actual prices, their relative levels, their ebb and flow, and their relationships with other economic phenomena don't cleanly lend themselves to theoretical niceties. The apriorist inversion of data and theory functions in economics not to explain things like this but to explain them away.[5]

Neither Marxist nor neoclassical analysis employs actual empirical prices as the primary data, the ultimate "given," and the value subsystem doesn't really refer to them save derivatively. Both traditions prescribe a category or set of prices that stand in for empirical prices and function as the data of economic/analytic investigation. Essentially, these prices are conceived to be prices that always and in every way obey the various laws of economics. Or, in behavioral terms, one conceives that if people's transactions were freed from all inessential, extraeconomic factors, then they would exchange at these prices. Such prices tell us how people would behave if they were acting purely rationally and not from ignorance, impulse, social pressures, and so forth.[6]

I'll henceforth adopt the convention of using *price* to refer exclusively to actual, empirical prices and *Price* to refer to those prescribed by economic theories employing the value subsystem. I'll also refer to empirical markets, reserving *Market* for the theoretical construct that normally stands in for actual empirical markets in economics discussions.[7]

Insofar as *Prices* are stand-ins for prices, a *Price* still only refers to that which was exchanged for a specific commodity in a specific *Market*. One needs a logical bridge, so to speak, or a common medium to use another image, which will serve to represent all *Prices* occurring as if in a single system. "Value" provides the bridge and the medium. Then different *Prices* will be part of the same system or, to use the economists' construct for that system, all markets will be part of the same *Market*. Or, in behavioral terms, all human exchange behaviors are thereby depicted as directly acting and reacting on one another, with all choices proceeding from the same quantitative value-maximizing logic and thus comparable.

Whatever further images one attaches to the concept of value, its logic is that it asserts a codetermining linkage between discrete *Prices* that may not be otherwise plausibly linked. One then constructs a "utility" or "labor-power" narrative to give a degree of empirical clothing to the value concept, but—again—those narratives are secondary and derivative of the methodological functions of the concept within high theory.[8]

Introducing value via this procedure is not without its own cost, however. If we put the best face possible on the matter, the logical situation is as follows: the concepts of value and *Price* are introduced as intervening variables in order to make plausible the claim that actual, empirical prices are genuine microcosms in the desired sense and obey the desired economic laws.

The Troubling Status of Value

But one has thereby created a substantial methodological problem to translate between the language of prices and the stipulations of the value subsystem, to translate from prices into values and vice versa. This classic "transformation" problem affects the neoclassical approach no less than the Marxist.[9]

The concreteness of the narratives surrounding the value subsystem imposes a great barrier to clarity in these matters. The imagery of labor or desirability is very powerful, so much so that one has to guard against its covering up fault lines in the analysis. Leaving aside the narratives, then, when one introduces any such term, including *labor-power* and *desirability,* as an intervening variable one has only added a new pronoun to the discussion, not a noun. Because it is an intervening, not an observable, variable its meaning is specified only by the logic/grammar surrounding it. The term has the grammar of a noun but only that, not, as with a noun, its own autonomously given meaning. There is a close analogy here to adding an unbound variable into a set of propositions or an extra (numerical) variable into an equation set. The meaning of the pronoun, unbound variable, or "unknown" is at least partially defined by the context in which it appears; if an expression in w is added to an existing equation set written only in $x, y,$ and z we know we're dealing with a number, and the operators accompanying the expression in w may tell us a little about what sort of number it is. But more is needed; we need a transformation procedure that reliably identifies the noun, binds the variable, or solves for the number.

It is at least arguable that Marx may have responded to this value/*Price*/price transformation problem somewhat better than the neoclassicals. I say "may" because two quite different resolutions of the problem can be appended to his work. I am not entirely persuaded, however. Recall that for him value and labor-power are near equivalents. In a passage we've cited before, he writes,

> The total labor-power of society, which is embodied in the sum total of the values of all commodities produced by that society, counts here as one homogeneous mass of human labor-power, composed though it be of innumerable individual units. Each of these units is the same as any

other, so far as it has the character of the average labor-power of society, and takes effect as such; that is, so far as it requires for producing a commodity no more than is needed on average, no more than is socially necessary. The labor-time socially necessary is that required to produce an article under the normal conditions of production, and with the average degree of skill and intensity prevalent at the time. ([1867] 1967: 46–47)

This passage is open to two interpretations, neither of which is fully adequate but one of which at least indicates a stronger approach. With the "average" labor-power and the "normal" conditions of production, with their "average" degree of skill and intensity, it may be possible to establish an unambiguous value unit. But if he understands that these "averages" and norms are established through the price system he is obviously reasoning in a circle; these are merely elaborate tautologies equating the terms *value* (of labor-power) and *price* (of labor-power).

There is another possibility, namely, that the working of the General Law serves to level and minimize the quantity of commodities consumed by laborers in order to produce labor-power; ergo, value is being depressed to a uniform social—not mathematical—average. This can also be assumed to be leveling socially both the degree of skill and the intensity of work, so that the prices of things and their values are empirically being forced to converge or even coincide.

On the other hand, this leveling is arguably being effected by the workings of the market, hence one is bringing prices into the leveling process itself. Again we're in a circle. *Value* and price must be defined independently or we're merely confusing ourselves with disguised synonyms.

The independence of the conceptions of price and value is the key here. Value is introduced as an intervening variable between what and what? Here's the rub—there aren't two observed variables bridged by value. There is only price. It is as if one introduced the concept of heat or temperature solely to "explain" the expansion and contraction of metals so that, in effect, *hotter* and *larger* were functioning as synonyms.

One needs one or more other observed variables to move out of the realm of synonyms and tautologies. The fact that under differential heat treatments metals become liquid, change crystal structure, and/or bond or unbond with other metallurgical elements—all of these and more serve to validate the concept of a common, hypothesized heat as central to each phenomenon. But by tying price and value only to one another (I'm ignoring the halfway *Price*) one only replicates the quiddities of the ancients, that people sleep because they have the dormitive faculty or laugh because they have the risible faculty, and so on, one explanatory variable—a value—for every behavioral category—a price. Methodologically, if one is to introduce the concept of value as an intervening, hypothesized variable in microeconomic analysis then one must have more evidence for it than prices transmuted into *Prices* transmuted into values, all on a one-to-one basis.

The analogy between heat and value suggests what is missing in the value subsystem. As long as the premodern world considered heat—like value—to exhibit an unspecified quantity ("more or less") not much could be done with it. But with the development of the concept of mass one could postulate a measurable unit of heat. A calorie or British thermal unit (BTU) is defined in terms of raising a unit mass of this or that substance by a fixed amount on a common scale, say, a mercury thermometer. This procedure, by uncovering the different coefficients of expansion of different substances and their differing volatility, fruitfully lent itself to codifying and then expanding our knowledge of how, when, and why, say, heated iron took this or that crystal structure, bonded this way or not with other elements, and exhibited different tensile strengths, hardness, brittleness, density, and other properties. Thus heat, introduced as a simple intervening variable, came with further analytical development to fruitfully connect hosts of observable variables and to that degree validate itself.

Unfortunately, the value subsystem precludes an analogous development of the concept of value. Marx allows that labor may vary by, say, duration and intensity, but the only way in which he relates these two terms is through the price system; that is, two labors of apparently varying duration and intensity are equal when their prices—of their wages or their output—are equal. We're still in a circle.

One could, in devising a neoclassical, subjective value theory, attempt to conceptually relate some empirical measure of the effort to earn a sum of money with some calculus showing the empirical circumstances under which the same amount would be spent. If a concept of value were employed in this way, whatever its other usefulness it would not be merely a disguised synonym for price. But historically the neoclassical school has been unwilling to confront the ideological and political implications of allowing that differences in the marginal utility of income to different persons within the population might be important (Dobb 1973: 167). As long as it does so, *value,* it may fairly be argued, is being used only as a disguised synonym for *Price,* itself a too well behaved substitute for unruly price. We need to do better than that.

Reformulating Value Theory

For the remainder of the chapter, I propose to sketch a modified value theory and in the following chapter to analyze some of its features.

I want to argue on behalf of a theory in which greater value is identified solely with the expansion of freely chosen human futures by men and women acting not abstractly but in their own societies. This is not an easy concept to unravel. But the key to that unraveling lies in our conception of a social labor-power in which learning is itself a dominant factor in the self-propelled expansion of its own productive powers.

For a start, this value theory represents a double break from traditional value theorizing. Because the future is always less than fully predictable, in this theory judgments and estimates about value can in principle be only tentative, conditional, and relative, never fixed and/or crystallized, even temporarily. Closely related, value can never be satisfactorily embodied in "things," although, I would argue, this has been the position of both Marxist and neoclassical analysis.

Marx's labor-power unit is ultimately measured, and thus represented, by a bundle of commodities, namely, the bundle necessary "under normal conditions" to reproduce the laborer. The imagery is of human effort, but the logic rests in the quantitative aspect of the bundle of things. More subtly, even the "subjective" value theory of the Jevons/Walras micro ultimately measures, and thus embodies, value in things, namely, in the things that are equivalently exchanged. Here the narrative is of human subjectivity, but the logic is a logic of the quantitative aspect of things. Our task here is to develop instead a value theory in which value is located in the condition of people themselves, that is, whether and to what extent they can and do realistically choose a freer future. Such economic choices can never be entirely free of things, but I want to focus instead on people's learning to evaluate the relationship between the exertions of their own human labor and the effects of such products on their own future. In this value logic, to the precise degree that the relationship between human labor and human usefulness is characterized by expanding social choice there is an increase in value, and not otherwise.

Thus, in the exposition that follows I propose that statements about value should ultimately be understood to be statements about the present or prospective expansion of the freely chosen capabilities of the social labor-power. The leading idea I want to theorize is that value discussions are always about the dynamic processes internal to the social labor-power itself, the products of the social labor-power having value only to the extent, and for the span of time, that they add to the social labor-power's present and prospective capacity for more freely chosen futures. In short, to ascribe value to something is always to make an estimate about the future, its truth or falsity is always contingent on that future, and its validity can only be vindicated in that future.

Our modern languages are not particularly adept at characterizing such a slippery, changing phenomenon as this value. As I argued in criticizing Sweezy's commodity theory, they tend instead to excel at classifying phenomena. But their very ability to classify things—fix their relationships—tends to make them less able to characterize qualitative change, especially continuous and conditional qualitative change. The value theory I propose to sketch is a theory about just such continuous, conditional, qualitative change within the social labor-power itself. Thus, the narrative and analytic development of value theory will of necessity take place close to the horizon of linguistic expressibility. We can, however, start with the simplest matters and thereby begin to shed light on value.

First of all, I see no way to avoid introducing value as an intervening variable (or pronoun), as one is using it in part to hypothesize that all, or nearly all, economic activity occurs in the same interactive behavioral medium, here the social labor-power per se. Whether such a hypothesis was plausible in the Victorian capitalism of Marx's or Jevons's time is open to debate; there already existed a world market for some commodities, but, as I argued earlier, that market hardly touched the final consumption behavior even of the English and Western Europeans, much less the rest of the world. At any rate, a universal market for virtually all goods and services is, if not the present reality, surely the present prospect. That there is an emerging system or systems of interactive empirical prices demands some such value hypothesis, but at the same time we have to avoid transmuting prices into *Prices,* that is, imposing greater order on the facts revealed by prices than the facts themselves will bear. Thus, in trying to recast value theory it is important not to overreach or, the same thing in other terms, not to fall back into apriorist methods and findings.

Second, economics and its predecessor, political economy, have their roots in the Enlightenment hope that humankind should increasingly escape the "tyranny of things and of people"; Adam Smith was after all a professor of moral philosophy. Accordingly, the association of value with social and individual well-being has always been close.[10]

Prices may just add up to facts on the ground, but *values* suggests something that is good for people to have more of and implies fairness in their dealings. Even in Marx, there is nothing intrinsically wrong with the production of surplus value; he objects to those who hog it. Accordingly, I would like to maintain that association here, namely, that the value pronoun represents that something or other in economic behavior, and ultimately in the social labor-power, that we want more of, not less.

Third, that something or other that is called value has historically been closely linked to the phenomenon of a price system or systems, that is, to those codified social behaviors involved in making and distributing price-denominated goods and services. Here we will keep that linkage but avoid creating value in the image and likeness of *Price*. Looking slightly ahead; if we are to argue that all actual prices in "final" sale/purchase involve a degree of constraint—a kind of extra "cost"—imposed by the producer/seller on the purchaser/consumer, then their value ought to vary inversely with that constraint, that is, to the extent to which there is a lessening of constraint in economic affairs there should be a corresponding increase in value. I'll follow this lead in a moment.

The program to be worked out here is to equate an increase in value with an increase in the capacities of (some part) of the social labor-power. On that basis value can be derivatively attributed to commodities, services, and quasi services produced in the past and present. One then conceives of the value aspect of the economy as comprising a relation within the social labor-power between its present capacities, the product of its past efforts, and the value of those in or to its own more freely chosen futures.[11]

Within this framework, it seems possible to me to reconstruct a value theory that will provide a useful tool of analysis and will also serve as a humane orientation to the way one should approach theoretical and policy questions regarding economic preference. Both of these aims are, of course, classic aims within the history of value theorizing.

Turning to the actual substance of the theory, we can elucidate it (a) with the aid of the doctrine of price relativity, (b) under the closely related assumption that all value assertions hold only for concrete durations of time, (c) combined with Schumpeter's famous observations on "creative destruction," along with (d) Pareto's concept of the sort of optimum economic situation now named after him. Our common medium of economic activity is of course the social labor-power acting through price-denominated sale/purchase-in-time.

In this theory of price relativity, empirical prices remain key pieces of evidence about the economy. But they are starting points for investigation, not part of the value subsystem. A price can be made to tell us something about its own origin and its relations with other prices, but that deciphering must have an empirical, not merely an apriorist, warrant.

Such price analyses can be prima facie verifiable only for specific situations, that is, for definite commodities in definite sale/purchase arrangements for definite durations of time. It is time for economics to stop pretending to be a kind of theology (Hobsbawm 1994: 547–48).

Accordingly, each such price is conceived only as an index of (money) value in relation to other prices, not a measure, as in conventional price theories. As an index it can be hypothesized to represent not a fully determinate past (or "microcosm") but a number of different scenarios; in other words, if milk today is $2.79 per gallon at the supermarket, we know or can discover the outlines of its productive and marketing history and can reconstruct different cost scenarios for feed, machinery, rent or interest, other farm costs, transportation and other costs to and from the processor/bottler, the costs imposed by the advertiser and taxes, and the place of milk within the supermarket's costing, pricing, and profit strategies. In addition, that milk was marketed within a definite environment of consumer demand in that duration and in that place.

Each of these historical prices is itself only an index of other costs, which, because each also lies within a range of indefiniteness, soon go beyond the horizon of our investigative ability. In the same spirit, we don't imagine that we can see the whole economy at once; all our perspectives are partial ones. I was going to say that empirical prices are like landmarks in a countryside otherwise unfamiliar to us and for which we are trying to provide some useful mapping. But the image of prices as depth markers in an estuary with an irregular bottom and ever-shifting channels does seem more apt.

What this implies is that unless we can show conclusively otherwise, we should theorize that each of the productive and transportation costs of that milk could have been different than they actually were for they, too, are only indices set within their own history. On the other hand, had we a practical or policy question in mind, further investigation of these prices of the component costs of the milk could in principle enable us to draw conclusions as to whether $2.79 represented a "reasonable" price under "normal" circumstances, had been distorted by special circumstances, and so forth. In other words, it might be possible under close investigation to show how that $2.79 came about, to determine why it lay in the range it occupied, and to evaluate whether at that price it had more or less value than some other possible price or prices.

Theoretically speaking, here a price is an indicator appearing within definite productive and distributive systems operating in a bounded span of time within a specific environment of constrained consumer demand within the social labor-power. To say that we know or can know more about that price prior to carrying out an investigation of those systems and that demand environment for that duration of time is to retreat back into price realism.

Naturally and Socially Imposed Constraints

It is often argued in introductory economics classes that the subject comprises the study of the allocation of scarce resources, with the implication, or at least the hint, that the resources are made scarce by nature itself. But a modern capitalist economy is at least arguably dominated not by natural but by humanly fashioned constraints. After all, Bristol-Meyers has the technical capacity to flood Europe and North America with virtually unlimited quantities of its toothpaste. The supply of toothpaste, like that of mass market beer, aspirin, autos, and most other commodities, is limited by institutional, not Mother Nature's, constraints. The point, then, is to analytically characterize those constraints.

Here, as so often, Schumpeter provides some useful theoretical guidance. In his well-known chapter on "creative destruction" in *Capitalism, Socialism, and Democracy* ([1942] 1962: chap. 7), Schumpeter, rather inadvertently I would imagine, has shown us in what manner all empirical prices are set under the same dominant constraint, namely, the existing property system as expressed in historically established prices of productive assets. His actual argument is that one of the virtues of capitalism is that profit-oriented firms will discard still usable capital equipment if newer, more cost efficient equipment that will lead to greater net returns is available. Extrapolating the effect of this "creative destruction," he argued that over time a capitalist economy would seek out those paths of economic change, marked by cost considerations, that comprise some calculus of least effort/best effect in the present while always remaining state of the art in its choice of productive (and presumably distributive) methods.

This approach is quite congenial to the present effort to reconstruct value theory without the value subsystem. But there are some problems.[12] What Schumpeter has done in fact is to underline the tension in his conception between the historical prices of productive assets and the likelihood that those prices will be validated by their subsequent productive effect. Put more simply, at one pole there is the historical-empirical price of the lathe and its operation, at the other the priced returns likely to be received in a determinate future span of time for the products of its operation. For Schumpeter, *creative destruction* refers to the normal practice of a capitalist economy to weight the decision on whether to scrap or maintain the lathe in favor of those future prices and not be bound by the prices paid in the past.

Agreeably to Schumpeter, his analysis is often seized upon to argue the virtues of "market capitalism" or some such equivalent expression over opposing or competitive economic systems because it will always shed unnecessary constraints on growth and efficiency. Any piece of property, in his view, may or will be creatively destroyed if it can be replaced with a more price productive one. Yet in making such a argument we again run afoul of logical/grammatical confusion. Here it is one of those classic cases of the older logic's Fallacy of Composition, that is, inferring from what is true in the individual case to the whole set of cases. Or—a more professorial image—if one is grading on a curve not every student can do better on the next test.

It does not follow from the notion that "any productive asset" will be creatively destroyed that "all productive assets" will suffer the same fate. As a practical matter and in a capitalist economy such as we have at present, the evaluation of the cost/benefit character of a productive asset is crucially dependent on the rate of interest and the empirical price(s) relationships at the period in time within which the asset is evaluated. We can take up these points in reverse order.

An Indian friend told me not many years ago that in his city they were only then scrapping cotton textile machinery that dated from mid-Victorian times, machinery, in other words, about a century and a quarter old. The equipment had been employed in the United Kingdom until the 1920s and then sent out to India, where it continued in productive use until the middle 1990s, at which point it was creatively destroyed. The price logic of that history is not difficult to decipher. Rising or prohibitively high productive costs in the English Midlands in the 1920s were decreasingly competitive with those of, very possibly, Japan. Thus, perhaps copying the migration of the cotton textile industry out of New England to the U.S. South in the same period, some of the equipment of the British industry went off to India, where, it seems plausible, the very low wages paid there underwrote the continuing use of quite ancient and arguably rather inefficient equipment. So went my friend's explanation, and there seems to be enough verisimilitude in it to serve as an illustration.

What the story illustrates is that what is destroyed and what is retained does not depend in the first instance on productive prospects per se but on the price relations holding between the old and the new. The continued use of relatively inefficient equipment may be underwritten by particularly low wages or other costs, while the benefits accrued by introducing more efficient equipment may be voided by price collusion between producers, by patent monopolies, by tariffs (or "Imperial Preference"), or by the fact that the existing equipment happens to be (empirically) priced so low that its money rate of return cannot be outdone by the better, technically more productive, replacement machinery. It is possible, in short, that existing price structures for productive assets may nullify the capitalist preference for new, "better" methods as opposed to old, "inferior," productive methods, as in my Indian friend's story.

One can see the bearing of this argument when one tries to maximize the operation of the principle of creative destruction. A whole capitalist economy cannot simultaneously subject every productive asset to its regimen. We can mentally divide productive assets into three categories, those that for historical reasons happen to be underpriced in terms of their profitable returns, those priced within what appears to their contemporaries to be the appropriate range, and those that are relatively overpriced. As long as assets remain within the first category, they will likely not be candidates for creative destruction no matter how crude and backward their technology or even their social and ecological effects. Schumpeter's analysis only bears on those assets passing or threatening to pass from the second to the third category.

The point is, of course, that the first category will never be empty. An economy based on property has an overriding concern to preserve existing, overall property values, so decisions to creatively destroy this or that asset will always made in a definite context of existing property values that will determine whether a new productive technique or system will enhance or threaten their net increment. There may be much or little creative destruction, but its upper limits are always fixed by the dominant imperative to maintain the existing system of property values.

This finding gets further bite from the manner in which modern interest rates and money supplies are managed by the several central banks in the advanced countries. As Greider (1987) has shown us so well—or rather reminded us so well—the several rates of interest in a modern economy, along with the money supply, are managed with the precise end in view to preserve existing property values. That very fact, of course, obviates much of the historical theorizing about the complex phenomenon of interest. The various central banks are very pragmatic and do not stand on theoretical ceremony; if one interest rate and its theoretical justification won't do it, then for that very reason they'll set another. If one level of money supply fails to do it, they'll try another. Those actions, in combination with the great variety and ease of ways to pass between liquid and nonliquid assets, place a very permissive threshold on the profit productivity of physical and social assets. Because the interest of the central banks—another bad pun—is to preserve property values per se, there is a built-in, adjustable tendency in a modern economy to place most productive assets within the first category, that is, to make sure that the tension between historical prices and anticipated returns is not so great as to "creatively" threaten the great bulk of those historically priced productive assets—the existing valuation of property. The form that this lesser tension takes is necessarily higher prices, preemptively slowed economic growth, and the delayed introduction of improved productive methods. These, I would argue contra Schumpeter, are characteristic of any economy that protects so-called property values. Creative destruction is, so to speak, the exception and can't be the rule.

A modern capitalist economy operates well within that band of tension created by the existence of historical prices for productive and other properties that will have to be validated by future prices even when the future productive setting is or may be radically altered.

Imagine now that we shift our conception of the economy. Before we conceived it to comprise the ensemble of priced productive assets that are the property of someone or other, that is, are de facto sheltered from too much exposure to the storms of creative destruction. Now conceive that the economy is more or less coterminous with the social labor-power and that we want to evaluate prices with respect to the value or values they represent to it. We focus on the degree to which a given price approaches the value of that commodity to the social labor-power or some part of it in that span of time, its value, that is, as simultaneously a freely undertaken input and a freely chosen output. When we imagine that the social labor-power could operate under different, lesser, historical constraints than those introduced into empirical prices by the property system, we can envisage whole menus of different pricing decisions and choices that would be dictated by our perceptions of value. This brings us to Pareto.

In a Pareto optimum, should any economic actor change, say, the way he or she distributes expenditures, that actor will suffer a net decline in economic well-being. Actors are theoretically assumed to exist in an economy of fixed productive assets and in instantaneous time. But such an optimum situation would change if there were different menus of empirical prices. To take a commonplace example, sport utility vehicles (SUVs) in the United States are classified under the regulations of the Environmental Protection Agency (EPA) as light trucks rather than passenger vehicles. Accordingly, they have been given a bye in meeting both air pollution control and road safety standards. Trucks operate under looser standards because presumably the EPA didn't want to wipe out at a stroke a substantial part of the trucking industry's capital assets. At any rate, the bye permits SUVs to be produced and sold more cheaply than if they had to meet passenger vehicle standards. No one, I think, seriously doubts that the SUV exemption is simply a device to help the auto companies and oil firms, in our terms, to protect and enhance their property at others' expense. Obviously, there are or could be devised prioritizing and price-setting modalities here, as in many other areas now tinged by property constraints, in which individuals had at least as much say as they do in the current corporately created "markets," and to each of them corresponds a different Pareto optimum.[13]

Unless our minds are singularly lacking in social invention, it does not seem impossibly difficult to conceive of pricing scenarios in which different projected optima for the development of the social labor-power would weigh more heavily in economic decision making and price setting than those corresponding to the present, or other, property system.

Technically speaking, insofar as we conceive of the economy in real time, true maximizing is out of the question; optimizing is the ticket or, more concretely, people would have to consider different scenarios for the future insofar as they could be precast by today's pricing decisions. We would realistically assume a great deal of uncertainty about the future effect of this or that price or price structure. We would also realistically assume that there would be conflicts within the social labor-power about which no permanent decision or consensus would or could be reached.

Ideally, one would want modalities in which the people who set priorities and make decisions would experience their effects, with that effective feedback operating in real time. To borrow an image from William James, we want the "moral equivalent" of the "free market." We want to be able to confidently expect that there will both social and individual learning curves as experience with the effects, intended and otherwise, of prioritizing and price setting accrues over time. Of course, unlike that free market, we would like to allow more diversity and tolerance in economic priorities.

I have been trying to sketch a situation in which, through the medium of pricing decisions, a modified principle of creative destruction would be tied to time-modified Pareto optima within an economics of price relativism. More directly, I have sketched elements of an economy in which price estimations are tied only to value costs and effects of various assets, independent of all pricing imperatives tied to the preservation of nonproductive effects, to a value calculus or calculi and not to property preservation. In practice, of course, no such black and white distinction would likely present itself, but the conception of price relativism doesn't call for that. It calls only for preferencing decisions that are always provisional and subsequently adjustable.

Granted, there would be monumental difficulties in organizing such an economy, and even more in overcoming the present dominance of property. But we have succeeded in defining *value* as that which increases as and to the degree that property constraints are diminished; *value* is identified here with the tension within the social labor-power between more freely chosen economic futures and those imposed by constraints emanating from even the best, most flexible, and most far sighted property system.

Value here still functions as an only partially defined intervening variable. It points ultimately to the gap between our present modes of quasi-constrained sale/purchase and the different menus of choices that could be made as and to the extent that those constraints were lessened. Thus, for each priced transaction at present we conceive that there is a set of different values corresponding to what that price would be or could be in the future if this or that degree or kind of constraint were removed, most notably those constraints directly introduced by property strictures and the social and related constraints that are ancillary to it.[14]

Value Expanded

Earlier we treated commodities as consisting of complementary quasi services linked to integral services in time. It follows from the previous analysis that commodities have value insofar as they may come to be employed to amplify the capacity of the social labor-power or any element of it. Thus, the value of a commodity is not historically determinate or even a historical given; it is validated only in the future. A commodity, no matter how laboriously produced or avidly desired, has value only to the extent that it will play a role in the future of the social labor-power. Insofar as there are different scenarios in which that commodity, service, or quasi service will so serve the social labor-power, to that same extent does it have values. In that sense, the value of a commodity, service, or quasi service is never ultimately crystallized but always relative to future validations. Value ultimately comes from the ways in which commodities enter the stream of self-development of the social labor-power. Permitting some bad grammar on my part, it can be said that the word *value* is always in the future tense and always in the plural.

Derivatively, we can say that commodities are also value shells and that to each quasi service there corresponds relative value, only estimable in the present but subsequently determinable as and to the extent that it becomes an integral service. The value here is only relative in that it can and will be validated when and as an integral service ensues. Its value is relative to that process only and carries no necessary implication as to whether it adds, subtracts, or leaves intact the quantum of value in the economy as a whole. I repeat: this use of *value* is only a derivative one.

Seen in those terms, the various stages or phases of the sale/purchase of an auto can be seen as adding (or removing) relative value to (or from) the commodity. I will employ the conception of a value shell for both senses of the variability of value, that is, that value may be added or taken from a commodity and that that value estimation is always only situationally warranted.

In this theoretical formulation the hypothesized relationship among price, actual prices, and value departs from the sort of theory associated with the value subsystem. Here both price and value have a dual utility/disutility logic to them. Both function in time but differently. Price represents the historical pull of past property values (costs) carried into the present and the future and demanding, as it were, to be made good. Value emphasizes the shedding or diminution of that sort of historical constraint in light of a less constrained future. Schematically, prices are in part validated or invalidated backward in time, and I think it apt to keep that implication. But value is most fruitfully thought of as the other, future pole of price, demanding that the worth or utility of a commodity or quasi service eventually depends on how it functions in the present and future. In that sense values are essentially confirmed or unconfirmed in forward time.

The following summarizes the argument about value that has been sketched here and has been developing since our earlier pages. The form under which constraint operates in a modern economy is the actual price system. As described earlier, "final" or consumer consumption occurs modally under different kinds and degrees of constraint, that constraint being significantly a projection through the medium of price of our present system of property, that is, the power of capitalist institutions and their allied political states over those who work and those who consume.

Each sale/purchase state should accordingly be viewed in both price and value terms as comprising (1) costs, monetary and otherwise, to the purchaser/consumer; (2) gains, satisfactions, utilities, and rewards; (3) through time; and (4) within a definite structure of externally imposed constraints. In an actual economy, the various prices for that commodity are all united in that structure of constraints: the price at point of nominal sale; additional prices coming due within the sale/purchase state; the monetary liens on the purchaser/consumer's labor-power; and the influence of the person's course, especially through the social identity of his or her income stream; its size, regularity, and security; and its future prospects. Here the sale/purchase state, as reflected in its several prices, reflects an economy of constraints.

All actual prices are anchored more or less firmly in time past, that is, they reflect the actual or projected costs in commodities, including labor-power, that entered into their production and distribution, and those costs are in part skewed by the property system, that is, a set of preexisting prices that, above and beyond their actual contribution to the creation of new commodities, are weighted toward the one-sided advantage of their owners. In the actual formation of prices, whatever else is true in an economy in which productive assets appear in the form of property, those prices will be pulled by that structure of preexisting property prices. At the same time, changes in productive methods and what is produced also react backward to revalidate or even destroy some of the preexisting property assets and their respective prices. But even this creative destruction occurs within narrow economic limits.[15]

The same breakdown can be given in value terms. The leading idea here is that the value of a commodity is given by the degree to which its production and consumption lead to a net decline in constraints imposed on people as producers-consumers. There is a studied, deliberate "vagueness" in this formulation that several further observations should clarify.

Value is conceived as a quantitative variable, but the means of identifying its quantity in any given context are inferential and indirect and one makes no claim that there is or even could be a unique decision procedure to which to appeal. Technically, value has intensive not extensive quantity (Cohen and Nagel 1934: 293ff.).

A given commodity at a given time has a variable, not a fixed or crystallized value. Its value is not a direct reflection of its price but something conceived to be an index of the complex tensions within its several price scenarios between constraint and freer choice.

Because there is no unilinear path or measure of the amplification of free choice, we can view the evaluation of the value of each commodity as a switching point into different futures and its value can in part be "measured" by that very role, that is, whether it points to futures of less tension between price and value, the same tension, or greater tension.

The relationship between price and value cannot be resolved by theoretical means; it is purely a question of practice. To the extent that one accepts something like the Enlightenment hope for our common human future, one would try at both the personal and social levels to lessen the price-value tension. Insofar as economists accept this narrative and/or are convinced through the scientific spirit that the arguments advanced herein are worthy of assent, then the object of analysis and policy is to assist in lessening price-value tension, that is, to lessen or even remove those sorts of things, preeminently property claims, that we know from experience arbitrarily constrain the activities of people. There is no menu of removals here; one calls only for a learning curve.[16]

I do not postulate that there exists or could exist a state of affairs in which the value produced by an economy was "maximized" or was being increased at the most "perfect" or "best" rate. Beyond self-deceiving conundrums and tautologies no one can read the future with certainty. Even the best conceived, well-motivated judgments of today may turn out to have a dreadful effect. As important, human beings are shaped in their preferences, knowledge, and moral attitudes by the existing political economy. To the extent that economics has been part of the "moral sciences" in the past and still has not shed that role entirely, the best one can do is do one's best, always in critical light of the evidence, to lessen price-value tensions. If there is to be a "progress narrative" it will not be mapped from outer intellectual space but laboriously created, step by hesitant step, down in the tangle of confusing events.

Paradoxically, the aggregate quanta of value are not a given in an economy. In the account given here the best one can say is that greater value should be an emergent feature of an economy and the decisions, procedures, and institutions within it.

The theory given here is simultaneously a modified labor theory of value and a modified demand-driven subjective value theory. Value is optimized to the extent that the tension between the two, as represented, say, in the actual prices one receives for one's freely chosen labor and pays for one's freely chosen consumption, is decreasing over time.

I want to close this brief presentation of a different value theory by again emphasizing that value questions are practical not theoretical. We would in the general case know that the value being produced and enjoyed in our society was near an optimum to the extent that people, acting under fewer constraints than yesterday, were less inclined to introduce changes—in the pricing system, in what was being produced, how, how much, and so on. There is no imputation here that what was decided today should be maintained tomorrow; perhaps it will even be seen as a mistake and a new start made. To again borrow from the tradition of historic value theorizing, one would like to work to bring about something along the lines of a Pareto optimum but an optimum decided on a somewhat less individualistic and, paradoxically, corporate basis, with no imputation that today's optimum will be satisfactory tomorrow.

8 | Amplifying, Confirming, and Proposing

The present study has been drawn most heavily from two major points. The first six chapters presented and analyzed sale/purchase-in-time as characterizing modern microeconomics. Then the first part of chapter 7 presented a methodological critique of the value subsystem, followed by a sketch of an altered theory of value. In this chapter I further analyze that altered microeconomics and theory of value. Thus the chapter title, as I want simultaneously to amplify the views presented there and show some of the ways in which they are apt to the investigation of modern capitalism. Finally, I want to indicate, if only briefly, how this analysis bears on the growth of fabricated society at the expense of "natural" or spontaneous society. The discussion is organized around the role, forms, expansion paths, and "ownership" of capital today as seen in the light of price relativism and our rejection of the value subsystem.

The Cost of Change

We should start with a negative observation, namely, that no analytical or investigatory loss is incurred by giving up the value subsystem and its associated doctrine of price realism within general equilibrium. What is most striking about both the Marxist and the neoclassical microeconomics is that they raise problems which are often of important theoretical interest but have little practical utility in economic investigation. This comes of the fact that neither the Marxist nor the neoclassical microeconomics satisfactorily effect the transformation between an apriorist world of *Prices* and values and the unruliness of empirical prices. The logical distance between exploring general equilibrium/price realist conditions and trying through partial equilibrium or other price-determinate models to understand the dynamics of actual markets or other changes for a firm, a product line, or even a specific, real-world economy is enormous. A general equilibrium cast within the value subsystem is not a sum of partial equilibria; methodologically, they are two different species entirely. In the latter, and not in the former, one makes difficult, often compromise methodological decisions such as how to construct variables and measure them, how to identify the actual conditions that would reasonably be modeled as an equilibrium, and, more importantly, the nature of possible findings that might falsify the equilibrium assumptions. In short, one has to "solve" the transformation problem between price and value, but this is precisely what cannot effectively be done within general equilibrium theory and its associated price realism and value subsystem, for the latter three are defined in such a way that in principle they cannot be falsified by price evidence. Simply by employing them one has swept aside the problem.[1]

Thus the question "what is lost in giving up the Marxist or neoclassical microeconomics and their equilibrium assumptions, price realism, and the value subsystem?" The answer is that very little if anything is lost! No criticism made in these pages even crowds, much less devalues, the use of quantitative methods, econometric procedures, and even price-determinate models in economic research, and no obloquy attaches to their employment. We merely accept as a theoretical principle that the meaning of no price is given a priori but must be searched for by a variety of, we hope, mutually supporting and over time correcting empirical investigations.

We do lose, of course, the ideological implications of those microeconomics, which depict analytically an absolute dictatorship of capital over "the proletariat" or, alternatively, a realm of superior, almost unlimited freedom for that "sovereign consumer." In foreswearing those dubious claims one instead has made a net analytical gain with the concept of a constrained and productive "final" consumption, which, regardless of its exact development in these pages, provides a more useful, nuanced, investigatory logic than those it replaces.

The Courses as Functional Units of Capital

The courses take on a special, though somewhat paradoxical, significance when we view them as functional units of capital. As a social organization of labor-power they have, for capital, several enormous advantages over their predecessors. In the first place, the course division of the work force into Managers and workers restricts the more and more decisive growth areas of knowledge and technique into a Manager course small enough to be especially rewarded and thereby its links to the capitalist property system drawn tighter. At the same time the amplification of their productive services and deployment in the economy and society can be more closely controlled. Further, in a democratic age the privileges of this "meritocracy" are more easily defended on functional grounds, that is, on grounds asserting—truly—the especially important role that cadres play in a modern, dynamic economy.[2]

The modern Manager course is not the product of the private sector alone. It is an institutional product of the intersection of business, government, and university and can also be usefully employed for the most part only within that intersection in which business is the dominant though not the exclusive power. In that sense, business has an oligopoly position with respect to the services of the Manager course. This sort of oligopoly is of at least equal, and probably greater, importance to capital than the sort winked at in the antitrust laws. It confers upon capital the ability to choose between different trajectories for its own growth and, to a significant degree, the pace of that growth. Analytically, the self-expansion of capital, now free of "the free market," becomes to a significant degree self-directing as well.

Second, the existence of a special managerial course has historically been associated with an enormous expansion and an equally enormous ramification of capitalistically usable knowledge and techniques; here oligopoly over scientific and technological knowledge paradoxically encourages growth and ramification. If as before we schematize the work of managers as multiplying the output of workers, then that multiplier is itself particularly susceptible to multiplication. Does it follow that as a strategy for capital growth the higher unit costs of investing in the education of a minority should generally lead to greater increases in capitalist value productivity than the same investment spread over more persons? We do not appear to have the empirical ability to test that particular thesis, but it is clear enough that it is that strategy that has been enacted by modern capital since the last decades of the nineteenth century.[3] Following the U.S. lead, manpower investments internationally have tended to be overly weighted in favor of the Manager course and to be associated with the "deskilling" of the rest of the work force, here meaning the removal from the worker ranks of the more important types of knowledge and skills necessary to guide industrial work both organizationally and technically.

It is only a metaphor, but one can say without great imprecision that Managers function as the producers per se in modern industry and the workers more as a kind of raw material for production. With true capitalist logic, there tend to be one-sided increases in investment in the former while the latter play a relatively declining role. To repeat, for the point is of cardinal importance, by virtue of modern cadres, capital has achieved a degree of selective self-pacing over its own growth.

Third, the productive system is commonly likened to an army. In that sense, by treating workers as the simple soldiers of production with a course possessing a technological but changing "oligopoly" the workers themselves may function almost as interchangeable units to be deployed now on this production front, now on that. The most significant productive feature of the erosion of crafts-based technologies in industry is that the labor force becomes more job mobile, which is more important in a modern economy than geographical mobility. I don't mean that there is frequent switching of jobs for an individual worker, but across the generations the modern work force is immeasurably more mobile than its predecessors, for not only crafts skills but also city-country differences, the separation of the sexes, and the withholding of children from the central economy, all once operated to compress the numbers, range, and adaptability of the productive services of the social labor-power more closely than now. Within the Manager-worker relationship these restrictions can be socially erased so that virtually all the social labor-power can be deployed to industrial and commercial uses, or preparation for such uses, in each generation.

Analytically, this also means that capital has achieved greater freedom to change its actual, empirical productive form, now appearing in the garb of the steel industry, now as auto manufacturing, and subsequently as communications or electronics. To view this phenomenon only under the rubric of the "mobility of financial capital" is to substitute a fetish form of analysis for the real thing. In a modern economy, the vast proliferation of financial procedures, credit forms, payment modalities, and investment opportunities is a reflex of the real economy based on a polyvalent modern cadre dominating an unusually adaptable work force. Basically, the empirical form of these things consists of changes in the use of a social labor-power organized by courses, which are themselves subsumed within capital's own growth circuit.

Fourth, and as already pointed out, the Manager-worker relationship, by bringing into social labor-power virtually the whole population of a modern country, creates the possibility for capital to advance to and hover at the very limits of its own possible amplification.

As long as the circuit of capital was not completed by integrating final consumption into it, capitalist institutions were limited in the numbers of people who could be brought into the work force, limited in the skills and educational changes it could impose on them, hence limited in the way it could make use of them, and limited in the modes of exerting social control over them. Its self-expansion was hemmed in by "the Market," as was its trajectories of growth and the pace of those trajectories. Earlier capital coexisted with a social labor-power of primitive productive characteristics, and capital's ability to alter those characteristics was also severely limited. Through sale/purchase-in-time and what I have elsewhere called Social Taylorism (McDermott 1991: 150ff.) the processes of final consumption are brought within the productive circuit of capital, quickly evolving into the purchasing/consuming/preparing/working ensembles we have called courses. The development of these modern courses in effect brings virtually all stages in the life of each person within that circuit of expanding capital, increasing the scale of its growth far beyond what could have been expected in the Victorian economy that both Marx and Jevons experienced.

It is not at all clear that the Manager-worker relationship as it has developed since Taylor in every case must be more efficient than, say, a work regimen in which the workers, each with a higher level of skills and knowledge, control the organization and pacing of the work. Whether or not that sort of microefficiency holds in the general case has to be established—or refuted—by means of appropriate empirical investigation.[4] But the division of the social labor-power into its contemporary courses brings nearly all aspects of the life of virtually every person in the society immediately and directly into the expansion of capital; it is this—let us call it macroefficiency—that serves to further confirm that the courses are the human elements of modern capitalism's ability to grow at an optimal pace.[5]

The Altered Role of Money

Theoretical constructions are always conditional on contingent events; historical change requires adaptations in theory. "The Market" in its several manifestations has become an obsolete construction; the dominant idea that auctionlike behavior should have a theoretically privileged standing to which other economic phenomena must be made logically hostage is no longer sustainable. As the present study has been at pains to show, modern markets have been shaped and engineered as much as or perhaps even more than the products that appear in them. An actual market, today especially, is no more "natural" than the credit card slips or electronic signals that change hands in it. As much as anything it is that which weighs against the existing microeconomics of both the traditional Marxist and neoclassical traditions.

Both the Marxist and neoclassical paradigms are predominately theories of exchange, having the effect of obscuring the degree to which formal exchange normally now occurs within and is subordinated to other kinds of economic behavior states, in particular to administrated processes of production and distribution, which have come to the practical and therefore theoretical foreground.

This shift from exchange to distribution further implies that there has been a substantial alteration in the role of money, an implication that is quickly and richly confirmed. As we have seen, the process of production and distribution of commodities from design through fabrication through empirical distribution, including the processes of final consumption, are manifestly steps within the circuit of productive capital (see chapter 3). They complete that circuit so that in fact as well as in theory commodities never drop out of the circuit, with even their "final" consumption occurring within the circuit itself.

Money still functions as a means of exchange and a unit of account, but it is only a temporary unit, for the commodity is normally a value shell, that is, a value in the process of change. The commodity still appears to be a crystallized, self-contained value, as we imagine it in the Market, but in reality it is only a phase in a circuit of expanding capital in which there is an enduring tension between processes of expenditure and delayed utilities: we buy and maintain the car with a view toward obtaining certain services from it over time. But there is no guarantee that to each present expenditure, nor even to the whole stream of expenditures, the expected future services can and will be enjoyed in the time frame expected. Probably they will be and the expenditure-return tension will be erased in time, but the tension will continue until that time has come.

Money-denominated prices function in general within the wider tension between price and value in a modern economy, that is, prices of exchange reflect past historical phases of the sale/purchase state, including prominently the property costs imposed *ante diem* by the producer/seller, but which will also live on in a future world in which those values may become undone. Costs by purchasers/consumers are incurred in anticipation of value, but the expenditure must be subsequently validated in real time and often it is not.

The widespread practical and theoretical use of the concept of "opportunity cost" provides further evidence of this tension between (historical) price and (anticipated) value. In employing an opportunity cost analysis in a given situation, we assume that quantifiable returns over time for alternate uses are reliably enough assured that one can make a warranted calculation of them, not a wild guess or a sheer speculation. We should here distinguish a purely technical computation of some sort, which is always more or less possible, from the social practice of regularly making those computations. In a purely technical sense, a fifteenth-century mariner-adventurer could guesstimate the differential returns to be gained between plying conventional cargoes of wheat and olive oil between Algiers and Lisbon compared to a voyage out to the Indies, hopefully to avoid uncharted shoals, unpredictable storms, and the surer attentions of pirates and disease so as to return with a cargo of fabulously valuable spices. It is a different thing today, as we can realistically assume that alternate investment opportunities are always at hand, all within the boundaries of conventional not daredevil behavior, and with some experience of the likelihood and scale of returns for each alternative. Even the expression, "alternate investment opportunities are at hand" underdescribes the situation. In a modern economy every commodity is in fact a "piece" of capital because of its location within one or more actual or possible capital circuits. It is precisely this that the conception of opportunity cost reflects. In short, the warrant for employing opportunity cost reflects a social reality in which the nature of the tension between (past) costs and (future) returns is well understood and whose calibration lies well within the range of common economic practice.

The Money Form of Value Superseded

The empirical worth of commodities is decided by their locus in one or more capital circuits and in light of the degree to which, for that reason, the commodity's (money) value is expected to grow. Empirically speaking, commodity production and distribution occur within and as conditioned by markets engineered to make the size and surety of returns as predictable as human artifice can allow. Commodities are made and sold with those returns in mind, and their empirical prices of exchange established to facilitate it. Literally, commodities and their services are capitalized, their historical prices of production being expectantly precoordinated (or subsequently adjusted) with the later, constrained purchases and consumption of consumers. Their money worth is established by neither of these two crystallized poles but by their changing relationships in time. Their worth is their value as capital, their (money) value within the capital expansion process, not their various historical prices nor various anticipated prices taken by themselves.

In Marxist terms, we can say that a modern economy has burst through the older "integument" of the Money form of value and exchange and reached a Capital form of value, meaning simply that the money price of a commodity is determined less by its crystallized historical costs of production, and less by what it will today bring in a market, than by the worth in money conferred on it by its place within different actual or possible circuits of capital. Crudely, its worth is evaluated by its function as a unit of capital, not a static element of property. Or, more generally, commodities in a modern economy never exit entirely all the circuits of capital, never appear, so to speak, shorn of that character in this or that market, and it is this phenomenon that dominates the establishment of both their value and their money value.

This finding again emphasizes that the capitalism that Marx knew and that even the Jevons-Walras generation of economists met was a capitalism still in its infancy and not fully liberated from the merchant-dominated capitalism that preceded it. In both of their microeconomics, trading categories predominate—money, market, and exchange—categories that can be used to characterize modern capitalism only as to the effect of distorting or at best delaying our understanding of it. The concept of "monopoly capital" provides an illustration. It expresses ultimately a narrative of competing merchant rivals, of commodities that can be monopolized because they have technical qualities that cannot be readily substituted for. It fits a narrative of "industries" consisting of relatively specialized firms that collaborate in producing and selling their one or a few products at finagled prices. It is only with difficulty that one can fit into such a monopoly scheme diversified firms, firms that engineer the growth of their markets through the advance of credit, or autonomous firms that nevertheless are historically partnered, for example, GM (engines, frames) and DuPont (fuel additives, and paints).

Understanding this further evolution in the forms of value changes our view of credit, especially consumer credit, in two ways. First, the increasing ubiquity of credit cards and credit purchases, along with the huge ramification in the different scale and modes of extending or receiving credit, should give us pause. To use a credit card is not to gain a discrete series of credit advances and incur an equally discrete series of payback obligations. To have a credit card is to have an instrument equally useful through a period of time to make any and all purchases whose costs do not exceed a certain time-adjusted balance. Moreover, the time period is normally fixed only on its past historic side—the date when one "got the card." The cards themselves have nominal termination dates, but the universal commercial practice is to renew them automatically as long as the relationships between credit advances and payments lie within certain parameters, parameters initially set by the size and surety of one's income. To have a credit card is to exist in an open-ended state of being able to enter into a wide range of sale/purchase relations. A credit card expresses a social practice keyed to the size and continuity of one's income stream, not the discrete purchases one makes.

Thus, the credit card is a social expression of the fact that the (money) value of our own commodity labor-power has also been capitalized, and in that respect it is a major institutionalized expression of a socially manifest expression of the shift from the Money form of value as the dominant form in which value appears to a situation in which value is almost universally capitalized, that is, to a Capital form of value.

Thus, the credit card is keyed to one's course identity, not just one's personal identity; one qualifies for it by fitting a certain socioeconomic profile and not, as in previous forms of consumer credit, because the creditor has direct reason to attest to the debtor's personal uprightness. In turn, the cardholder's income stream is in a socially manifest way "measured" within the series of payments of income, payments for commodities, and liens against future income, with the whole coordinated by the policy practices of the credit card issuers seen in light of their relationships with the commodity producers/sellers. In short, a credit card socially manifests the tension between past expenditures and future earning, and, to the extent that the Visa and Mastercard statisticians can do so, the cards actually try to calibrate that very tension. In another sense, the card issuers function as a special institution coordinating the income stream of purchaser/consumers with the capital needs of corporate business.

A further manifestation of a historic change in value form comes in the macroeconomic shift from commodity money (the "gold standard") to credit- or bank-created money, the former the exemplar of the Money form but the latter designed to take account of the need to expand and/or contract the supply of money so as to make sure that the economy's performance will not needlessly threaten historically established property values. Again, in the tension between money price and capitalized (money) value, the value pole more heavily determines the kind and quantity of money that circulates within an economy, and in fact nowadays that quantum is normally designed to bring about a steady inflation-free expansion of economic activity, that is, one in which the threat to the deflation of property values is minimized.

This shift from the Money form to the Capital form of value raises interesting questions about the nature of capital itself as it is revealed in a modern economy.

What Is Capital?

As we know from the Cambridge capital controversy and kindred debates, the concept of "capital" is elusive and not at all trouble free. One needs the concept so as to be able to make comparative judgments about the (money) value of productive assets, but, as we saw with the concept of utility value and labor-power value, postulating a unitary substance called capital seems to press against the margins of metaphysics.

Marx characterized capital as self-expanding value ([1867] 1967: chap. 4). On the narrative level his meaning is sufficiently clear. He cites the development, beginning in Europe in the sixteenth century, of distinct classes of persons, organizations, and social institutions devoted to making money, not as an end in itself, as with a miser who hoards it, but as a continuing process of making money in order to make more money. At a somewhat different level, he cites the "magical" phenomenon of invest-ment, that is, spending money as a way of increasing it.

Yet there is a peculiar analytical gap in his views on the subject. Value is for him virtually equivalent to labor-power, but this conception is only incompletely and erratically related to his definition of *capital* as "self-expanding value." As he writes, "labor-power is the substance of value" ([1867] 1967: 46). Accordingly, he treats the expansion of capital as a process of capitalists extracting surplus value via the wage system from the workers' exercise of their labor-power. In Marx, that possibility arises because, while labor-power is paid for at its value like any other com-modity, that is, the cost of its production and reproduction, it is capable of producing value beyond its own cost of production; it creates new, additional value. The capitalist pays only for the value of labor-power and so is in a position to garner the newly created surplus.

Clearly, there is a gap in Marx's analysis. If by nature capital expands as a residue of something else, it cannot be *self*-expanding. Something else must be expanding; in Marxist terms, capital would be only the phenom-enal form of that something else. But what is that something else?

Clearly, it must be labor-power, but it can't be, at least in Marx. His concept of labor-power doesn't permit that inference; he's already identified labor-power, all labor-power, as having at any given time a crys-tallized or fixed value, to repeat, the "socially necessary" cost of its production and reproduction. Moreover, the fact that the value of labor-power can be crystallized, as in "a (definite) bundle of commodities," is the pivot of his whole theory of value, surplus value, exploitation, and the rest. Thus, the conundrum: if fixed at every given time, then not expanding at any time; if expanding, then not fixed.

As far as I can tell from Marx's writing, nowhere does he address this conundrum. In his system, the social and narrative meaning of "self-expanding value" is both central and clear, but at the analytical level it remains just as central but is by no means clear.

In its narrative dimensions, the Marxist economic scheme is presented as a theory of production, with labor-power at its heart, the "labor theory of value." But analytically, in fixing the value of labor-power as he does, via the wage-for-work exchange, Marx's theory is in fact an economics of exchange, not production.[6] In the logic of his position, he implicitly allows the market abstraction to interrupt the (notional) circuit of productive capital so that the value of labor-power and the value of some bundle of commodities are made identical; again, not narratively identical but, more importantly, analytically identical. Narratively, we can actually see change in the value of labor-power, but analytically there is no logical room for that obvious change in the scheme.

This shift, however important analytically, is also very subtle, and we have met it before. It is another instance of mercantile categories creeping into an ostensibly supply-dominated approach to economic theory. In Marx's case it comes of the fact that the capitalism of his era had only partially evolved away from the merchant-dominated capitalism of the previous era. But now we appear to be at a historical point in which we are— or can be—less blinded by the "naturalness" of trading categories in economic analysis. The concept of the social labor-power provides the formal analytical conception that corresponds to this historical change— and it is the key to the expansion of capital.

As already indicated, the concept of the social labor-power includes all those capacities to work, trained as well as natural, in an entire economy or, better, society. The value of commodities, including that of labor-power itself, comes only in their role as complements to the expansion of that labor-power. A given commodity or class of commodities, no matter how dearly produced in terms of human effort and natural resources or however ardently desired, has value only to the extent that it adds to the capacity of that labor-power, that is, to the expansion of its productive services or quasi services. As before, that expansion does not have an absolute character. All such expansions are only relative and perhaps only temporary and situational, for to the degree that a tool, or a substance or an effort or a skill or a bit of knowledge, has been superseded, for good reasons or bad, its former value is eradicated. Value attaches not at all to the past but is, as before, validated or disconfirmed as futures unfold.

From this it follows that the historical values of a commodity can be entirely reduced to the role of that commodity and its quasi services and services at some definite extent of time in the history, the present or the anticipated future of the social labor-power. In this new perspective, the values of commodities have—ultimately—only a labor-power component, that is, they represented at some point or points in time a resolution of some price-value tension within the social labor-power. Consistent with this standpoint we can define the universe of goods and services, that is, "the economy," as consisting solely of dated labor inputs that are being constantly revalidated (and devalidated) by their complementarity to the needs, actions, and changes of the social labor-power.

These formulations provide the key to relating value theory to Marx's old formula about capital as self-expanding value. The self-expansion of capital is the social and institutional form taken by the self-expansion of the social labor-power but as constrained by the past historical prices that must be made good to sustain the existence and health of the property system. Analytically speaking, the expansion process of capital is thus the ultimate expression of the price-value tension we have been discussing.

From this point we reaffirm the economic and dynamic definition of *property*. Property consists of goods and services whose money price is expanded, preserved, and protected to at least some extent without regard to their contribution to the expansion of value.[7]

Again we see the tension between price and value as it is socially manifested. In fact, this is the deep root of that tension; it comes of the contradiction—a contradiction of true, classical Marxist proportions—between prices ultimately imposed by the need to preserve historical property "values," irrespective of their contribution to the growth of the capacity of the social labor-power, and the other value-enhancing possibilities and paths of the social labor-power freely choosing and rechoosing its own course of development. In a modern economy, property" is ultimately not a set of legal arrangements about "ownership" per se; owning and the attributes of owning are, again in Marxist terms, the phenomenal form of the deeper system of constraints imposed on sale/purchase-in-time by the operation of the contemporary capitalist production and distribution system. In that sense, we could replace the foolish old epithet "Property is theft!" with the appreciably more accurate "Property is constraint!"

Because the rate(s) of interest in a modern economy is prescribed with a view toward preserving property, it becomes impossible to discriminate between the, as it were, "true cost" of producing things and the additional costs levied by the owners who control the paths between production and (final) consumption. Thus, the centrality to modern capitalism of the sale/purchase-in-time; the sale/purchase state is the modal locus in which constraint is exercised. Even the ability of capitalist firms to discipline their employees by administrative means is a function of the latters' constrained place in the network of sale/purchase arrangements linking wages to consumer commodities.

In this discussion I would emphasize the word *arbitrary*. There are often occasions when the past imposes unavoidable constraints on our present economic activities. Consider the farmer's adage "One must work if one is to eat." In my use of *arbitrary,* I refer only to those constraints (or that degree of constraint) imposed on prices that represent a tribute to property and entirely aside from returns keyed to value productivity, that is, to the expansion of the productive services and quasi services of the social labor-power. We sometimes can make realistic calculations around this distinction, but not entirely. It is, for example, almost surely the case that patent protections make pharmaceutical prices too high while the ready availability of workers with little political "clout" just as surely lowers the prices of processed chicken in the United States, and textiles worldwide, below where they "ought" to be. Whatever the calculable technical range of indeterminacy to a given set of prices, the property system adds an economically arbitrary component.

Seen in this light, while one can distinguish profit from (economic) rent in a putatively competitive economy, it is impossible to do so in our contemporary one. Even, or especially, when taking into account Schumpeter's "creative destruction," there is no unambiguous way to assign a (money) value measure to productive assets that are actually destroyed (or preserved), or technologies pursued (or not) for no other reason save that capitalist institutions believe that the chosen alternative is more likely to be more price profitable or pari passu more enhancing of the property position of the dominant firms, their chief beneficiaries, and their social-political allies.

The "real productivity" of capital is an analytical chimera because in the last analysis there is a systematic effort among business firms and their central bank allies to preserve "historical values" per se. If a theory of general equilibrium in time could be satisfactorily formulated and with methodologically testable transformation criteria then perhaps on different plausible assumptions about rates of growth we could estimate "natural" rates of interest or the "normal" profit. But such constructions have no bearing on an economy in which sale/purchase-in-time is coordinately constrained by one side, all the way from the nominal price in the retail shop to the value of money as determined by the central bank.[8]

There is yet another reason to conceive of capital as the social labor-power acting under constraint, with increases in value calibrated to increases in labor-power-productive services. It comes of the fact that the productive contributions of the social labor-power are becoming more socially manifest over time. There has been a historic trend in modern capitalist economies to supplement or even replace natural resources in the production and distribution of commodities. It takes various forms. Obviously, one form is the growth of materials science, which, for example, has allowed petroleum-based fibers to replace "natural" ones in the textile and clothing industries. Here the role of nature in providing materials is vastly altered by human artifice. The fabled growth of services at the expense of manufacturing gives us still another form in which human artifice and labor replace natural endowments in the provision of commodities. Relatedly, economic growth in a modern economy seems to be increasingly keyed to its superior organization, including in this its organization of intellectual resources and improvements in transportation and especially communications. As we say, a really modern economy consists predominately of people, not things.

This point serves to give analytical support to the growing awareness that we have pushed some natural resources to their limits. These include, most importantly, fresh water, petroleum, forests, and the favorable temperature and quality of the atmosphere. In principle if not in practice, "we" understand that the era of free gifts from nature is drawing to a close so that our balance with nature will have to tend toward zero; we can use natural resources only to the extent that by human action we do not over time diminish or degrade them. These things suggest a trajectory in economic affairs in which the only resource whose services can be expanded without limit is the social labor-power. In that sense, labor-power comes over time to occupy a greater, and natural resources a smaller, role in providing goods and services.

In these senses, too, our social labor-power theory of value becomes more and more an emergent, empirical characteristic of a modern economy. The identification of capital expansion with the (constrained) expansion of the social labor-power here functions as a description of an actual secular process. The practical dominance and importance of the social labor-power, even as constrained and distorted in its growth by capital, are already the central elements in the growth of a modern economy. It constitutes the primary fructive element and the only productive component whose use expands, not reduces, its further and continued availability.

How Should We Evaluate Capital's Performance?

It is a good investigation that successfully answers the questions it set out to answer but a better one if in the process equally important questions are unearthed or even just usefully redefined.

We have argued that in a contemporary economy there is reason to view "the self-expansion of capital" as comprising the self-expansion of the social labor-power but as constrained in its activity and path of development by "property," that is, as we have defined it, by claims to authority over the direction of the economy and society and the rewards pertaining to them, which are, at least in principle, nonproductive.

Thus, the question is: How should we evaluate the performance of capital? becomes, under our theory of value, How do we optimize the free development, the self-chosen expansion, of the powers of the social labor-power? In stating the question in this way I am not reintroducing either morally or ideologically, and certainly not analytically, the traditional labor theory of value associated with Adam Smith, David Ricardo, and especially Karl Marx. As for the moral and ideological issues, Schlatter ([1951] 1973) has convincingly argued, I think, that that classical view comes down to little more than repotted Locke, namely, that "man" is entitled to the fruits of his own labors for no other reason than that he has mixed part of himself with nature's free gifts; those fruits thereby become his "property," that is, extensions of his self, as in the Latin *proprius,* meaning "pertaining to the self."

If one conceives of a society and an economy as a simple aggregate of individuals, each acting and reacting more with nature than with each other, the Lockean view has a certain plausibility, Robinson Crusoe writ large. But once we allow that every individual is born into an existing society and is significantly shaped by it, Lockean simplicity loses its charm. Am I, for example, entitled to earn more than you because I work harder? The answer isn't and can't be open and shut. Perhaps in the course of my life—or course—it has been socialized in me that hard work will bring a socially guaranteed reward—a career, a title, status, a good salary with "perks"—while others will have learned early in their course of life that their ambitions will be frustrated, their efforts sterile, their work socially undervalued, and perhaps even their calling viewed as conferring low, possibly even demeaning status. The point of course is that none of our personal attributes can be entirely severed from the efforts of others such as our parents, teachers, and mentors and the often unknown men and women of the past who contributed to the shaping of the society we were born into and which has shaped us. There is no Einstein if there was no Newton, no Newton without Descartes, and no Descartes without those unknown ancient workmen who codified a practical knowledge of construction shapes and the unknown scribes who extended and preserved that knowledge across the centuries.[9]

Analytically, of course, the classical labor theory of value rests on the discredited value subsystem, synonyms, and tautologies, lacking a solution to the problems of value-price transformation.

The value theory presented in this study argues for a moral equivalent of the legendary "market." This is not a market as in "market socialism" or "deregulation," one must add, because under modern conditions arguments and conceptions of a "free market" function in fact to inure people to economic necessity. Globalization, it is typically said, requires freer trade, that is, that we should accept as iron necessity whatever happens as private firms, with government assistance, go their own way on their own say-so where and when they want. In fact, this magical transmutation of the rhetoric of freedom into a rhetoric of obedience to necessity has long been the hallmark of market theorizing, especially since its rebirth a century and a quarter ago more or less simultaneously with the growth of economic institutions possessing significant power over labor and other markets.

By the moral equivalent of the market I mean that one wants to shape a program of economic change and reform that confronts the "sovereign consumer" not merely with the chance to buy or not to buy but with the issues involved in to make or not to make. Market conceptions inevitably, it seems, limit themselves to treating economic actors as transcendent, ahistorical, suprasocial individuals. Moreover, they assume, as in the value subsystem, that economic value itself is unambiguous, constant, and equally available to each and every Individual. The sort of moral equivalent I have in mind rejects both of these points. First, of course, it accepts that the economic actor as we meet him or her is a socialized person armed not only with socially conditioned needs and information but with socially created blinders to his or her experience and consequently judgment. The moral equivalent of the market, if it is to contribute to individual and social freedom, must be organized in such a way that there is learning and feedback between individuals, groups, and institutions so that the consumer comes over time to value the good or service not per se but in the wider context of its social, ecological, and other costs and benefits. Simultaneously, those consumers must have at hand the ready power to punish in significant ways economic institutions that are not sufficiently responsive to not the sovereign consumer but the sovereign citizen.

This view of the matter also implies that value questions can't be answered by appeals to this or that theory; if we take seriously the idea of the moral equivalent of the market, value preferences, that is, the value preferences of individuals and groups of people and ultimately of an economy taken as a whole, can only be answered by looking to see what people prefer when they possess the best practical information as to the costs and consequences of those preferences with respect to other possible choices. Values, ultimately, don't exist in philosophic space, and they really can't be imposed. They have to be discovered in critical practice. Just as we allow the novice to make mistakes as part of a learning curve based on trial and error, economic arrangements must be such that the actors can and will be confronted with the consequences of their choices and hence allowed the possibility of learning from them. I grant that it is easier to say this than to specify how to embody it in a scheme of new economic arrangements, but what is the alternative?

The existing economic mechanism works visibly and powerfully to shape the consumer market and hence to shape consumers en masse to fit its needs not theirs. The tobacco companies give only one instance of the power that modern economic institutions routinely exercise against—or within—government and against the consuming public. Like the home insulation companies, auto companies, tire companies, and chemical companies, big tobacco has long produced and distributed a product that menaces the health, indeed the lives, of its customers. What is striking about big tobacco is not that there have been steps taken against them in recent years, but that it took so long for scientific studies of tobacco to break through industry smoke screens, that so little has been done to date to check their ability to target children and adolescents, and that even the fines they've suffered will be amortized through the tax and regulatory systems. Under an agreement with the states' Attorneys General and the Justice Department the companies have been given an exemption from antitrust prosecution in order to jointly raise their prices for the purpose of paying their fines!

If one wants to preserve, even widen, areas of social spontaneity and diversity, if one wants to avoid the worst effects of fetishized experience, if one, in brief, wants to prevent, as I put it earlier, the victory of property over society, then clearly one must set about to do that in those terms and under that banner. Historically speaking, the strategies of progressivism and social democracy at the turn of the twentieth century were to coexist with the property system of corporate capital by ameliorating its effects through schemes of partial regulation, countervailing institutions like trade unions, and an objective science and social science. That strategic vision has obviously failed. Today government regulators are typically industry representatives, the trade unions are staggering, and the voices of "objective science and social science" are, as in the case of tobacco, more often than not drowned out by the hired scientists and other experts put forward by industry. In short, the present dominance, both nationally and internationally, of the big firms has placed us right back where our ancestors stood over one hundred years ago. We must confront the task of making a humane economy in light of that hundred years, that is, in light of the historic failure of the trio of government regulation, trade unions, and objective social science to sustain themselves against the corporate counterattack exemplified by the Reagan-Thatcher years.[10] If there is a lesson in this failure, it is that the evolution of constraining property relations now threatens the very existence of freely chosen social relations, for those are the ultimate terms of today's dilemma. It is in the name of a threatened society that we must radically revamp our economic priorities, which is to say our economic arrangements and institutions.[11]

On the Tension between Prices and Values

The value system advanced here seems required in order to provide a consistent microeconomics for modern sale/purchase, that is, for sale/purchase-in-time. As such it is incompatible with both so-called free markets and a program of state ownership of producer assets. As we have seen, in value terms those hoary conceptions represent not alternatives but mirror images of one another. Both—pointedly—don't measure up to our standard, the moral equivalent of the market, because both lack or block the social learning connection between producing and consuming that in principle exists within the social labor-power and of which any system of propertied capital, state or private, is a truncated and distorted expression.

To put the matter another way, if we continue to accept the immense advantages and flexibility of price-denominated production and distribution of goods and services, then those prices should lean more and more heavily over time toward being social labor-power prices and not property prices. They should be weighted to reflect the present and future needs and desires of the social labor-power in some manner democratically organized—value—and not to preserve property values established in the past and nonproductively projected into the present and the future. Without "going utopian," what I have in mind is clearly a further projection and amplification of familiar present-day pricing policies that incorporate such things as energy consumption taxes, fair wage requirements, and health and safety regulations, in short, price-influencing policies that attempt to incorporate into empirical prices what economists typically call negative externalities, that is, the costs that are normally excluded or minimized in a pricing system in which the preservation and expansion of property values is sovereign and imperative. The public, too, should earn the benefits of its own considerable contributions to so-called private investment, that is, to pay discounted not premium prices, for example, for drugs and other pharmaceuticals developed at public expense, for timber and cattle companies to pay full price for public lands, and, of course, for the citizenry to play a direct, immediate role in the investment/planning processes of private firms that is fully commensurate with their financial contributions both direct and indirect.

The famous American socialist Eugene Debs is reputed often to have ended his appeals for socialism with a particularly fine peroration. I've always admired Debs, but I also like the irony of quoting a socialist on behalf of the ideas, ultimately hostile to state socialism, that I have presented here under the rubric of microeconomics. Debs's coda is entirely appropriate: "If I could lead you into the promised land," he told his audiences, "I would refuse to do it, for if I could lead you in, others could lead you right out again. You must learn that there is nothing that you cannot do for yourselves." Or, in microeconomic terms, the transformation of prices and values does not have an ontological solution, for it is not at all an ontological problem. It is a wholly practical problem and one whose progressive resolution is increasingly overdue.

Notes

1. The category "quasi-compulsory" or the related "partially constrained" consumption, some of whose forms I just listed, is an oxymoron in contemporary economic theory, but the phenomena in question have to be subjected to analysis and theoretical codification if we are to formulate a microeconomics apposite to a modern not a Victorian economy.

2. The argument in economics that unique prices are codetermined rests on the mathematics of solvable equation sets whose solution conditions must generally be fixed; generally a variant of static equilibrium. But fixed solution conditions coexist uneasily with an economy designed, so to speak, to yield perpetual qualitative change in productive conditions, products, and of course the productive qualities of the working population. I agree with Frank Hahn that general equilibrium theory, based on mainstream microeconomic analysis, is well-nigh unassailable on its own terms but that those very terms explicitly exclude the characteristics most visible, most important, and, indeed, most desired in a modern economy, namely, change and growth. See Hahn 1981, especially p. 132.

3. Following Schumpeter, it is useful to distinguish the narratives we give in clarification of fundamental propositions in economics from their analytical content, that is, from their formal properties and thus their role within the inferential apparatus. See Schumpeter 1954, 1053ff. ("Appendix to Chapter 7: on the Theory of Utility"), where he is interested in distinguishing the inferential/analytic dimension of utility theory from this or that (psychological) narrative. See especially footnote 2, page 1057, and page 1058, where he argues that "the utility theory of value has much better claim to be called a logic than a psychology of values."

Yet even while one distinguishes the narrative from the analytical dimensions of a theory they cannot be entirely separated. A theory must be "interpreted," meaning technically that the meaning and the initial and boundary conditions of at least some of its terms and propositions must be specified in terms of some body of material purported to provide their "meaning" and "evidence." Persuasive narratives can be presented in place of an articulated interpretative procedure, but, as I will argue, they may not be quite consistent with the theory being offered. For this argument, see the following sections.

4. Proposition set 1–8, hereafter *Inst* {1 + 8}, is obviously not a complete representation of the axioms of neoclassical microeconomics; significantly, I have omitted the stipulation that buyers and sellers always act to maximize utility. We'll return to this issue later.

5. The import of this distinction will become clearer as we proceed.

6. In a general equilibrium model one both incorporates and discards time through the device of assuming that markets for the future delivery of future goods and services both exist and are cleared in the present through time-discounted prices. This point does not gainsay but in fact emphasizes the instantaneous nature of exchange per se.

Analytically speaking, if one allows that the exchange of certain goods or services extends over real time intervals one thereby opens up the logical possibility that two or more prices for the same goods might obtain within the interval, that is, those prices would not be mutually conditioned and hence some supply/demand functions characterizing those exchanges would be discontinuous in some interval within the interval, hence also nondifferentiable in that interval. Alternately, one can overcome these barriers to general equilibrium analysis by assuming futures markets, conditional contracts, and other logical and narrative devices that make future uncertainty calculable. Uncertainty about the future or another's price behavior under different circumstances can be accommodated by means of this gambit—but only as long as the uncertainty has what one might call an underwriter's or actuarial character, that is, is at least notionally calculable. Even random futures could in principle be so accommodated but clearly not all possible future behaviors. For this point, see also Arrow and Hahn 1971: 33ff., 122ff.

It should be observed that in introducing analytical constructs such as futures markets, time discounted prices, the reduction of complex exchanges to simple, one-to-one affairs, and such the fabled elegance and simplicity of the basic microeconomic theory is being compromised. The point is that no theory that purports to deal with complex, many-faceted realities can be simple and unidimensional. One must incorporate the complexity somewhere, though it need not be in the axiom set. It can be incorporated instead in the theory's transformation rules, that is, the rules governing the logical development of the theory from the axioms or, alternately, in the rules that "interpret" the theory in relation to its purported meaning and evidence. It is in this last, the rules of interpretation, that the elegance of the neoclassical microeconomics is, as it were, "paid for," often in the form of ad hoc interpolations such as futures markets, assumptions that market information comes without cost, or omnipresent insurance and even reinsurance schemes, or is painted out by means of the expression "ceteris paribus." In any event, choices about which level of analysis to incorporate this or that complexity are generally governed by considerations of methodological convenience, not of the innate superiority of one choice over the other.

7. This is not sufficient condition, obviously, but necessary one. In the strict sense, as used here, to say that Q is the necessary condition for P is to say that Q being false implies that P is false as well.

8. This observation brings out the fact that the initial definition of *exchange* in the previous section was not analytically innocent. The very definition assumed that all of the PC's services, including unforecastable future potential services, were alienable en bloc at the initiation of the sale/purchase, closing off the possibility of serial transfer. Hence it appears that proposition 4 (fully transfer en bloc), proposed as an additional assumption, also contains a repeat of the initial definition, albeit in disguised form.

9. Note that this is not the familiar "unequal exchange," that is, an exchange of unequal values. We point instead to an inequality of the seller and the purchaser within the sale/purchase interval. Again duration of time is critical. If a sale/purchase is conceived to occur instantaneously, then the free and equal relationship of the neoclassical view at the inception of the sale/purchase is the same relationship at its conclusion; a trivial inference. But if there is a positive interval of sale/purchase one may not assume that the relations between seller and purchaser cannot change within that interval. Thus, even if, along with the neoclassicals, we accept that the purchaser initially bought the car or PC or microwave or health plan in a free and equal relationship with the seller, it does not follow that this free and equal relationship will necessarily extend throughout the entire interval of the sale/purchase, that is, that interval in which all of the purchased (potential) services of the good in question are transferred to the purchaser. In fact, and as we can readily observe, the symmetry of the sale/purchase relationship may change to the detriment of the purchaser once the initial purchase occurs *and because of it.*

10. The microeconomics in positive time that was just outlined does not require a utility-maximizing assumption; it purports to be a formal scheme adaptable to the ways different sellers and purchasers actually behave; to what degree a utility calculus is involved depends on further empirical investigation of different sets of such sale/purchase relationships. This observation serves to bring out a feature of the implicit logical structure of *Inst* {1 + 8}. By characterizing exchange relationships as instantaneous, one precludes the possibility of examining the relationships themselves to discover possible further characteristics. Instead one must exogenously impute that exchange is symmetrically utility maximizing.

From the standpoint of theory construction, one is here assuming that the set of economically admissible exchanges is entirely comprised within the set of elementary utility-maximizing exchanges, that is to say, one is *interpreting* the proposition set *Inst* (1 + 8} as valid for that field of logical objects and further claiming that all economically significant exchanges are in principle reducible to elements of the field. One need not make these additional assumptions for the microeconomics-in-positive-time just described.

11. In *Dur* {1 + 10}, length of time is not specified, presumably varying with the different cases from a moment or so into several years—as for a health plan. Analogously, for instance, to say that the seller and purchaser are formally unequal or partially constrained in the modal transaction is merely to indicate that different degrees of inequality and constraint are possible in the modal relationship, occasionally nil, more often varying from slight and substantially inconsequential, on up to serious levels of one-sided compunction. Similarly and consonant with social science and mathematical usage, the incidence of advances and liens may be considered as parameters varying within the sale/purchase relationship from zero to one, nil to compulsory. Technically, the sale/purchase relationship—between producer/sellers and purchaser/final consumers—is given here as a complex dyadic relationship, x S/P y in which the left-hand member ranges over one or more sets of varying size while the right-hand member is a unit set. The relation x S/P y includes, indeed emphasizes, the possibility of its nonsymmetry. In contrast, in exchange, x E y, the relationship is necessarily symmetrical and both members are unit sets.

12. Theories dealing specifically with the pricing/selling behavior of firms are comprehensively reviewed and analyzed in Lee 1998. This interesting study also contains an extensive bibliography of both pricing theories and empirical pricing practices.

13. Note that if the elemental exchange relationship is necessarily symmetrical, as is requisite in *Inst* {1 + 8}, then every sum of several such relations will yield only a symmetrical relation. To introduce the necessary nonsymmetry some additional stipulation would be required, which would necessarily nullify stipulations 2 and 3 of *Inst* {1 + 8}. On the other hand, *Dur* {1 + 10} incorporates the subcase in which x S/P y is symmetrical and x ranges over unit sets.

14. Imagine that for some arbitrary time, t, one arranges the possible set of sales/purchases-in-time in the whole economy in sequential order by the length of their time intervals. If we examine that sequence as the intervals diminish, we can hypothesize that they will diminish toward a limit of zero time, the familiar instantaneous time of neoclassical exchange. But can the limit of this time-interval sequence fairly represent the key properties of the elements of the sequence of which it is the limit? Or, equivalently, can one formally and without distortion reduce sale/purchase-in-time to exchange-in-instantaneous time?

Unfortunately for the hypothesis, the formal properties of sale/purchase relations don't hold at the limit but only up to the limit. Sale/purchase-in-time relations are normally asymmetrical, though they include symmetrical relations as a subcase, that is, they are *n-to-one* relations where n ranges over the positive integers. Neoclassical exchange relations are necessarily symmetrical, *one-to-one*. Thus, the extrapolation of the positively timed relations to the limit of zero time introduces a formal change in the nature of the microeconomic relationship between seller and purchaser. The neoclassical "exchange" does not represent but instead distorts the logical properties that seem to be required for sale/purchase-in-time. The different logics entailed in "exchange" and in "sale/purchase-in-time" will in turn entail different and noncompatible inferences as one further develops the respective micro theories.

Note that if this analysis holds, we have gone beyond the familiar argument of heterodox economists. Their argument says, in effect, that neoclassical economics constructs an ideal world, and the real world isn't really like that and doesn't really work that way. To use our earlier distinction, this sort of objection lies in the narrative realm. But if the arguments just discussed are valid, they say something stronger, namely that there is a formal theoretical gap between microeconomics-in-instantaneous-time and the microeconomics-in-positive-time that has been sketched here. That in turn implies that the neoclassical "micro" cannot be adjusted—not even "in principle"—to comprehend the sort of commodity practices now so typical of a modern economy.

Technically, the objection is not to the body of neoclassical theory itself. Having so thoroughly explored the hitherto unknown logics of *exchange, equilibrium,* and *utility,* it marks an advance in economic understanding and is a remarkable scientific achievement combining the most rigorous analysis and creative human imagination. It calls to my own mind the similarly remarkable effort stretching from Peano through Bertrand Russell and Alfred North Whitehead to explore the limits of *system* in mathematical knowledge.

But for the neoclassical enterprise, its own rules of interpretation require that it both allow and forbid economic transactions that fill non–zero time intervals, or, equivalently, that the very effort to find narrative analogues to its formal, logical features must introduce inconsistency into the theory itself.

15. For an elementary discussion of this point, see Copi 1967: 187ff. The following is a trivial illustration of the point. Assume in each case the false proposition, All geometrical figures have four sides. Then (a) assume truly that, All triangles are geometric figures. This implies the false proposition, All triangles have four sides. The inference is perfectly valid, but the falsity of the initial assumption carries over into the falseness of the inferred proposition. If we instead (b) assume truly that, Squares are geometrical figures, then a valid inference implies the true conclusion, Squares have four sides. On the other hand, from a premise (c), All n-sided figures are geometrical figures, one is left with the valid conclusion, All n-sided figures have four sides. Its truth or falsity is indeterminate until one specifies the range of values that n may assume.

More simply, in formal logic, where $\supset$ designates material implication, p ranges unrestrictedly over propositions, and F designates any false proposition, the expression, $(p)[F \supset p]$ is a tautology.

16. The reference here is to the quality "expressive completeness," namely, the capacity of a group of defined concepts and propositions to fully characterize a circumscribed body of empirical material. Expressive completeness is one of the conditions for a group of defined terms to yield, in the context of a group of axioms, inferential completeness, that is, to yield as theorems all the "true" propositions about the circumscribed body of material. There is no question of trying for an inferentially complete microeconomics in this present study, but we ought to try to reach expressive completeness. My point is that the Jevonian/Walrasian microeconomics exhibits weak expressive completeness in the form of open-ended, ultimately indefinable expressions such as "all things holding equal." Thus, it has a kind of delphic quality that belies its heralded theoretical parsimony to a degree that appears to be unacceptable in scientific work.

17. "Americanism, in is most developed form, requires a preliminary condition which has not attracted the attention of American writers who have treated the problems arising from it, since in America it exists quite 'naturally.' This condition could be called 'a rational demographic composition' and consists in the fact that there do not exist numerous classes with no essential function in the world of production" (Gramsci [1925–34] 1971: 281). (The prison writings of Gramsci date from the period 1926–35 and were for the most part only published after his death in 1935. I do not know that any part of them can be dated more precisely.)

18. Marx, too, appears to have believed that, at least in the very long run, "society" was self-correcting. In the Marxist view, there is a contradiction—a fundamental, unresolvable social opposition—between the claims of property and those of society that in the long run will inevitably result in the victory of society over property. As he phrases it in the *Manifesto*, "Society can not live under this bourgeoisie, in other words, its existence is no longer compatible with society" ([1847] 1968: 45).

19. It is puzzling that the practical importance of this point less seldom engages the interest of contemporary left-leaning critics of modern society who remain, one must admit, partial to "viewing with alarm" the social influence of capitalism. For example, the foremost historian of modern European socialism sees not a secular trajectory to refabricate the contours of society to capitalist institutional advantage in the way I claim but instead merely a more diffuse "*fin-de-siecle*" turmoil reshaping the planet at enormous speed" (Sassoon 1996: 776; see also my review and critique of this otherwise excellent study in McDermott 2001).

This rather passive, nonprescriptive reaction to the totalizing effect of business enterprise on modern society is itself extremely noteworthy. There was an enormous literature in the last half of the nineteenth century and the first, say, third of the twentieth that tried to understand and cope with that very phenomenon. It was a subject that preoccupied such (American) luminaries as John Dewey, Herbert Croly, Thorstein Veblen, the Lynds, Charles Beard, Carl

Becker, John R. Commons, Selig Perlman, and later Gardiner Means, William Appleman Williams, and a whole host of equally distinguished researchers. All worried about the prospect of business domination, and all more or less confidently proposed various new doctrines, institutional innovations, social and political actions, and so on to stem and reverse the business tide. Sassoon's position is, I think, not at odds with other contemporary critics, who seem to accept implicitly that the broad programs of control over big business proposed by their predecessors have failed and that society must accommodate itself to business imperatives rather than vice versa. For an introduction to that older literature (and history) one could hardly do better than to consult Kolko [1963] 1967; and Wiebe 1967.

Chapter 2

1. But, like the neoclassical "micro," the Marxist version, too, is not free of conundrums, particularly around its value theory. We will address that issue in chapter 7.

2. I say "virtually" because, while "labor power" is bought and sold like any other commodity, is utilized just like any other producer commodity, and in fact is the most important producer commodity, it is not produced as one. It is produced outside the capitalist economy per se and even somewhat independent of it.

For Marx, the quantity and value of goods and services that are devoted to the production and subsequent maintenance of the labor force are strictly determined by powerful economic processes, but the actual consumption of the goods and services that enter into its production is theorized to go on outside the economy per se in a realm of essentially private consumption—thus the anomaly. Labor-power is the supremely productive force for the Marxist economy, but its actual productive characteristics—its relative size within the population, the level and distribution of its skills, its technological and other, related culture—fall within and are determined in the last analysis by the private world of "final consumption." As he writes,

> The maintenance and reproduction of the working class is, and ever must be, a necessary condition to the reproduction of capital. But the capitalist may safely leave its fulfillment to the laborer's instincts for self-preservation and of propagation. All the capitalist cares for, is to reduce the laborer's individual consumption as far as possible to what is strictly necessary and he is far away from imitating those brutal South Americans, who force their laborers to take the more substantial, rather than the less substantial, kind of food. (Marx [1867] 1967: 537)

Obviously, a central constructive point of the present study is to revise Marx's commodity theory to make good this omission and more concretely to link the changing consumption of the labor force with its changing productive characteristics.

3. See the afterword to the second German edition of volume 1 of *Capital*, dated 1873. Marx writes that, irked by the tendency of some of his contemporaries to derogate the work of Hegel, "I therefore openly avowed myself the pupil of that mighty thinker, and even here and there, in the chapter on the theory of value, coquetted with the modes of expression peculiar to him" (ibid.: 29). The word *coquetted* is apt; his introduction to commodities and their characteristics in the chapter in question is overelaborate, often indirect, and somewhat stilted, with sometimes obscure signals as to his meaning. The style is very different and more difficult to decipher than his often crystal clear, always vigorous prose in the later parts of the volume and in his histories and other short works.

4. If we were to employ Hegelian terminology we would talk of the four dimensions as "reflexes" of one another.

5. This, of course, is analytically akin to the nonmonetary economy theorized in modern general equilibrium analysis, although there a numeraire takes the place of cattle or tobacco.

6. The conundrums cited in chapter 1 are philosophically related to the argument of the foregoing paragraph. In both cases one creates what I believe are insoluble theoretical problems by introducing a full, formal separation between a putative structural realm and the empirical/historical manifold.

7. The process of "abstracting," say, from a particular dog, Fido, to the point that Fido is a vertebrate involves a process of ignoring or eliding Fido's particular characteristics, of going from the (observed) particular to more and more abstract (or "dumb") general terms, as represented in the progression Fido, spaniel, dog, canine, mammal, vertebrate. In the first step, all of the animal's unique characteristics—size, color, personality, habits—are put aside to focus mentally on those few that define its breed. Continuing on, the differences between dogs, wolves, foxes, and such are put aside so as to locate Fido in the canine family. Then all the characteristics of canines are put aside save those that are shared with all mammals, and so on. Aristotle, who appears first to have identified the processes of abstraction per se, clearly seized upon the fact that Greek and presumably all modern European languages are classificatory in their structure, that is, via the grammatical relationship between nouns and adjectives. In a sense, Fido can be seen as an ensemble of many descriptive adjectives; "abstracting" makes the implicit claim that the adjectives (or characteristics) are clustered within one another in a definite, naturally given order so that the investigator can remove them like Sweezy's "one at a time" as if nature itself directs it.

Imagine, for example, a set of concentric rings, with each ring representing a group of characteristics of Fido, the inner one representing his unique characteristics, then surrounding it one for his spaniel characteristics, then another for the canine ones, then for mammalian, and so on. Here abstracting means to start at the center and empty progressively all of the rings save the outer one. It will be relatively empty compared to the initial situation or, in Marx's words, "dumb." From the nature of the case, *to abstract* means to shed meanings, nuances, and characteristics and shed "species" characteristics to gain the "genus," the emptiest ring of them all, the "dumb" generality.

It is a classic complaint against the logic of this position, and of Aristotle's own views on formal logic, that they raise mere classificatory grammar into a metaphysics, that is, impose the structure of language onto reality itself. Moreover, classification equals location fixing in a static logical space, hence in principle it is inadequate to cope with issues of change and time. In my view, Sweezy traps himself into Aristotelian Marxism, basically by employing a theory of language that is too primitive. For a more elaborate critique of abstraction, see the excellent Cassirer [1910] 1953, especially the opening chapters.

8. "All the linen in the market counts as but one article of commerce, of which each piece is only an aliquot part" (Marx [1867] 1967; 109).

9. "Every useful thing, as iron, paper, etc. . . . is an assemblage of many properties and may therefore be used in various ways. To discover the various use of things is the work of history" (Ibid.: 43).

Rudolf Hilferding, one of the most celebrated Marxist theoreticians, underlined this point about the social-material character of commodities in a very striking way. He writes, "In order to be exchangeable a commodity must conform to certain fixed and definite standards; a specific weight for a given volume, a particular color, aroma, etc. Only then does it constitute the 'type' or brand suitable for delivery. The 'type' used in coffee futures trade in Hamburg was of inferior quality. Accordingly, all superior brands of coffee were adulterated by adding black beans, kernels, etc." ([1910] 1981: 167).

10. "The total labor-power of society, which is embodied in the sum total of the values of all commodities produced by that society, counts here as one homogeneous mass of human labor-power, composed though it be of innumerable individual units. Each of these units is the same as any other, so far as it has the character of the average labor-power of society, . . . that is, so far as it requires for producing a commodity, no more time than is needed on an average, no more than is socially necessary. The labor time socially necessary is that required to produce an article under the normal conditions of production, and with the average degree of skill and intensity prevalent at the time. . . . In general, the greater the productiveness of labor, the less is the labor-time required for the production of an article, the less is the amount of labor crystallized in that article, and the less is its value" (Marx [1867] 1967: 46–48).

He continues, "A commodity may be the product of the most skilled labor, but its value, by equating it to the product of simple unskilled labor, represents a definite quantity of the latter labor alone. The different proportions in which different sorts of labor are reduced to unskilled labor as their standard, are established by a social process that goes on behind the backs of the producers, and, consequently, appears to be fixed by custom. For simplicity's sake we shall henceforth account every kind of labor to be unskilled, simple labor; by this we do no more than save ourselves the trouble of making the reduction" (51–52).

11. "Whoever directly satisfies his own wants with the produce of his own labor, creates, indeed, use-values, but not commodities. In order to produce the latter, he must not only produce use-values, but use-values for others, social use-values" (ibid.: 48).

12. This formulation would obviously have to be modified slightly in order to cover service commodities such as haircutting, auto repairs, investment advice, and so forth.

13. For the history of local vegetable production within and for New York City in the latter part of the nineteenth century, see Linder and Zacharias 1999.

Chapter 3

1. In many cases, of course, Victorian markets were so local and special in nature that they cannot really be included under the General or Money form of exchange. This would have been the case even when goods were exchanged for a price rather than by barter. I presume that there was a true national market for cloth and perhaps stove fuel (coal) but not so for clothing, food, and housing, all of which were provided subject to local peculiarities and together presumably making up a considerable proportion of consumers' expenditures. It is this phenomenon, I think, that seems to have reinforced the idea that how and to what end consumers consumed commodities was a more or less private affair, that is, a set of discrete private processes with only limited and unsystematic feedback into the larger economy. Obviously, that standpoint hardly fits what we can readily observe in a modern economy.

2. As we saw with respect to the services of, say, the PC or the auto, consumption of those services by the purchaser occurs within the sale/purchase state as conditioned by various relationships to other parties, to wit, the producer, often the credit agency, the producer of ancillary equipment, various dealers, the repairmen, and so forth. There is an analogous institutional conditioning to the consumption of welfare state services, a subject to which we shall shortly turn.

3. I will use the expression "constrained consumption" to signify a range of constraint pressing on consumer behavior. Agreeable to social science usage, we can conceive of such constraint as a parameter ranging from zero to one, from absolute freedom to absolute compulsion. On the face of it, most consumption of welfare state services lies somewhere between those two extremes.

4. The strategy behind GM's innovations in making and marketing cars is

lucidly described in the memoirs of its dominant figure in the 1920s and 1930s, Alfred P. Sloan (Sloan 1964).

5. In the more compact U.S. cities of the 1920s, public transport was readily available and not yet challenged by the commuting auto user. Accordingly, the earliest phases of auto marketing emphasized the pleasures of the road. I recognize that this concept might astound the present-day driver, whose daily commute is a nightmare of crowded roads, half-crazed speeders and weavers, and oversized sport utility vehicles. But during the 1920s–1930s special roads were designed and built so as to encourage auto owners to use their cars strictly for pleasure. Called "parkways," the word lingers in our usage, but it originally referred to roads that were designed to give the motorist the experience that he or she was within a park with an always pleasant, restful, bucolic vista. An early example of this sort of road construction is provided by the Bronx River Parkway in Westchester County, New York, whose deliberately winding course was conducted through a corridor whose trees and shrubs were laid out to hide from view the urban landscape behind them. Trucks and vans were excluded so as not to spoil the motorists' Sunday outing "in the country." Of course, a combination of sharp curves with tree trunks right at the shoulder of the road made for a notoriously dangerous roadway. Although several times reconstructed for safety reasons since the 1930s, the Bronx River Parkway still retains much of its early shape and charm. The Hutchinson River–Merritt Parkway system, which connects New York City with New Haven, Connecticut, has much the same character, again in spite of considerable modern reconstruction aimed at making the system a bit safer. A modern, parallel route, the Connecticut Turnpike, also connecting New York and New Haven, shows the difference in post–World War II highway construction. Very wide, straight, and utilitarian, paralleled by commercial signs and highway sprawl and filled with trucks and tractor-trailers, the turnpike was engineered simply to move traffic, mostly commercial, at relatively high speeds.

6. In classical and neoclassical exchange, market theory postulates an absolute equality, the product of free choice, between buyer and seller, hence the old warning, Caveat emptor! "Let the buyer beware" (of what he or she is buying), as in the general case the seller retained no legal or other obligation to the buyer subsequent to the point of sale. The gradual evolution of consumer protection laws and kindred court decisions is further testimony that the old formal equality between buyer and seller has been socially altered by the exigencies of modern products and modern buyer/seller relationships. Of course, the law lingers behind the reality and only slowly catches up. Formally speaking, however, it is conventionally accepted that the seller does retain significant obligations to the buyer after the initial sale is consummated, at least to the point where it is evident that the seller's representations about the product were responsible and relatively realistic.

7. The reader may satisfy himself or herself on this point by noting that one will spend just about as much money to operate a car over its lifetime as

one spent at its initial purchase. In that sense, the "purchase price of the car" has a somewhat fetishlike character, severely obscuring the cost of the services provided by the car. This social bifurcation between the commodity per se and its services, especially with respect to time, is a prime characteristic of modern commodity form, a point often advantageously obscured by marketers.

8. Technically speaking, a car or air conditioner or CD player or PC is only one element in a system that delivers the services we want to enjoy. Modern marketing strategies focus our attention on the thing itself, but there is no call for economic analysis to accede to this fetishism.

9. It is often the case in modern marketing that the commodity comprises both the item and the service. For example, in recent years auto leasing has become increasingly popular. The manufacturer both builds the car and leases it to the consumer, the terms of the lease including leaving the maintenance and repair of the vehicle in the hands of the auto manufacturer. Here the "package" is the commodity, not the auto or the leasing services.

10. Michael Meeropol has pointed out that there is a striking parallel here to the sale of capital goods in, say, mid-nineteenth-century Britain. A locomotive or coke oven would yield its full services to its purchaser only over time, and in that period the purchaser might well have to seek the manufacturer's assistance for spare or replacement parts, and of course complementary producer goods such as coal or rails would have to be acquired. But such sale/purchase states were then by and large limited to capital goods and were not, as now, ubiquitously present in retail sale/purchase. What the parallel suggests is that goods for final consumption have been taking on more and more of the economic characteristics of capital goods, that is, goods that are in the normal case productively consumed. In both cases the original sale, whether of a capital good or a consumer item, constitutes only the sale of some quasi services for the item in question, and thus also incorporates an advance—an "investment"—on behalf of eventually obtaining an integral service.

11. In the sale/purchase relationship between a modern corporate seller and a person or family, there is a multidimensional one-sidedness analogous to what we found in the administrative relationship. For example, if one has warranty problems that is precisely the sort of complex encounter one engages in with the company representative. It is perhaps simpler for our purposes just to point out that your unreliable new car or crotchety PC may constitute a multiheaded disaster for you but it is only an infinitesimally small blip on the producer/seller's screen.

12. A theory that purports to have scientific value must also prove fruitful beyond its initial ambit; it should lead the investigator to discoveries not understood and anticipated prior to its formulation. A microeconomics based on sale/purchase within commodity form will prove to do just that (see the following section).

13. Sloan 1964 is indispensable for this narrative.

14. The classic account of these changes in general business practice is Chandler 1962. See also Chandler and Daems 1980 for the historical spread of these practices beyond the United States.

15. See, for example, Stern and El-Ansary 1982. In a personal conversation a researcher on the apparel industry, and friend, Prof. Ellen Rosen, pointed out that nature's (and Vivaldi's) traditional four seasons have grown to six, perhaps seven, under the pressure to give the selling of clothing more of a flow character. My own inquiries at a few upscale women's and men's shops in the Boston area confirmed it. To winter, spring, summer, and fall have been added "cruise" for that winter holiday in warmer climes and two transitional seasons, as yet unnamed, between spring and summer and, especially, between summer and fall.

The home furnishings and apparel industries appear to reach a degree of tacit agreement on what colors will be featured in a given year or even a given season. This makes sense, for it would entail great waste and significant losses if, say, the shoe and dress firms prioritized lines with directly clashing colors or designs or the rug manufacturers featured Victorian next year while the furniture makers went modern. By and large, I think post-Keynesian price theory is right to shift the focus from the behavior of the (single) firm. The work of industry associations and long-standing corporate cooperative relations seems to be of increasing importance, as in the complementary relationship between GM and Dupont, which, among other things, pioneered antiknock gasoline and durable auto paint colors (Sloan 1964).

16. See, for example, the interesting essay on Herbert Hoover's work as Secretary of Commerce in the Harding and Coolidge administrations on behalf of "associationism," that is, encouraging cooperative relationships between businesses in the same industry. To encourage exports, Hoover presided over standardization efforts for industrial products and specifications and, as if belying his later reputation as the "Great Individualist," won exemptions from antitrust regulations so that U.S. firms could collude in the their overseas operations (Rothbard 1972).

17. Manufacturers normally consult with their distributors and advertising firms as to what to produce, in what volume, and with what design and packaging. Even in the book business is this true, so that we now find major publishers consulting with bookstore chains such as Barnes and Noble and Borders as to in what numbers to publish a given title, what its dust jacket should look like, how its advertising campaign should be pitched, whether Oprah or some other media multiplier might take it up, and so forth.

18. This observation is sometimes less trivial than it appears. It is chronically the case that low-wage workers face transportation difficulties that help to maintain their low place in the productive system and, of course, their low wages. Outside of a few major cities and other favored areas, the "private" automobile is the centerpiece of our social transportation system, that is, a system not only terribly expensive in comparison with mass transit but one in

which the especially heavy capital costs of transportation fall directly and individually upon the traveler.

It is also chronically the case that poor children who feel shabbily dressed often avoid school and, more striking, when given a proper breakfast they do better than their less well fed companions. In each case, the role of consumer goods in improving, or lowering, the productive qualities of workers and future workers is socially manifest.

19. There are also numbers of "hobbies," do-it-yourself materials and tools, especially for home repair and maintenance; and other consumer items whose normal consumption enters as a matter of course into the coproduction of further services.

Chapter 4

1. For example, the metatheory behind the Jevons/Walras microeconomics is drawn from English philosophy of the eighteenth and nineteenth centuries, drawing prescriptive and psychological tenets from both natural rights theorists such as Locke and the utilitarian tradition associated with the Mills and Bentham. Both traditions posit a conception of human nature as transcendent, that is, not fundamentally conditioned by historical time, place, and circumstance. Thus, in spite of the vast sophistication with which the theory has been developed in the past century, the customary formulation of the initial conditions for calling the theory into play and the boundary conditions that limit its claimed scope are often left, as we have seen, to the unsatisfactory "all else holding equal."

2. It is a theoretical lapse on Marx's part that he sometimes can be read to say that use-values are predicated of the thing and not on the social relationships within which the thing is set. "The utility of a thing makes it a use-value. But this utility is not a thing of air. Being limited by the physical properties of the commodity, it has no existence apart from that commodity. A commodity . . . is therefore, so far as it is a material thing, a use-value, something useful" (Marx [1867] 1967: 44). This formulation is relatively innocent because he seems to have in mind solely the case in which all of a commodity's use-values or services are transferred, and at once, to the purchaser: "To become a commodity a product must be transferred to another, whom it will serve as a use-value, by means of an exchange" (44).

3. "In the laborer's circulation, L-M-C, which includes his consumption, only the first member falls within the circuit of capital as a result of [the previous exchange of labor-power for money {JM}]. The second act, M-C [the exchange of money for the laborer's consumption goods {JM}] does not fall within the circulation of individual capital, although it springs from it" (Marx [1885] 1967: 77).

4. See ibid.: chap. 20; and Marx [1894] 1966: chaps. 8–9. For further dis-

cussion, see, for example, Sweezy's treatment, following Bortkiewicz, in Sweezy 1942: chap. 7. As Schumpeter points out, Marx's arrangement of three distinct Departments provides one of the earliest attempts at theorizing a general equilibrium model for the economy as a whole (Schumpeter 1954: 391, 965–66).

5. "The greater the social wealth, the functioning capital, the extent and energy of its growth, and, therefore, also the absolute mass of the proletariat and the productiveness of its labor, the greater is the industrial reserve army. . . . But the greater this reserve army in proportion to the active labor-army, the greater is the mass of the consolidated surplus-population, whose misery is in inverse proportion to its torment of labor. The more extensive, finally, the lazarus-layers of the working class, and the industrial reserve army, the greater is official pauperism. *This is the absolute general law of capitalist accumulation"* (Marx [1867] 1967: 603).

6. For a remarkable observation on this point, see ibid: 229, n. 2.

7. If one retains Marx's demand theory as is and yet tries to give an account of consumers' consumption, one must erect a whole new theoretical apparatus that from the nature of the case will be logically independent of the theory itself. Baran and Sweezy's (1966) analysis of "monopoly capitalism" as having radical tendencies toward overproduction, and consequently of the necessity for wasteful production and thus wasteful consumption of consumer goods, including those for the working class, provides a case in point. Marx's theoretical apparatus calls for capitalist production to oscillate continually and wildly from under- to overproduction while always subjecting the workers to the General Law. There is really no room in Marx's theory for excessive consumption goods to be regularly steered to the workers. What Baran and Sweezy argue is not particularly erroneous; in fact there is a core of truth in it. But it is an add-on, a paste-up, not an extension of the logic of Marx's commodity theory and one often in contradiction to its findings. If one wants a "Marxism" adequate to the modern economy, one must—for better or worse—try to repair that system at its foundations not engage in paste-ups.

8. A more critical (and commonsense) theory of advertising would much deemphasize the purely symbolic realm in favor of analyzing the wider behaviors of the producer/advertiser in altering and improving the market channels for the product. Advertising per se—the manipulation and broadcast of symbolic appeals—is typically aimed at a target audience that previous market research has ascertained is particularly susceptible to it; as in tobacco and beer advertising to the young. Then, (1) the example of the targeted audience will act as a small multiplier, that is, will cause others to buy the product as well; and (2) it will influence distributors and retailers not only to stock the product but to feature it in their ads, in their premier display spaces, and—this is often tied to the ad campaign—in temporary price reductions directed toward getting others to buy it and hopefully initiating a habit of buying it. This provides still another, often very significant multiplier of sales. Then, (3) based

upon the larger economic returns to the mass producer, the advertised product will be better financed to continue in these ways to multiply its sales at the expense of its rivals—unless, of course, the rival producer/advertisers are doing the same thing. In truth, much advertising is purely defensive in orientation, especially for commodities that are relatively uniform such as patent medicines, beer, tobacco, gasoline, and so forth.

Note that in this thumbnail analysis the much heralded symbolic character and power of advertising does not assume an independent role but is submerged within social-material strategies and behaviors on the part of producers, distributors, advertisers, dealers, and potential purchasers who can be identified as particularly vulnerable.

9. Marx himself did not give an extensive treatment of services commodities and yet, in writing about them, he comes close to the element, "quasi service": "A service is nothing more than the useful effect of a use-value, be it of a commodity, or be it of labor" ([1867] 1967: 187). For his wider treatment of services commodities, see also "The Costs of Circulation," chapter 6 of the second volume of *Capital* ([1885] 1967).

10. Marx [1867] 1967: 3. The inner quotation is from his own *Critique of Political Economy,* published in 1859.

11. Even in a great modern city such as New York, until the 1830s the production and distribution of fruit and vegetables was quite haphazard. Only from the 1880s on were these items supplied other than locally (see Linder and Zacharias 1999). My mother, growing up in the decade prior to World War I in a working class district of Brooklyn immediately across the East River from Midtown Manhattan (Greenpoint), recalls that dairy goods, poultry and eggs, and fruit and vegetables were normally bought directly from farmers coming in from nearby Queens, which was also located within New York City. Much of this produce was sold from the farmer's wagon, not in shops. Throughout Western Europe, as we know from numerous World War II memoirs, locally produced meat, poultry, eggs, dairy products, fruits and vegetables, wine and beer, though not grain and bread, were the norm until after 1945.

12. Ford did not design his Models T and A to supersede what a horse could do. It was not a demand for improved transportation to which he responded; whoever makes that claim authors one more false "progress narrative." Urban dwellers were at the time sufficiently clustered that walking to work or using mass transit would do; but farmers were locked in isolation by distances, muddy or snowy conditions, and poor roads. Ford seems to have built the Model T, for example, in order to create a brand new utility, namely, to end the traditional isolation of the farmer (Jardim 1970: 118ff.).

13. The reader will have noted that this discussion refers almost exclusively to the producer/user relations in industry, and not to the final consumer/retail level. In this it fits with my interpretation of utility or use-value as representing indifferently a band of services and not a unitary phenome-

non. On the other hand, this interpretation is also consistent with our discussion of Marx's theory of worker demand discussed earlier.

14. See chapter 7.

15. On all questions regarding "property," I've found Schlatter [1951] 1973 both very helpful and very stimulating.

16. In a recent essay, I offered the following, admittedly very crude calculation, which complements this very point, namely, the degree to which investment in a modern economy is a social not a private phenomenon: "In 1997, US Net Private Investment less Inventory Adjustment was $818.3 billion. But, so-called 'corporate welfare,' in which government directly underwrote private investment, came to $75 billion (1996; the conservative Cato Institute), or $167 Billion (the liberal Nader group), or $150 billion (*THE BOSTON GLOBE;* July 7–9, 1996). If we add their average, about $130 billion, to total public sector outlays for education (564.2 billion), federal outlays just for Research, Natural Resources Development and Training and Employment ($32.2 billion), and state and local outlays just for Highways, Natural Resources, and Waste Disposal ($55.6) billion) it would appear that for every dollar advanced in private investment ($818.3 – $130 =) 688.3 billion, government advanced about ($130 + 564.2 + 32.2 + 55.6 =) $782, that is, about a dollar and change. (See *STATISTICAL ABSTRACT OF THE US.* 1998, tables 715, 251, 543, and 500 respectively.)" (McDermott 2001: 114, n. 8).

Even these unsatisfactory figures (and this short list of functional outlays) demonstrate that private investment outlays are roughly equaled by public sector outlays, which necessarily complement them. One cannot argue that all of these public sector outlays redound to the exclusive or preponderant benefit of private firms, nor that they are intended to, nor that private interests determine their levels and trajectories. Such claims are woefully beside the point in any case. Without these public sector investments, private investments wouldn't yield the productivity, the scale, the technological level, and hence the "earnings" of a modern economy. If, for example, government doesn't constantly modify the productive characteristics of the labor force, one doesn't even have a modern economy; one has an "underdeveloped economy." Modern "capitalist" investment has an ineradicable bilateral character. In short, as a self-contained economic entity the concept of a purely "private sector" entitled by "hard economic logic" to its own self-generated "earnings" points only to an analytical fragment. Whatever their purely ideological functions, concepts of an autonomous "private sector" or of "private enterprise" are only fragments of an integral economic system.

It is not at all beside the point to observe here that the public has an obvious "property"-based right to an appropriate share in the strategic direction of corporate activity. The public provision of investment give that public extremely powerful levers with which to win acceptance of its property rights should it care to exert them.

17. Again one must be struck by the dramatic way in which the analytic

introduction of real time plays havoc with our familiar and "natural" economic categories. Actually, as we know from modern physics, there is no reason to believe that reality corresponds to our Euclidean three-dimensional or other "natural" frameworks.

18. Thus, the microwave, for example, also plays the same role of constant capital for the complementary producer/sellers: the semiprepared food manufacturers, the microwavable dishes makers, and even the popcorn producers. As one can see, analysis of contemporary property relationships fits no older template.

19. "A commodity is therefore a mysterious thing, simply because in it the social character of men's labor appears to them as an objective character stamped upon the product of that labor; because the relation of the producers to the sum total of their own labor is presented to them as a social relation, existing not between themselves, but between the products of their labor. . . . There it is a definite social relation between men that assumes, in their eyes, the fantastic form of a relation between things. In order, therefore, to find an analogy, we must have recourse to the mist-enveloped regions of the religious world. In that world the productions of the human brain appear as so many independent beings endowed with life, and entering into relation both with one another and with the human race. So it is in the world of commodities with the products of men's hands. This I call the Fetishism that attaches itself to the products of labor, so soon as they are produced as commodities, and that is therefore inseparable from the production of commodities. . . . The Fetishism of commodities has its origin . . . in the peculiar social character of the labor which produces them" (Marx [1867] 1967: 77).

20. One unfortunate—indeed, anticivic—effect of so many popular and academic views of advertising is that we come to accept that people are in general rather gullible, greedy, and not at all admirable. Such is the cultural and intellectual influence of business that modern political Elites routinely assume something like this and as a result can find even more reasons to excuse their opportunism, their failure to take the "longer view," and their reluctance to take up "unpopular" or "controversial" causes.

Chapter 5

1. As before, I here assume an "economic" paradigm in social analysis. It is best to clarify just what is entailed in that assumption. Most important of all, I am not assuming a two-level model in which economic factors provide the "base" and other things merely the "superstructure." In fact, as already indicated in the discussion on abstraction (chapter 2), such a distinction is methodologically illicit and the source of endless muddle. Instead, I am merely projecting one step further Gramsci's observations about "Americanism." In modern U.S. society, and in those societies that copy it, economic

organizations, economic developments, and one's role in the economy are of unique importance—because the society just is that way. One of the meanings of a "modern" society is that in it a special deference is given to the economy and its institutions. They are permitted more leeway than others for even their most antisocial behavior. They are given first call on resources, and less control on how they will be deployed, while institutions such as "family," "education," "science," "government," the "media," and "culture" accept as a major part of their own roles deference and service to the "economy." Only the military and, mainly for ceremonial purposes, the churches are more or less free of this obligation to defer. In fact, as opposed to sentiment, the churches spend much of their time trying to cope with hostile social, economic, cultural, and moral influences coming from the economy.

This one-sided deference is not an instance of an absolute law of social organization. Granted, how one makes one's living must influence every society but ours is an extreme case—and growing ever more extreme in my view—of a virtually idolatrous deference to the economy, that is, to the needs, desires, power, and contributions of a world made up of very large, diversified, often international corporations. To assume, as I do in the text, that the economic has far greater causal influence on society and culture than they have on it is merely to reflect one of the characterizing features of our historical time and place.

2. The poorness of the "labor force" as a measure of those who might successfully hold a job is illustrated by the U.S. "manpower" experience during World War II. It turned out that for every five workers considered to be in the labor force just before the war there was a sixth whom the count skipped over. In 1939, just prior to the war-induced expansion of the U.S. economy, the labor force was measured at 55.6 million, breaking down into 45.7 million employed, 9.5 million unemployed (17.2 percent), and .4 million serving in the armed forces. However, at the peak of the wartime expansion 66 million persons were counted in the labor force (54 million employed, .7 million unemployed (1.06 percent), and 11.4 million in the armed forces). Obviously, that difference of (66.0 − 55.6, or) 10.4 million persons, isn't to be accounted for by population growth. Most of those 10.4 million potential workers were around in 1939 but weren't being counted for no better reason than that the economy wasn't interested in them and/or wasn't acting in a way that attracted them to seek work. Basically, for every worker taken into the armed forces another person, previously statistically invisible, stepped forward to replace him or her. Thus, the 1939 statistics measured only about 84 percent of the labor force that was then available for work. But even that 84 percent is suspect. At the peak of the wartime expansion only about 40 percent of adult women had entered the labor force; the current percentage is about half again as high. Thus, even the 1944 figure of 66 million is 5 to 6 million shy of the number of persons who either came forward to work in the paid economy or—with a weakening of sexist practices in the employment market and social

structure—arguably would have come forward offering to work for wages. See *Historical Statistics of the United States* 1972: series D1–25.

3. Statistics on worker productivity abound, but those on Manager productivity can be hard to come by. Part of the difficulty comes from the fact that many managerial posts are filled based on criteria other than productivity. It may be that a particular job occupies a bottleneck in the production process and thus must be kept out of the union's hands. Firms are also loathe to fire managers because it has adverse effects on the esprit de corps of the managerial echelon itself. Thus, failed or underperforming managers may not be fired but can be slipped sideways into a sinecure where they can be maintained until early retirement. Moreover, insofar as upper-level managers measure their success in terms of the number of their subordinates, the managerial echelon is in perennial danger of overstaffing. Some productive work requires workers with degrees, but there is a tendency in U.S. industry, now changing, to include all degreed workers along with their college fellows in the managerial echelon. Estimates of managerial productivity would have to be analytically teased out of these complexities. To add an even further complexity, there also appear to be great differences in the size of the managerial echelon in different industries and different advanced countries.

Of course, none of this precludes research into managerial productivity. The paucity of managerial productivity studies is, if not a deliberate oversight, an eminently convenient one on the part of business researchers, who do, one must note, hold worker performance to a harsh standard of pure and unadulterated efficiency. For a review of these issues, see Gordon 1996; and Reich 1998.

4. The spirit, if not the text, of this industrial division is found in Frederick Winslow Taylor's *The Principles of Scientific Management* ([1911] 1967) in his account of his dealings with the workman Schmidt (43ff.). By citing Taylor I don't wish to imply that modern management was invented, like the light bulb, by a single creator. It is just that Taylor appears to have been the most important proselytizer for the wider change in manager-worker relations that was sweeping U.S. industry in the period just before and following 1900. Taylorism, as it's come to be called, was clearly only one expression of the contemporary "trustification" movement wherein the quantum jump in size and complexity of these new protocorporate firms required a radical rethinking of management strategies and techniques.

In this discussion, for heuristic reasons, I've momentarily oversimplified the "industrial" division of labor by collapsing two ultimately different kinds of managers into one, that is, by ignoring the Sloan's and Chandler's distinctions between managers with strategic/entrepreneurial functions and those, mostly middle-echelon types, who carry out the relatively rote work of administration. This distinction is of sufficient importance and yet of enough complexity that I've left it to a later place in the chapter.

For a more nuanced analysis of the three-way division of labor typical of modern corporate and related institutions, see the analysis of "corporate form" in McDermott 1991: 21ff. It includes both extensive quotation from Taylor's peremptory, even derisive relationship with the stereotyped "dumb Dutchman," Schmidt, and consideration of the wider technological, product, productive, and marketing developments that together shaped division of labor within the twentieth-century corporation. There, as here, I acknowledge the depth and extent of my borrowing and learning from the work of Alfred Chandler, especially Chandler 1962.

5. I will often collapse the categories Manager and Technological Specialist into the single term *Manager*. This reflects the U.S. industrial practice of including both in a "managerial echelon," distinguished from the "production work force" or, if a union is present, the "collective bargaining unit," by systematically different terms and conditions of employment (rate and kind of pay and benefits, tenure of employment, access to promotion, and so on). This point will be elaborated later in the chapter. In this locution some managerial echelon people directly manage workers (line managers) while others (staff) contribute to the systems that keep the work going (accounting, quality control, design, plant layout, routing, etc.) or perform scientific/technological tasks calculated to increase output while lowering the wage costs of the workers themselves. My own preference is for the French term *cadre*, which includes the state and private sectors, both staff and line. On this subject, the work of Dumenil and Levy (1996: pt. 5) is especially useful.

6. For Marxist theory, we must address two extremely important issues. On the one hand, Marx's reduction of different complex labor-powers to uniformly simple ones rested on his assumption that markets for goods, services, and labor-power were or were becoming more and more homogeneous. But in the economic universe that began to take shape in the 1880s we can see the evolution and spread of diverse, often noncomparable markets for different sorts of labor-power no less than for other commodities. For example, it takes about as much time, expense, and effort to produce a master's degree in English as one in electrical engineering, although for many years the latter has carried far more earning power than the former. On the other hand, a nursing degree is likely to bring a much lesser return than one in marketing, although most people would agree that nurses, of which there has been a shortage, are at least as useful as marketers, who always seem to be quite plentiful. More generally, it is not at all clear that credentialing (with degrees, certificates, etc.), which tends to increase the wages and benefits of the credentialed employee, has any economically significant link to increased productivity on the part of the employee. Consequently, and absent evidence to the contrary, the conditions necessary to technically reduce different employments to a uniform productive/monetary standard are not present in the various modern labor-power markets. This is itself a reflection of the evolution of modern cap-

italism toward creating and modifying distinct markets to suit its own interests rather than being subject to the putative discipline of a claimed universal
market.

At the level of his historical materialism, Marx also understood that the
reduction of complex labor-powers to simple ones was an actual historical
process characterizing the capitalism of his time. Uniform, simple labor-power
formed his standard for labor-power because he believed that the processes of
proletarianization were the most significant development of his era. The
reduction of complex to simple labor-powers was thus not solely a technical
matter but a crucial historical development bringing in its train a mortal
threat to capitalism.

But we are now in an era with seemingly disparate labor markets for different kinds of labor-power and with evident tendencies that labor-power productive skills and capabilities are ramifying, not simplifying. Further, it
appears to be the case that resources devoted to the reproduction of social
labor-power are growing or at last stable, not following the downward path
called for by the General Law of Capitalist Accumulation. Whether this is the
case worldwide is debatable, but it is beyond debate in the developed
economies. Thus, if we wish to analyze contemporary capitalism the analytical reduction of complex to simple labor-powers, even if it were possible to
carry out, would amount only to a technical exercise lacking in
historical/material warrant for its importance.

In chapters 7 and 8, I will argue that Marx's labor theory of value, the foundation of the reduction being discussed, is, as currently argued, purely and
simply untenable. But, independent of those arguments, neither in the analytical nor in the historical/material dimensions is the Marxist reduction of
complex to simple labor-powers any longer sustainable. Even if it were, it
would be of only marginal significance to the trajectory of capitalist change.

7. An oft-cited and widely esteemed analysis of deskilling is in Braverman
1974: 389–401.

8. See, for example, the excellent Stone 1973. For Marx, see Marx [1867]
1967: 164ff. As to the persistence of the master-servant template, in the
United States it was only in the 1960s that hospital and nursing home workers came to be recognized in law and practice as employees bound only by the
terms of their contracts and not servants owing an extracontractual obligation
to—as they used to be called—"their patients."

9. Analysis of courses/channels is not at odds with the concept, nor,
indeed, the existence, of social mobility. It does, however, reflect the over-
whelmingly evident but universally overlooked fact that most people don't
change their class/status group in a lifetime, that is, that social immobility is
a more prominent feature in a modern society than social mobility. Obviously, the study of different courses must at some point address social mobility issues but not here and not now.

10. I have come only with difficulty to understand that a course is not a kind of class, notwithstanding the economic paradigm I'm employing. The differences are in fact quite considerable, but let me characterize only four at present.

First, class is a function of markets, and courses correspond to a capitalism that has evolved beyond them. In mainstream sociology, *class* is defined in terms of Max Weber's "market situation." In the last analysis, too, Marx's *class* is defined in terms of "the market," specifically the market for labor-power where one class exclusively purchases its use (the propertied) and another exclusively sells it (the propertyless). "The Market" and its analytical consequences have little place in a modern corporate economy.

In the second place, in a class paradigm one as it were deduces the characteristics of the different classes and their occupants from that class equals market matrix. This seems to be an effective procedure in a class paradigm featuring only two or possibly three classes. From the nature of the, say, two- or three-class paradigm the social and cultural differences between the classes will be exceptionally severe and readily discernible not only to observers but within the classes themselves. When the propertyless suffer such dire deprivation, as they do in the paradigm presented in *The Communist Manifesto,* it is relatively easy to link the strictly economic term *class* to associated characteristics in the social, political, and cultural realms. But in more complex societies featuring courses the association is not all that clear, either empirically or paradigmatically. For example, some very rich persons today are also very politically influential (corporate leaders), but some are not (pop stars). Similarly, some of the very poor are radically deprived in cultural terms, but, as in Thompson's *The Making of the English Working Class,* some are not.

My sense is that we should treat a course as constituting an actual subsociety with a common culture and common values. That is, in class analysis one tries to infer that because different members of the same class have the same abstract *kinds* of experiences they will predictably react in similar ways. Alas, that's always been a more obvious inference for the class analysts than for the class participants. But in the manner in which we have analytically constructed the concept of a course we have tried to show, especially for the higher courses, that people within the courses share (or overlap) experiences, not just kinds of experience. That is, members of the Elite course form a definite subsociety, with shared prep school, university, and even graduate school experiences and shared or overlapping roles in big institutions; Thus, from the nature of the case they have been and will be frequently brought into face-to-face contact with one another, will intermarry, will share mentors, and so forth. In short, their social and other traits will be manifestly tied to their economic ones. A similar account, albeit watered down, fits the Manager course and so forth. I estimate that it can be shown, on this basis, why and how it is that the higher courses are so much more politically and culturally potent than the lower. If possible, I intend in a future book to go beyond the somewhat narrow economic concept of courses and develop more fully an analysis of their political, cultural, and social actions.

Finally, in at least one respect courses have a greater affinity to premodern societal divisions such as estates, ranks, orders, and even castes. Unlike classes, which the dominant intellectual traditions accept are mainly constructed through contractual and market relations with only a very limited role for a political authority such as the state, the courses are each significantly constructed and actively maintained through government action. This has taken such diverse forms as the funding of education, labor union regulatory systems, professional certification, research subsidies for science and technology, and the administrative relationship. As I have pointed out elsewhere (McDermott 1991, 1991–92) and emphasized here, we increasingly live within a society whose outlines are socially fabricated so that, for example, life course differences must be considered constitutive of it, not just one possible—and thus erasable or otherwise alterable—outcome.

11. The social (and economic) capacity to buy a preschool experience for one's child has taken on an enhanced importance as the managerial ranks have become more open to non-Elite persons and more demanding from the technical point of view. It tends to give the favored child better access to the more prestigious public or, usually, private primary schools, which in turn increases his or her chances of access to one of the more prestigious public or (usually) private secondary institutions and the elite-connected mentors found there.

One is not arguing that it is solely the quantity of money that provides course privileges for a young child. The social standing and even the (high) culture of the family can skew the odds that the boy or girl can get into a "better" preschool and can aid considerably in the transition to "better" primary, secondary, and undergraduate institutions and thus prechannel the candidate into the "right" institutions and the "right" type of graduate education. The level of (high) culture enjoyed by the boy's or girl's family is important. All school tests are skewed to certain cultural norms, and the boy or girl who is already acculturated to those norms will do better on them as a rule than their counterparts not so well capitalized. To a very great extent, more than I think is popularly acknowledged, an intimate familiarity and knowing comfort within a certain kind of liberal, humanist, and secular culture, somewhat cosmopolitan in character, is "the coin" for entry into and continued equal participation in the upper-middle and higher classes in the United States today and, probably more so, those of the other capitalist powers. It is, however, an important reality, but even more an important myth, that this culture can be embraced by persons and families of modest means, especially when aided and abetted by those public elementary and secondary schools that have traditionally acted as conduits for the elite colleges and universities.

12. It is appropriate to digress here to again emphasize the centrality of the

manager-worker division. For reasons that I do not understand, the deeply modal division does not occupy the absolutely fundamental place it ought to occupy in all employment discussions. One simply does not understand industrial organization, industrial practice, industrial law, or even the role of unions if one overlooks the distinction. I can say that with equal assurance as a labor studies scholar, an industrial historian, an economist, and even a former shop steward for my union. Yet, to take a particularly egregious example of the neglect of the distinction, one might look even cursorily at typical U.S. productivity statistics in manufacturing that merge total employment hours, that is, those of both the managers and the workers. But managers normally have much greater job tenure than workers; in actual industrial practice managing is a fixed not a variable cost of doing business. Hence, if there are, say, two managers and eight production workers and times go bad, one of the eight workers is much more likely to lose his or her job than one of the two managers. But then productivity should fall by about one-eighth. When times change and that worker is hired back, productivity should then rise by about one-seventh. There is a certain verisimilitude in our simple example because, as far back as I can remember, the onset of bad economic times has been marked by a sharp decline in labor productivity and the return to good times by dramatic rises in the same. Considerable ink is normally used to analyze these two phase shifts, much of it wasted because of the failure to understand that in modern industry two quite different classes of employees, workers and managers, have a differential impact on output. Workers produce; the role of management is not normally to add their bit to that production but to act as a multiplier of it. It is precisely this difference in modal productive roles that conventional discussions of labor productivity too often obfuscate.

13. The modal modern manager-employer relationship, including much of its historical development, is analyzed at length in McDermott 1991–92.

14. This was not always the case, nor perhaps was it usually the case before, say, the 1890s and the consequent move to professionalize the management function. But from the more or less simultaneous birth of the modern university, modern science-linked technology, and the modern corporation, "promotion from the ranks" has been much diminished. Business firms maintain different entry points for managers and workers. Thus, low-level managerial posts that perhaps in an earlier time could be taken by workers now fall to the lot of persons coming in from management or technical degree programs at the colleges and community colleges.

Somewhat countering this change, many companies encourage their employees to obtain further schooling as a condition for promotion, sometimes even promising promotion and pay raises ahead of time for those who will complete a given course of study. Some companies even partially subsidize further education for their employees and may even allow them time off from the job to take their classes. In my own twenty-odd years of experience teaching evening college students, I found that this sort of further schooling is typically granted to junior managers or perhaps to workers whose work is especially technology oriented. Regardless, whether one must enter management through a different portal or detour to it through a continuing education program, this further confirms that there has been a clarification and ramification of the different courses/channels in occupational life.

15. I knew Harry Braverman; he was both my editor and friend. There is much in his 1974 book that is excellent, but he does leave one with the impression that a modern worker doesn't get much chance to exercise any sort of skills. My own experience and observation argue that a machine operative in a contemporary setting has a job requiring high stamina, reasonable intelligence, a "knack" for mechanical things, a substantial measure of common sense, and good personal reliability. Basically, the idea is that the worker's personal, productive characteristics must far exceed what is minimally needed to do the job so that (a) the job itself will be done reliably, and (b) the worker will have the wit, skill, and initiative to correct and adjust the flow of material to maintain the machine-set rhythm of the production process. If the productive characteristics of the individual workers were only marginal, their lapses would show up in marred product, disruptions of the pace of the work, lower output, more accidents, even greater lateness and absenteeism, and so forth. The human tragedy of this mode of work is that it is absolutely necessary that the worker's productive qualities be far superior to the actual work he or she is to carry out. Chaplin's famous *Modern Times* misses the point of mass machine production as Charlie plays a bit of a bumbler in the film. A wonderful film, it is one of those artistic products that Plato so roundly criticized in that its artistic invention is in the service of falsification, here of the industrial experience of the ordinary, "unskilled" worker.

It is to the point here to observe that one of the most effective of all techniques workers can use in conflicts with management is "to work to rule," that is, for each worker to carry out only those tasks specifically required by the job description prescribed by his or her managers. When the "hands" do only what the "brains" tell them to do, very little can be accomplished!

16. McDermott 1991–92 provides an analysis of the complex employment relationships of what we have called here Regulars, that is, between the employee, employer, union, and government. Unfortunately, in that discussion I had yet to understand the important differences between classes and courses and the consequent lessening relevance of market-based classes to a modern economy. The characteristics of modern employment need to be analyzed in the five-termed relationship mentioned in the text and cannot be adequately rendered in the binary relationships employer-employee and propertied-propertyless. At issue here is not the importance of social stratification and frontiers of conflict between different social strata. To cope with these issues in a modern economy, both practically and analytically, one has to go beyond the binary or ternary logic of elementary class analysis.

17. The wartime evolution and crystallization of U.S. union-management relations from the stormy events of 1938–39 to the relatively peaceful postwar pattern is narrated in the excellent Lichtenstein 1982.

18. Managers who don't have "line" responsibilities are usually echeloned into an organizational structure in parallel with "line" managers and with corresponding pay and benefit scales.

The "fixed" costs associated with managing are very high. In U.S. manufacturing in the 1990s, for example, roughly one-third of all employees were located within the managerial echelon and received about half of the payroll.

19. Something like the center-periphery distinction has been developed by Gordon et al. (1982) in terms of primary and secondary labor markets. An excellent analysis in its own right, the distinction is based mainly on the sociological character of the workers, primarily pointing to the overrepresentation of women and people of color in the poorer paying, poorer working conditions found in the secondary labor market. (At present, young, school-age workers would have to be added to the picture.) By and large this way of drawing the distinction was intellectually (and morally) animated by the sociology of discrimination and inequality rather than the wider study of the relations of production that we have been subsuming under the concept of commodity form. What I conclude lies at the bottom of this bifurcation of the sociology of discrimination in work from the wider study of productive relations per se is the tendency, notable among left-wing analysts, to limit the meaning of relations of production strictly to the single dimension of the propertied and the propertyless, that is, of owners and workers, viewing its differentiated empirical consequences as of very much lesser importance than that abstract difference itself; I fear we are again dealing with echoes of the old "proletariat." Yet such a one-dimensional, "structural" analysis is far too limited and sterile a schematic even to describe much less to analyze a modern economy whose main industrial, economic, and employment line of conflict is between manager and worker, not owner and worker. In a real sense, the evolution of the modern management echelon has served not only to quicken the profits of owners but to keep them well away from the firing line of what one might call the modern industrial class struggle. But to show this one must analyze the ensemble of relations of production, not just the propertied-propertyless relation per se. The steady expansion of the Marginal course to include large numbers of white, male, or other (formerly) privileged sociological categories of workers also lends support to this position.

20. At present almost one in four farm managers and operators in the United States, for example, do not live on those farms and presumably commute to work (*Statistical Abstract* 1999: table 675). These would predominate in the larger farms that produce the largest share of farm products and are organized under modern labor-management relationships. Exclusive of imports , roughly 20 percent of the fresh fish sold in the United States is produced in factorylike ponds or enclosures, not from the open sea, by laborers

working under modern management systems and not by traditional fisher-men. On the other hand, much of the fish caught at sea is caught by fleets of smaller boats working in tandem with "mother" ships that take, clean, and either freeze or can the product at sea. Again we meet the industrial division of labor already familiar to us in factory, farm, and office (table 1160).

Chapter 6

1. In the past decade, for example, an investment in a Ph.D. in English would arguably have led to a poorer return than an MBA in Finance. It is not prima facie clear in the 2003 economy whether an investment in a college degree from a low-prestige institution will perform better than an apprentice-ship in a skilled trade such as plumbing.

2. Along with game theory, which was developed largely in association with the defense industry, Becker's and similar work by others was among the main influences on the extension of cost-benefit analysis to hospital care, environmental protection, safety and health legislation, and other social ser-vices, even to the extent that Becker might be called the godfather of the edu-cational voucher movement and the other attempts to introduce price-com-petitive criteria into the world of public education. These last are truly ironic because, as indicated, Becker's original analysis of education was done largely in nonmonetary terms.

3. As we know in practice, wage setting tends toward anarchy, the wage level for a particular job depending variously on custom, geography, the pres-ence or absence of a union, or even the social prestige of the occupation in question.

An official of my union once explained to me that the ebb and flow of ado-lescent hormones determined the wages for State University of New York (SUNY) professors in the 1970s, as follows. In the city of New York, most unionized teachers were averse to strikes but not so those who labored in the junior high schools. These teachers much preferred wintry picket lines and aggressive policemen to restless adolescents; hardened, apparently by these cruel alternatives, their militancy did succeed in winning raises. Naturally, that meant that there had to be a corresponding adjustment for each level of educational employee in the city—elementary school, high school, and city university. But when the latter got raises we SUNY workers had to have them, too, lest the prestige and competitive posture of the state university suffer.

The union official's story is amusing, but it also has, as far as I can discover, a significant measure of truth. Keynes's old observation that wages tend to be unusually inelastic on the down side merely hints at one dimension of the peculiarities of wage determination ([1936] 1964: 267ff.).

4. Alfred Marshall is characteristically frank and open about the unrealis-tic nature of this point ([1890] 1930: 95–96).

5. Just such a thesis is argued in Bowles and Gintis 1976 (see especially chapters 4, 5, and 6).

6. Appeals to snobbery and exclusiveness, however, also have a significant impact on wealthier and, presumably, better-educated consumers. See Stiglitz 1987.

7. This submersion of public services within the network of commodity practices makes privatization more readily possible. Medicare and Social Security, for example, pioneered and developed the "market" for mass medical and retirement plans, devised different commoditylike "packages," gained costing information, developed administrative structures that are now advanced on the learning curve, and so on, without which such areas would still be terra incognita to the private sector. Moreover, as in education, the presence of a vast funding system in which "customers" are already constrained to purchase has proven immensely attractive to the private sector as an unexploited line of business with a guaranteed customer base.

The most dramatic model for government creation of a commodity market was probably the fast-food business. It was the military that first perfected the technologies of purchasing, preparing, standardizing (portioning), costing, distributing, and serving a great variety of all kinds of foods on a truly mass basis. It also helped to prepare the market by familiarizing millions with a mass-produced food product. Less well known, site manufacture of housing, as opposed to craft fabrication of individual houses, was also pioneered by the government (Baxandall and Ewen 2000: 37ff.). These observations also serve to confirm the value of the conception of commodity form, that is, as a constellation of convergent social practices.

8. This is not always without lag, as we know from the import, via the Immigration and Naturalization Service, of large numbers of both well- and undereducated workers on behalf of U.S. industries and employers.

9. "While the United States spends less on primary and secondary schools than most advanced countries, it devotes 40 percent of its education spending to colleges and universities" (Sassoon 1996: 764). On the other hand, both the "brain drain" the United States now imposes on other countries' economies and its import of low-wage agricultural, manufacturing, and domestic service workers, often illegal but winked at by the authorities, testify that the system is only "more or less coherent."

10. This sort of cooperation is itself borrowed from the customary arrangement between the military and its suppliers. Since World War II, "tech" representatives from the producers of weapons systems often serve on the ship or air base while combat operations are being carried out. In fact, it was as a tech representative for Lockheed and other aircraft firms that a civilian Charles Lindberg flew combat missions during the fighting in the South Pacific in that war.

11. It has been suggested to me, in a private correspondence, that the university system may be splitting into several levels so that the higher courses

are coming to be associated with only the high-prestige institutions and so forth. The anecdotal evidence is not at all clear, but the hypothesis that the Manager course is being split in two would represent a sea change in corporate employment practices and thus, derivatively, in the social structure.

12. If a peevish note creeps into my presentation here it comes of the fact that from early college through graduate school my problem was not to defer income on behalf of a richer tomorrow but of simultaneously earning enough income to (help) pay living costs and (entirely) pay school costs. I remain deeply grateful to New York City's taxpayers, as without the then free city college tuition I could not have afforded to finish college when I did and without the subway I could not have squeezed in the necessary studying; to this day, when I ride the subway, I feel a certain pressure to be reading Hegel or at least Dostoyevsky. Later, in my roughly two decades of teaching mostly older, returning students, I saw how difficult it was for them to afford (the relatively low) state university tuition and how much potential study time was consumed in driving to and from home, job, and school. The concept of a human capital is much too sanitized to grasp these realities for the working student, who is, after all, not that rare a species. More generally, it neglects the fact that a student works to prepare for work, an undertaking more arduous and stressful than a simple "investment."

13. In the latter decades of the nineteenth century and the first few of the twentieth, the United States passed from its position as a relatively minor player among the world's industrial powers to the preeminent place it still enjoys. What is most remarkable about this great shift was that at its beginning the United States lacked what was then a state of the art social labor-power. That is, both the then declining but still powerful British economy and the German one threatening its supremacy possessed vast reservoirs of highly skilled workers, especially in the metal trades. By way of contrast, the U.S. takeoff into industrialization seemed fatally limited not only by the lack of such reservoirs but by the fact that its potential industrial population was going to be drawn, as was even then evident, from an immigrant population, largely agrarian and increasingly non–English speaking.

Clearly, this departure from what was then state of the art industry in high-flying Germany and Great Britain required a simply enormous effort to transform a crude aggregate of foreign-born, mostly agrarian immigrants into a social labor-power made up, analytically, of highly adaptable individual labor-powers able to fit themselves into different complementary roles. Or, as we put it earlier, to create a social labor-power with a wide menu of quasi-productive services. The size and rapid growth of mass education in the United States reflects this vast social-industrial development in both its terms: adaptable workers and polyvalent, managerial-technical cadres. See Bowles and Gintis 1976; and McDermott 1992: 300–308.

As already suggested, it is irrelevant whether the vast expansion of the educational system occurred solely or even largely due to "economic" motives—on anyone's part.

14. Managerial strategies that emphasize "quality circles" and other devices intended to quicken the cooperative exchange of information between managers and workers and their joint learning curve coexist in industry with fully programmed work modes, as in fast food, the sewing trades, the assembly of electronic and electrical goods, chicken and beef processing plants, data entry, and so forth.

While it may be true that in the "ideal" learning situation the learner learns enough to do away with the need for a mentor, in the real world learning is too often a matter of inducing in the student an exaggerated sense of his or her own incapacity. We now understand how destructive this has been for female learners, but it is no less widespread and destructive for those in the lower courses generally, as I can testify from direct experience as both learner and mentor.

Chapter 7

1. I am often told by neoclassically oriented colleagues that they eschew all value theory as fatally tainted by "metaphysics" or prescriptive prejudices on the part of the would-be value theorist. As we'll see, there's something to that. But on the other hand there is no economics and no economic analysis whatsoever unless one allows or admits that certain classes of human exchange actions are in principle quantitatively comparable. But as soon as one makes this point explicit, rather than implicit, one has adopted the fundamental proposition of value theory.

2. Continuing the analogy to philosophical epistemology, price "nominalists" would take the position that the price ratios between things can only be explored by means of empirical studies. No analysis of concept-prices, however acute, however "deep," can reveal anything further about real world prices. Later in the book I will argue for price nominalism or, equivalently, a theory of price relativity.

3. The Marxist model is of an economy in which the meager quantity of commodities going to the workers is governed by the Absolute General Law of Capitalist Accumulation, hence that the workers' consumption of commodities has no significantly free dimension, their quantity being so limited that qualitative choice among consumption items is vitiated. Marx, of course, wanted to show that the apparent freedom of a free market economy is illusory and that both capitalists and workers act according to imperatives disguised as choices. In that precise sense, Marxist microeconomic behaviors are always governed by imperatives.

This finding itself rests on Marx's equilibrium model of an economy, where there are three Departments producing, respectively, (I) producer goods, (II) workers' consumption goods, and (III) capitalist consumption goods. The controlling features of the model are the rates of surplus value and the organic composition of capital in Departments I and II only, with Department III (capitalist consumption or "luxury" goods) playing no role. Simplifying somewhat, the rate of surplus value, that is, the relative share of net product going to the capitalists and the workers, is governed by the General Law, while the absolute quantity of net product is controlled by the organic composition of capital, which is more or less equivalent to the capital intensity of the production process, itself a function of the technological state of the art. In brief then, the dynamic of such an economy one-sidedly rests in the necessary consumption both of the workers and of the productive process and the fact that luxury goods, goods that could possibly be consumed in the free choice mode, are only peripheral to the economic dynamic. See von Bortkiewicz [1907] 1984: 217. For a closely related analysis, see Sraffa 1960: 7, 8.

At the other end of the spectrum is the Jevons/Walras microeconomics, which makes the explicit assumption that final consumption occurs in the mode of free choice and that all nonfinal or productive consumption is purely derivative of that. Thus, my formulation that with their narratives included the two microeconomics, otherwise identical, are mirror images of one another.

4. Penrose ([1950] 1980), among many others, has examined this phenomenon. I find this older book still topical because of the breadth of her knowledge about business practice. For a more recent and more comprehensive examination of business pricing policies, see Lee 1998.

5. On a busy intersection near me, there are two gas stations, directly across the street from one another, whose prices I've been noting for about a half dozen years. One consistently charges a higher price for each grade of gasoline, and both seem to have about the same number of customers.

Technically speaking, there is no "law" in that much heralded "law of supply and demand." One can as easily cite as many instances of its failure as of its fulfillment. The proposition represents a sometimes useful observation or guide to action, not really much more empirically reliable than "Boys will be boys!" or "March comes in like a lion but goes out like a lamb." Economists who are convinced they are really dealing with a law here should understand that they are dealing with a prescription and not at all with a description. Their confusion on this point seems to me to be inexcusable.

6. Even if only briefly, we must again comment on this particular mare's nest. The terms *rational* and *irrational* are a methodologist's nightmare, particularly in microeconomics, where one assumes "rational" behavior of a certain not to be exceeded type, that is, where the behavior is claimed to be "perfectly rational" or, equivalently, "maximizing." This common usage exhibits a deep logical-grammatical confusion and is always illicit, as can be shown upon even the briefest reflection. One can say that something is "red" or "not red," "rectangular " or "not rectangular" merely by directly examining the situation

and more or less ignoring wider, contextual questions. Or, in logical-grammatical terms, *red* and *rectangular* are simply (one-place) predicates. *Rational* and *irrational* are often employed with the same sort of logical grammar, as in "If the buyer behaved with perfect rationality." But *rational* is not a (one-place) predicate; it is a (two-place) relational term like, say, *heavy*. Both point not to a predicated quality of single objects standing alone but to the place of two objects when they are ordered by the appropriate comparative relation.

One can no more say of a weight that it is "perfectly heavy" than of an action that it is "perfectly rational." Even when one says of something that it is "the heaviest," the meaning is merely that that weight is heavier than each of the other weights included in an indicated comparison; there is simply no meaning to a claim that there exists or might exist a weight whose heaviness lies outside any and all comparing functions. And there can be no such thing as a weight that is perfectly heavy, that is, cannot be exceeded by any other conceivable weight under any circumstances. But just that sort of claim about *rational* or *maximizing* or some other logical-grammatical synonym lies at the heart of every statement of abstract equilibrium conditions, whether partial or general. College presidents who claim that "excellence" is their institutional standard (or the good medieval St. Anselm, who "proved the existence of God" with an analogously devious construction), like economists who employ *perfectly rational,* need to be reminded from time to time that a superlative is merely the upper boundary of some definite comparative.

7. Disguised tautologies lurk everywhere in economics. Both Marxist "prices of production" and neoclassical "marginal" *Prices* are explained as being the prices that would obtain if a market or the whole economy were in equilibrium. But *Price* and *equilibrium* are simply the two terms of the same tautology; *Prices* are necessarily Prices in equilibrium. Technically speaking, *Price* and *equilibrium* are not synonyms but interdefined terms.

8. See Schumpeter's characteristically succinct account of the historical evolution of utility theory leading up to (and beyond) the Jevons/Walras microeconomics. At various times that theory has been cast in terms of utility (meaning really useful), pleasure, happiness, hedonic tone, satisfaction, ophelimity (desirability), anticipation or expectation, preferences (both cardinal and ordinal), and latterly in indices of indifference, substitutability, or opportunities foresworn, taking forms as simple as points of indifference between choices or, indeed, even complex indifference surfaces. Schumpeter's account correctly sees that what I have called the value subsystem needs to be purged as far as possible of psychological excrescence in order to explicate it as a logic. Even his account, however, underplays the fact that the term *value,* however carefully purged of undesirable psychological features, is still a coded term for certain human behaviors or, when the analyst is being really careful, a term whose exact psychological meaning need not be specified save that it is the omnipresent, universal something that decisively conditions, or should condition, all human economic behavior (Schumpeter 1954: 1053ff.).

9. The more familiar " transformation problem" in Marx's *Capital* was initially identified by Boehm-Bawerk (1896) and then defended against by von Bortkiewicz ([1907] 1984). Both contributions are reprinted in Sweezy 1942, and there is an almost limitless number of books and articles defending Marx. The transformation problem is the problem of consistently transforming value equations in which the Departments I, II, and III may have differing rates of surplus value into price equations in which each of the three has the same rate of profit. In general, the transformation solutions proposed only work for relatively trivial cases and a general solution has not been forthcoming nor, in my view, from the terms that establish the problem, is it ever likely to be forthcoming.

10. Again some of my neoclassically oriented colleagues would like to claim that their science is value free, that is, until they employ their science to analyze "trade union monopoly" or "government regulation," at which point their professional moral abhorrence of "waste," "inefficiency," and offenses against "liberty" comes tumbling out.

11. This conception of commodities as dated labor-power is borrowed from Sraffa 1960 (chap. 6), but the similarities in the two conceptions are only skin deep. The linkage between the value theory to be developed here and the work of Amartya Sen is closer, both intellectually and, especially, morally.

12. In the text I have elided Schumpeter's own emphasis on the way "creative destruction" is tied to the business cycle, but the elision introduces no essential distortion into our present discussion.

13. The classic conception of "the Market" is that it is a way of achieving maximal unconstrained feedback from the "sovereign" consumer. Theory aside, modern concentrated and coordinated industries construct rather than obey their markets. The classic problem with statist central planning mechanisms is that they discriminate against final or consumer satisfaction. The old Soviet Union was a marvel for the consumer; it most wanted to please the military but had political and other barriers to effective feedback from other consumers. I do think human ingenuity can do better than reinventing either of these trolley cars.

I am not arguing for a "best system." On the other hand we have had roughly two centuries of experience with the relationship between democratic political structures and private property, thus some idea of its strengths and weaknesses. I think it not difficult to list the sort of things that make that relationship more sensitive to citizen feedback and learning and those that dampen such feedback and incremental learning. Thus, even without going beyond what are in point of fact premodern political arrangements, such as constitutionally structured democracy through elected representatives, it should not be technically imposing to greatly strengthen those arrangements. In a future book I would like to explore what might be required to make a quantum democratic leap beyond the rather tatty democracy and economic priority setting we now enjoy.

14. What we have succeeded in doing is in giving an economic, not legal-historical, definition of *property*. In this sense, the institution of property consists of social and legal structures and procedures that assign "value" to goods and services at least in part independent of their future value, that is, some useful index of their contribution to the expansion of the social labor-power. Equivalently, it represents the set of phenomena that impose on future price relations, price relations enacted in the past that may be contraindicated from a productive standpoint. By definition, then, economic property is literally counterproductive, representing a drag on, not a goad to, the development of the productive powers of the social labor-power.

The relationship between economic property, as defined here, and this or that actual system of private or quasi-socialized property is obviously a complex one, and judgments about it cannot rest on simple inference. It is in principle conceivable that a given system of (legal) property and its ascribed values in a given period of time would correspond to or approximate a Pareto optimum with respect to the social labor-power, but that would have to be argued to the skeptic and not, as at present, assumed by the faithful.

15. The shift in the logic of "property" is most interesting here. If we conceive of an economy as fundamentally just a simple aggregate of individuals, a Lockean property is the logical (and moral-political) bridge that assures that their individuality will take primacy of place in the actions of the economy. This is Popper's and Hayek's "freedom." But if we conceive that an economy is a social phenomenon, that is, a structured aggregate of individuals, a "system," then that logic of property constrains the individuals in the economy from freely altering their relationships. In the first, property reflects a logic of freedom for the individual. In the second, it is precisely coterminous with the constraints operating on individuals.

16. If we apply a hard-nosed realism to the matter, the current appeals to allow the "free market" or "free enterprise" maximum leeway in the name of "freedom of choice" in fact advance the fortunes of the larger companies at the expense of the smaller. The deregulation of the interstate trucking industry almost immediately changed an industry made up of small, at best regional firms into oligopoly. Airline deregulation also led to failure of the smaller, weaker carriers and merger of the survivors into megafirms. Relaxation of the rules governing television and radio bands has had the same effect, along with a decrease in "public service" programming, an increase in the percentage of air time devoted to advertisements, and the greater frequency of using shock effects, violence, and other antisocial phenomena to gain temporary ratings advantages. Even the selection and presentation of the news is now heavily dependent on whether it will draw as large an audience as some other form of "entertainment."

One must acknowledge that government "bureaucracies" are often smaller and more responsive than those of the bigger private firms; citizens can often change their political representatives via the ballot box or change their behavior through the courts, but CEOs and boards of directors are much more self-perpetuating and much better insulated from "outside pressures." "Statism" is a lesser evil than business gigantism and collusion, though hardly a superior way to make for a genuinely freer economy. Again I plan to take up these issues in a future book.

Chapter 8

1. If, for example, in an empirical investigation of a more or less self-contained economy one assumes that employment is at an equilibrium level but then observes steadily rising wages across the board, one would normally use the latter fact to look again at the equilibrium assumption. Here the inconsistency of the assumption with the finding aids in developing a more useful, accurate model. In general equilibrium theoretical work, the relationship between premise and implicate is reversed. One assumes (or wants to assume) equilibrium and adjusts terms, propositions, and results to maintain it.

2. The expression "the class struggle" seems too vivid to describe the competition and often outright conflict between the several courses for reward and privilege. Probably that comes not of its literal meaning but of its association with images of fiery *sans-culottes* and rough-hewn Bolsheviks storming this or that barricade. On the other hand, the several courses do represent a multidimensional structure of privilege and authority, and between them there is obviously system conflict along many of those dimensions.

The major active front of class-related conflict in a modern society is not between labor and capital but between Managers and the several worker courses. One can reduce that latter pairing with the former in that the managerial course or its near equivalent, the professional, managerial and (university educated) technical or upper middle class takes its authority and extra reward from its special closeness to the Elite. Politically speaking it is foolish, however, to make that reduction. In a modern economy the special power and wealth of the Elite are not socially manifest, as they were, for example, in the Age of the Moguls in the latter part of the nineteenth century when one could readily identify the monopolies, the figure, the power, and the ostentation of a Rockefeller, a Morgan, a Gould, or a Belmont. The corporation as an institutional form obscures the empirical identity of those who actually guide it and those who reap its richest rewards. The social conflation of the Elite and the Manager courses into the colloquial "manager" has much the same effect, namely, to insulate the Elite to an important degree from everyday industrial and related disputes. In concrete industrial and commercial life the direct front of contact and therefore of potential conflict is between Managers and the lower courses. This includes not only on-the-job disputes over wages, hours, and work conditions or differences over consumer issues but also the nature of people's access to social services, typically funneled through the administrative relationship, and of course conflict over social mobility issues. Practical conflicts over social mobility are not usually fought on the frontier between Elite and Manager. The parents who square off over mobility-related issues on the school committee and in similar precincts are more likely to represent the different, codified interests of Manager versus Regular or Marginal.

It is interesting that this obvious point about social and class conflict does not find its way into the social science literature in those terms. Truth to tell, social scientists generally belong to the Manager course. One could argue, not without reason, that those social scientists who tend to think of themselves as either politically liberal and/or scientifically detached, would be ideologically embarrassed to have to view themselves as relatively privileged and as part of the very group that in our society struggles hardest in an everyday way to preserve, even extend, the structures of social privilege.

3. The one-sided development of the Manager course also carries with it the imperative for Managers to impose an often draconian discipline on the worker courses, itself a costly procedure in terms of workplace injury, absenteeism, strikes and slowdowns, poor quality control, and so forth. On the question of whether it would be more profit productive for capital to pursue wider and more even development of the productive capacities of the social labor-power in its entirety, see Bowles, Gordon, and Weisskopf 1990, especially chapter 7.

4. Bowles, Gordon, and Weisskopf (ibid.) argue the case against "Taylorite" microefficiency.

5. As previously remarked, there is a paradox, social and legal in nature, in the existence of the courses as the deployable elements of modern capital. Courses are more akin to orders, castes, and other such premodern social formations than to classes per se. That is, the older orders, estates, and castes were not based, as are classes, on "free," individually entered contractual relations between persons, thus not directly administered by government. Not so the courses. Course boundaries and identities are in good part maintained and even administered by means of state action.

The courses unite a lifetime in one ensemble of relationships. I agree that there are obvious differences between a medieval estate, an Indian caste, and a modern course, most dramatically in that there was lesser movement in and out of those older social orders than we believe is true—probably correctly—of the modern courses. Nonetheless, it is striking that the tendency of the modern capitalist property system is to re-create at least some of the features of those premodern sociopolitical orders or, in equivalent terms, to introduce greater administrative and other kinds of constraint not only into this or that day's activities but into the shape of one's lifetime. Here we see that modern property, in its youth a plausibly liberating social and political influence, now acts primarily to constrain, not liberate, the texture and quality of everyday life.

6. It is very easy to overlook this jump in Marx's logic and, in fact it is typically overlooked. Examine closely, for example, Sweezy's summation of

Marx's view as I cited it in chapter 2. The jump occurs within the following excerpt: "Marx . . . selected the forms of the capital-labor relation that arise in the sphere of production as the most important for modern capitalist society. . . What is the nature of this capital-labor relation? In form it is an exchange relation? . . ." And so it is. The Marxist sphere of production receives its analytical determination from his sphere of exchange, not vice versa. Marx's narrative of capitalist production was both pioneering and masterful, but it is embedded in an analysis of exchange relations and Marx never seems to have resolved the paradox. To escape the paradox logically requires that the workers' "final" consumption must occur within the continuous circuit of capital, not as an interruption to it, that is, within the sphere of production and not in a different sphere, that of circulation, that is, exchange. In fairness to Marx, the paradox was not resolvable in the underdeveloped capitalism of his time.

7. This thesis is consistent with the line of argument of the so-called Cambridge capital debates. For a summary, see Dobb 1973: 247ff. My text takes the position that there is no "natural" rate of interest and that profit is, to use an older locution, a deduction from wages, that is, from payments to members of the various courses in exchange for their actual productive accomplishments. This, however, would also have to include payment deducted in the form of opportunities foresworn for the growth of the social labor-power, in other words, a conception of lost "opportunity cost" directly predicated on the social labor-power per se.

8. There is no question that the actions of these banks are calculated at least in part to preserve "historical values." Obviously, other factors enter into these actions as well in order to keep the economy "prosperous," employment or unemployment restrained, social conditions acceptable, or the nation's competitive position "advantageous." But that "in part" is all that is needed to support the conclusion that modern profit collapses into (economic) rent. Once modern economies gave up commodity money there remained no determinate meaning to the orthodox linkage between the "rate of saving" and the "investment rate." The practice of creating money and credit by fiat breaks the old hypothesized determinate tie between demand and supply of money and necessarily introduces the possibility of both qualitatively and quantitatively different growth paths for any economy, any commodity, and any human productive resource.

9. Ironically enough, modern cost-benefit analysis confirms this very point, if sometimes bizarrely. Findings as to cost and benefit vary enormously depending on what one assumes prior to the analysis itself. A workman who loses an arm in an accident at the age of sixty would be "entitled" to only the equivalent of five years' worth of modest pay—if the injury is viewed under the rubric of loss of income; on the identical standard, a surgeon would presumably win a higher award than a machinist, and both be awarded more than a laborer. If we think it important to encourage new technology, we would view the poisoning of a chemical company employee as of less moment

than that of a food worker and so forth. The point is that in such calculations the ultimate findings are hostage to one's initial assumptions. The resulting calculations have more the character of a dance routine than an investigative procedure.

10. In my view the Reagan-Thatcher years were the consequence not the cause of the defeat of the social democratic/progressive trio described in the text. Given the social ubiquity of modern commodity production it would be an anomaly if business firms and industry associations had not expanded their participation in the entire political process, not just in electioneering. To give an example, I worked as a lobbyist for a progressive organization in the state capital, Albany, New York, during much of the 1961 and 1962 legislative sessions. There were many bills presented there, some of obvious importance to business lobbyists, about which they had only marginal interest and often on social issues no worked out political positions. That clearly is not true today. The business community has become vastly politicized in the intervening years. Bills of interest to the business community today are as likely as not to have been initially drafted by the firms or associations most interested and then put into the legislative hopper by friendly and/or dependent legislators. As for social issues such as abortion, education, or welfare, today well-planned, well-informed, business-generated positions dominate the discussion.

11. I do not want to leave the impression that fundamental economic reform is a mystery that confounds our present-day intellect. Each of the following proposals has been bruited about in economic discussions in recent years, and taken together they would go a long way toward altering in the requisite manner an economic mechanism now too often socially dysfunctional. In no particular order, then, consider the following.

Some years ago Michael Harrington proposed a barrier to companies that want to flee their present locale and relocate, say, overseas. They would be required to file a social and economic impact statement, modeled on the environmental impact statements now in the law, that is, to specify what the social and other effects of their leaving would entail. If the impact were estimated to be largely negative, they would automatically be disallowed the tax and other advantages pertinent to the move. At present, by contrast, companies that flee are not untypically allowed generous tax write-offs not only on their abandoned property and producer assets but often on the "customer goodwill" they leave behind. Typically, runaway companies can also "double dip." A company going from locale X to Y is often fully paid by Y to come even as X pays most of the costs of the going. Harrington thought, and with reason, that we as a public have no obligation to subsidize this sort of corporate roaming.

One could easily generalize this idea along the following lines. A charter of corporate behavior document could be legislated covering the social and related responsibilities of big firms. It would, among other things, include making their private records into public documents. Then companies that were found to have behaved in violation of the charter, could be excluded from all tax benefits, regulatory assistance (as in their labor relations), government subsidies, and consular assistance (for their overseas dealings). They would not be coerced into signing on to the charter, but those that refused would forego the benefits of public and government assistance. The point is that most modern firms operate, as we've seen, in a deeply social mode; even if society exacted only a fair price for its assistance and cooperation this would radically alter the nature and practical functioning of the economic system.

At present it is customary to fine companies if they violate the law, as in fouling streams and estuaries or, as today, "cooking the books." As with tobacco, these fines are often then amortized via the tax system. Given the social impact of the big modern firms, criminal penalties should be applied when the occasion merits it. Executives who knowingly endanger the public should be excluded from the right to continue in their position or to take another like it. In the extreme case, boards of directors might be removed and the directors similarly forced to give up their other directorships for a term of years or even permanently. In the more extreme cases—asbestos-producing firms, tobacco firms, Ford Motor Company, and Firestone Tires today—more severe criminal charges could and should be pressed against identifiable executives. One recalls that during the Napoleonic wars the Royal Navy hanged an errant admiral "pour encourager les autres." Penalties considerably short of that should "encourager" more responsible behavior on the part of our corporate steersmen.

More generally, while the different managerial specialties have been professionalized in the purely technical sense, they have not been in the moral sense. A doctor or a lawyer has a prescribed legal responsibility to his or her patient/client and to the organized profession. Some analogous legal prescription should fall upon every person in the management echelon. In fact, it should be illegal and punishable for any business executive to hide or otherwise conspire in corporate actions that he or she has reason to believe will be socially harmful; equivalently, every person in management should be legally required to be a "whistle blower" if he or she believes it appropriate. A negative protection for whistle blowers is not enough, either for the public or for the responsible manager. Both are best protected if whistle blowing is both a protected right and an imposed obligation. Taking one thing with another, a resocialization of the management professions that emphasizes the moral obligation of competence-based self-policing of one's own performance, which is the hallmark of professionalization, and not just their status as the firm's flunkies, is long overdue.

Again, one need not willy-nilly impose such a system upon a recalcitrant "private sector." Firms that are unwilling to sign consent agreements embodying such changes could reasonably be denied all gifts and assistance from government.

One could go on with ideas about closing up the differences between the courses, about restricting access to U.S. markets for foreign firms that, for example, would not sign appropriate consent agreements or that violate them. (We impose sanctions at present on foreign firms that deal with Cuba but less often on those that exploit child or slave labor.) There is really no mystery to these things; some reforms will work well, some poorly, others will have to be discovered on the basis of experience. But the key to that experience is to act on the principle that, ideology aside, a modern economy is a deeply social phenomenon in which society provides perhaps half of all investment and underwrites and often guarantees the profitability of the rest. One wants not aggression against the "private sector" but an end to excessive public forbearance. Basically, the deeply social nature of a modern economy provides society not only with rights to demand business acquiescence but with exceptionally powerful means to exert those rights.

Bibliography

Arrow, Kenneth. 1981. "Real and Nominal Magnitudes in Economics." In *The Crisis in Economic Theory,* edited by Daniel Bell and Irving Kristol, 139–150. New York: Basic Books.

Arrow, Kenneth, and F. H. Hahn. 1971. *General Competitive Analysis.* San Francisco: Holden-Day.

Averitt, Robert T. 1968. *The Dual Economy: The Dynamics of American Industry Structure.* New York: Norton.

Baran, Paul, and Paul Sweezy. 1966. *Monopoly Capital: An Essay on the American Economic and Social Order.* New York and London: Monthly Review Press.

Baxandall, Rosalyn, and Elizabeth Ewen. 2000. *Picture Windows: How the Suburbs Happened.* New York: Basic Books.

Becker, Gary. 1975. *Human Capital: A Theoretical and Empirical Analysis with Special Reference to Education.* 2d ed. New York: National Bureau of Economic Research.

Bell, Daniel. 1973. *The Coming of Post-industrial Society: A Venture in Social Forecasting.* New York: Basic Books.

———. 1981. "Models and Reality in Economics Discourse." In *The Crisis in Economic Theory,* edited by Daniel Bell and Irving Kristol, 46–81. New York: Basic Books.

Bell, Daniel, and Irving Kristol. 1981. *The Crisis in Economic Theory.* New York: Basic Books.

Boehm-Bawerk, Eugen von. [1905] 1984. *Karl Marx and the Close of His System.* In Eugen von Boehm-Bawerk and Ladislaus von Bortkiewicz, *Karl Marx and the Close of His System* and *Boehm-Bawerk's Criticism of Marx,* edited by Paul Sweezy. Philadelphia: Orion.

Bortkiewicz, Ladislaus von. [1907] 1984. "On the Correction of Marx's Fundamental Theoretical Construction in the Third Volume of *Capital.*" In Eugen von Boehm-Bawerk and Ladislaus von Bortkiewicz, *Karl Marx and the Close of His System* and *Boehm-Bawerk's Criticism of Marx,* edited by Paul Sweezy, 197–221. Philadelphia: Orion. Originally published in Eugen von Boehm-Bawerk and Rudolf Hilferding, *Boehm-Bawerk's Criticism of Marx,* 1949.

Bowles, Samuel, and Herbert Gintis. 1976. *Schooling in Capitalist America: Educational Reform and the Contradictions of Economic Life*. New York: Basic Books.

Bowles, Samuel, David M. Gordon, and Thomas E. Weisskopf. 1990. *After the Wasteland; A Democratic Economics for the Year 2000*. Armonk, NY, and London: M. E. Sharpe.

Braverman, Harry. 1974. *Labor and Monopoly Capitalism: The Degradation of Work in the Twentieth Century*. New York and London: Monthly Review Press.

Cassirer, Ernst. [1910; 1923] 1953. *Substance and Function* and *Einstein's Theory of Relativity*. Translated by the Swabeys. New York: Dover.

Chandler, Alfred D. Jr. 1962. *Strategy and Structure: Chapters in the History of the American Industrial Enterprise*. Cambridge and London: MIT Press.

Chandler, Alfred D., Jr., and Herman Daems. 1980. *Management Hierarchy: Comparative Perspectives on the Rise of the Modern Industrial Enterprise*. Cambridge: Harvard University Press.

Cohen, Morris R., And Ernest Nagel. 1934. *An Introduction to Logic and Scientfic Method*. New York: Harcourt, Brace.

Dobb, Maurice. 1973. *Theories of Value and Distribution since Adam Smith: Ideology and Economic Theory*. Cambridge: Cambridge University Press.

Dumenil, Gerard, and Dominique Levy. 1996. *La dynamique du capital: Un siecle d'economie americaine*. Paris: Presses Universitaires de France.

Gordon, David M. 1996. *Fat And Mean: The Corporate Squeeze on Working Americans and the Myth of Managerial "Downsizing."* New York: Free Press.

Gordon, David M., Richard Edwards, and Michael Reich. 1982. *Segmented Work, Divided Workers: The Historical Transformation of Labor in the United States*. New York: Cambridge University Press

Gramsci, Antonio. [1925–34] 1971. *Selections from the Prison Notebooks*. Edited and translated by Quintin Hoare and Geoffrey Nowell Smith. New York: International Publishers.

Greider, William. 1987. *Secrets of the Temple: How the Federal Reserve Runs the Country*. New York: Simon and Schuster.

Guttmann, Robert. 1994. *How Credit Money Shapes the Economy: The United States in a Global System*. Armonk, NY, and London: M. E. Sharpe.

Hahn, Frank. 1981. "General Equilibrium Theory." In *The Crisis in Economic Theory*, edited by Daniel Bell and Irving Kristol, 123–38. New York: Basic Books.

Hayek, Friedrich A. 1944. *The Road to Serfdom*. Chicago: University of Chicago Press.

Hilferding, Rudolph. [1910] 1981. *Finance Capital: A Study of the Latest Phase of Capitalist Development*. Translated by Morris Watnick and Sam Gordon. London: Routledge and Kegan Paul.

Historical Statistics of the United States: Colonial Times to 1970. 1972. Washington, DC: Government Printing Office.

Hobsbawm, Eric. 1994. *The Age of Extremes: A History of the World, 1914–1991*. New York: Vintage.

Jardim, Anne. 1970. *The First Henry Ford: A Study in Personality and Business Leadership*. Cambridge: MIT Press.

Jevons, W. Stanley. [1871] 1970. *The Theory of Political Economy*. Harmondsworth, UK: Penguin Books.

Keynes, John Maynard. 1920. *The Economic Consequences of the Peace*. New York: Harcourt, Brace and Howe.

———. [1936] 1964. *The General-Theory of Employment, Interest, and Money*. New York: Harcourt, Brace.

Kolko, Gabriel. [1963] 1967. *The Triumph of Conservatism: A Re-interpretation of American History, 1900–1916*. Chicago: Quadrangle.

Lacey, Robert. 1986. *Ford: The Men and the Machine*. New York: Ballantine.

Lee, Frederic. 1998. *Post-Keynesian Price Theory*. Cambridge: Cambridge University Press.

Lichtenstein, Nelson. 1982. *Labor's War at Home: The CIO In World War II*. Cambridge: Cambridge University Press.

Linder, Marc, and Lawrence S. Zacharias. 1999. *Of Cabbages and Kings: Agriculture and the Formation of Modern Brooklyn*. Iowa City: University of Iowa Press.

Marshall, Alfred. [1890] 1930. *Principles of Economics: An Introductory Volume*. 8th ed. London: Macmillan.

Marx, Karl. [1845] 1968. *The Theses on Feuerbach*. In Karl Marx and Frederick Engels, *Selected Works*. New York: International Publishers.

———. [1847] 1968. *The Communist Manifesto*. In Karl Marx and Frederick Engels, *Selected Works*. New York: International Publishers.

———. [1857] 1968. *Preface to a Contribution to the Critique of Political Economy*. In Karl Marx and Frederick Engels, *Selected Works*. New York: International Publishers.

———. [1867] 1967. *Capital*. Vol. 1. New York: International Publishers.

———. [1885] 1967. *Capital*. Vol. 2. Moscow: Progress Publishers.

———. [1894] 1966. *Capital*. Vol. 3. Moscow: Progress Publishers.

McDermott, John. 1991. *Corporate Society: Class, Property, and Contemporary Capitalism*. Boulder: Westview.

———. 1991–92. "Free Enterprise and Socialized Labor." *Science and Society* 55:4 (winter 1991–92): 388–84.

———. 1992. "History in the Present: Contemporary Debates about Capitalism." *Science and Society* 56:3 (fall 1992): 291–323.

———. 1999. Review of *How Credit Money Shapes the Economy*, by Robert Guttmann. *Review of Radical Political Economics* 31:3 (summer 1999): 146–48.

———. 2001. "One Hundred Years of ???" *Review of Radical Political Economics* 33 (2001): 99–115. Review essay on *One Hundred Years of Socialism: The West European Left in the Twentieth Century*, by Donald Sassoon.

Means, Gardiner. 1962. *Pricing Power and the Public Interest: A Study Based on Steel.* New York: Harper and Brothers.

Penrose, Edith. [1950] 1980. *The Theory of the Growth of the Firm.* White Plains, NY: M. E. Sharpe.

Popper, Karl. [1957] 1967. *The Poverty of Historicism.* New York: Harper and Row.

Reich, Michael. 1998. "Are U.S. Corporations Top-Heavy? Managerial Ratios in Advanced Capitalist Countries." *Review of Radical Political Economics* 30:3. (summer 1998): 33–45.

Ricardo, David. [1817] 1971. *On the Principles of Political Economy and Taxation.* Harmondsworth, UK. Penguin Books.

Rothbard, Murray. 1972. "Herbert Hoover and the Myth of Laissez-Faire." In *The New History of Leviathan,* edited by Ronald Radosh and Murray Rothbard, 111–45. New York: Dutton.

Sassoon, Donald. 1996. *One Hundred Years of Socialism: The West European Left in the Twentieth Century.* New York: New Press.

Schlatter, Richard. [1951] 1973. *Private Property: The History of an Idea.* New York: Russell and Russell.

Schumpeter, Joseph A. [1942] 1962. *Capitalism, Socialism, and Democracy.* 3d ed. New York and Evanston: Harper and Row.

———. 1954. *History of Economic Analysis.* London: Allen and Unwin.

Sloan, Alfred P. 1964. *My Years at General Motors.* New York: Doubleday.

Smith, Adam. [1776] 1970. *The Wealth of Nations.* Harmonsworth, Middlesex: Penguin. This edition contains only books 1–3 of the original.

Sraffa, Piero. 1960. *The Production of Commodities by Means of Commodities.* Cambridge: Cambridge University Press.

Statistical Abstract of the United States. 1998. Washington, DC: Government Printing Office.

———. 1999. Washington, DC: Government Printing Office.

———. 2000. Washington, DC: Government Printing Office.

Stern, Louis, and Adel I. El-Ansary. 1982. *Marketing Channels.* Englewood Cliffs, NJ: Prentice-Hall.

Stiglitz, Joseph E. 1987. "The Causes and Consequences of the Dependence of Quality on Price." *Journal of Economic Literature* 25 (March 1987): 1–48.

Stone, Katherine. 1973. "The Origin of Job Structures in the Steel Industry." *Radical America* 7:2:19–65.

Sweezy, Paul. 1942. *The Theory of Capitalist Development: Principles of Marxian Political Economy.* New York and London: Monthly Review Press.

Sweezy, Paul, Ed. [1949] 1984. *Karl Marx and the Close of His System* and *Boehm-Bawerk's Criticism of Marx,* by Eugen von Boehm-Bawerk and Ladislaus von Bortkiewicz. Philadelphia: Orion.

Taylor, Frederick. [1911] 1967. *The Principles of Scientific Management.* New York: Norton.

Walras, Leon. [1926] 1977. *Elements of Pure Economics*. Translated by William Jaffe. Fairfield, NJ: Kelley.

Wiebe, Robert H. 1967. *The Search for Order, 1897–1920*. New York: Hill and Wang.

Yellen, Samuel. [1936] 1974. *American Labor Struggles, 1877–1934*. New York: Monad.

Index